LEARNED IGNORANCE IN THE MEDICINE BOW MOUNTAINS
A Reflection on Intellectual Prejudice

VIBS

Volume 199

Robert Ginsberg
Founding Editor

Leonidas Donskis
Executive Editor

Associate Editors

G. John M. Abbarno
George Allan
Gerhold K. Becker
Raymond Angelo Belliotti
Kenneth A. Bryson
C. Stephen Byrum
Harvey Cormier
Robert A. Delfino
Rem B. Edwards
Malcolm D. Evans
Daniel B. Gallagher
Andrew Fitz-Gibbon
Francesc Forn i Argimon
William Gay
Dane R. Gordon
J. Everet Green
Heta Aleksandra Gylling
Matti Häyry

Steven V. Hicks
Richard T. Hull
Michael Krausz
Mark Letteri
Vincent L. Luizzi
Adrianne McEvoy
Alan Milchman
Peter A. Redpath
Alan Rosenberg
Arleen L. F. Salles
John R. Shook
Eddy Souffrant
Tuija Takala
Emil Višňovský
Anne Waters
John R. Welch
Thomas Woods

a volume in
Lived Values: Valued Lives
LVVL
Richard T. Hull, Editor

LEARNED IGNORANCE IN THE MEDICINE BOW MOUNTAINS
A Reflection on Intellectual Prejudice

Craig Clifford

Amsterdam - New York, NY 2008

Cover photo: ©Craig Clifford

Cover Design: Studio Pollmann

The paper on which this book is printed meets the requirements of "ISO 9706:1994, Information and documentation - Paper for documents - Requirements for permanence".

ISBN: 978-90-420-2498-4
©Editions Rodopi B.V., Amsterdam - New York, NY 2008
Printed in the Netherlands

For Mallory

I at least was young and unaware
that what I thought was chosen was convention.

Seamus Heaney
"Station Island"

CONTENTS

LIST OF ILLUSTRATIONS		xi
FOREWORD		xiii
ACKNOWLEDGMENTS AND DISCLAIMERS		xv
INTRODUCTION: Attempts: Philosophy as Essay		1
ONE	A Good Intellectual Is Hard to Find	7
TWO	Mind Forg'd Manacles	15
THREE	Running and Being	31
FOUR	The Queen's English, or That Awful English Language	35
FIVE	Wine of Wyoming	45
SIX	Wit and the Art of Conversation	49
SEVEN	The Fish	59
EIGHT	"A Minor Regional Novelist"	63
NINE	Wana	77
TEN	Culture Vultures	83
ELEVEN	Centennial	101
TWELVE	The Sweet Science and the Competitive Spirit	105
THIRTEEN	The Halfe Ars'd Angler	115
FOURTEEN	Blood Sports and Haute Cuisine	123
FIFTEEN	Bread and Wine	147
SIXTEEN	Idols of the Academic Theater	151
SEVENTEEN	Westward I Go Free	167
BIBLIOGRAPY		171
ABOUT THE AUTHOR		179
INDEX		181

LIST OF ILLUSTRATIONS

Figure 1.	Trail to South Gap Lake, Snowy Range, Wyoming	14
Figure 2.	View of Snowy Range from Mirror Lake area	30
Figure 3.	Wine bottles near Centennial, Wyoming	44
Figure 4.	Little Laramie River near Centennial, Wyoming	58
Figure 5.	Longhorns in bluebonnets near Glen Rose, Texas	62
Figure 6.	Ranch near Centennial, Wyoming	76
Figure 7.	Bass Performance Hall, Fort Worth, Texas	81
Figure 8.	Kimbell Art Museum, Fort Worth, Texas	82
Figure 9.	Centennial, Wyoming	100
Figure 10.	"The Sweet Science."	104
Figure 11.	Trout, Medicine Bow National Forest, Wyoming	114
Figure 12.	On the "Chiantigiana" between Siena and Florence, Italy	121
Figure 13.	Vineyard on Mosel River in Germany	121
Figure 14.	Prosciutto di cinghiale, Montalcino, Italy	122
Figure 15.	Grilled rack of pork, Stephenville, Texas	122
Figure 16.	Highway 130, Centennial, Wyoming	170

All photographs by Craig Clifford except for figure 5, which is by Kathryn Jones (used with permission).

FOREWORD

I first met Craig Clifford in a graduate seminar I offered at the State University of New York at Buffalo. This particular course was designed to initiate some discussion among students of varying persuasions, chiefly Continental and Analytic. Craig resigned from the class after a particularly heated discussion that gave off little light, and we progressed to being fast friends. I will leave the details of that transformation for another time.

A previous version of this work was considered for publication by the Value Inquiry Book Series, and rejected as too personal. One of the motives I had for creating this series, Lived Values, Valued Lives, was to give works that were highly biographical a voice, for I think that biography often illustrates how individuals manifest their values in the actions and characters they perform and develop.

The Lived Values, Valued Lives Series is comprised of biographies, loosely defined, that express and explore how values appear in and shape human lives. The series aims at provoking readers to engage in reflective exploration of the values expressed in the decisions, actions, and thoughts of philosophically reflective individuals. From one another's narratives we can learn much and come to consider possibilities that might otherwise never occur to us.

The series aims at readers of all ages looking for inspiration not only for course papers but also for their lives. The value of thoughtful reflection, not conversion, is the aim.

Craig Clifford's book is one that may make readers uncomfortable. Many of us go through a kind of professionalization that creates the attitudes this book criticizes; its greatest value, thus, may be the stimulation of that kind of puzzlement that precedes development of a more mature and realistic view of one's function in the world.

Craig Clifford, besides being an accomplished essayist and gifted teacher, is a champion archer, a painter of considerable talent, a guitarist and singer of Western and folk songs, an accomplished home renovator, and a superb chef. He himself thus stands as an answer to the regional snobbishness that initially inspired this work.

Richard Thompson Hull
Lived Values, Valued Lives Special Series Editor
Tallahassee, Florida

ACKNOWLEDGMENTS AND DISCLAIMERS

Joan Didion ends the preface to *Slouching Towards Bethlehem* with this disclaimer: "Writers are always selling somebody out." This book, by necessity, is about friends, enemies, acquaintances, colleagues—fellow intellectuals of many persuasions. It's also about a number of public figures who exhibit the characteristics I wish to criticize, but a great deal of the experience on which I base these reflections is personal. I've spent my entire adult life among intellectuals, at times almost exclusively. I know whereof I speak because most of the people I've associated with have been intellectuals. I know whereof I speak because I speak of myself.

Unavoidably, the characters in this book are heroes and villains—and I mean them to be. Many of them are public persons, persons of the intellect, persons who live and die by their remarks and their tastes and their world views and their thinking—and thereby fair game for the intellectual sniper. But many of them are persons with whom I've shared friendship, bread and wine, professional competitiveness, cultural one-upsmanship, moments of truth, the passage of mortal time. For that reason, I've done my best to blunt the personal thrust of my argument, when I feel it ought to be, by exercising the "creative nonfiction" license to fictionalize, not so much for the sake of creativity, but for the sake of friendship, privacy, decency. As well as my memory and my own repetitions of the tales can be trusted, everything in this book really happened; every remark was actually spoken. But sometimes I take the liberty of mixing up the locations and the personal identities, in one way or another, to save a few folks open harassment and embarrassment, although many of them may see themselves in these episodes nonetheless, even in some of the episodes that really didn't involve them. I imagine, too, that some folks will see someone else in all of the villainous roles and agree wholeheartedly with my criticisms, even though they themselves were the basis for those criticisms. So be it. Ultimately, my subject is intellectual prejudice, not my friends or enemies, or myself.

I also make an effort to conceal the identities of some very fine folks in Wyoming whose acquaintances I made during that summer many years ago when the idea for this book was sprung on me high in the Medicine Bow Mountains. They are private persons who have not signed away their privacy to the public arena of intellectual logomachy—I respect their privacy and them.

I couldn't have written this book without the help of many good people and several welcome twists of fate. To the many friends at home and in faraway places who read parts of the manuscript and contributed enthusiasm or advice, I owe much gratitude. And especially those of you who responded with your own personal reflections and experiences on the subject—you helped to convince me that my words were about more than myself. Most of all I must thank my finest reader, who has the uncanny ability to pounce upon the very sentences I had felt uneasy about but was too lazy to rework, and the wisdom to let the stubbornly idiosyncratic ones, about which we once would have fought like cats and dogs, alone. Thereby, she assures that if I am hanged, I will be hanged not for mere laziness but for my true writer's self.

I'd like to point out that a couple of passages of this book, the comparison of tennis and boxing in chapter 12 and the final passage of chapter 14, made their original debut in the unacademic but unslick pages of the *Fort Worth Star-Telegram*, back when Tommy Denton was the op-ed editor and, later, the editorial page editor. The openness of a number of op-ed editors to serious philosophical reflection and consciously literary word-tinkering has been responsible in part for luring me away from standard academic writing. Also, part of the passage in chapter 10 about *High Noon* and the discussion of the TV chefs in chapter 14 were adapted from papers I delivered at meetings of the Popular Culture Association, an organization that, as academic organizations go, is remarkably devoid of the kind of stuffiness I decry in this book. Finally, a few passages in chapter 12 were adapted from a book I co-authored with Randolph M. Feezell, *Coaching for Character: Reclaiming the Principles of Sportsmanship* (pp. 9–24, copyright ©1997 by Human Kinetics, adapted with permission from Human Kinetics, Champaign, Ill.).

Lines from Elizabeth Bishop's "The Fish" quoted as an epigraph to chapter 7 are used by permission of Farrar, Straus and Giroux, LLC. (Excerpt from "The Fish" from *The Complete Poems, 1927–1979* by Elizabeth Bishop. Copyright © 1979, 1983 by Alice Helen Methfessel.) Lines from Kinky Friedman's "Highway Cafe" quoted as an epigraph to chapter 11 are used by permission. (Copyright © 1973 by Glaser Publications. All rights administered by Sony/ATV Music Publishing, LLC, 8 Music Square West, Nashville, TN 37203. All rights reserved.)

On the subject of giving credit where credit is due, I should say a word about my use of "sources." On one level, this is clearly a scholarly work; it is not, however, a book of disinterested scholarship but one of thinking and storytelling that come from gut and muse and pressing necessity. For that reason, and others, I decided to scrupulously avoid scholarly citations in the body of my text. Indeed, the writers I quote and talk about are by and large the writers I wish to emulate; and most of them, though learned as the day is long, weren't, or aren't, big on documentation. The apparatuses of academic scholarship have their place, but in the personal essay, however philosophical and scholarly, quotations serve not as documentation but as occasions for reflection. However, for the sake of giving credit where credit is due and on the outside chance that these pages may spark someone to go off and read some of the works I admiringly or disapprovingly refer to, I include at the end of the book something of a personal, eclectic record of the books and other writings that played a direct role in this endeavor. In the bibliography, I also cite the English translations of Greek, German, and French works that I've heavily depended upon, although I admit to having freely tinkered with those translations in such a way that no one else should be held responsible for the versions that appear other than myself. In a few cases, I cite only a German edition, either because no translation exists or because I've made no use of it if it does.

Finally, I'd like to thank Dick Hull for having the courage and insight to create a home for works of this kind. This book is overtly philosophical, but it is far afield from the norms and expectations of academic publishing and perishing; and it is equally out of sync with the demands of the publish-and-profit expectations of commercial publishers. In a sense, the series in which this book appears returns philosophy to the thoroughly unacademic conviction of Socrates, who believed that what really matters are the lives we live, and that to live them well we had best examine them.

Craig Clifford
Stephenville, Texas

INTRODUCTION

Attempts: Philosophy as Essay

> How should one write, what words should one select, what forms and structures and organization, if one is pursuing understanding? (Which is to say, if one is, in that sense, a philosopher?) Sometimes this is taken to be a trivial and uninteresting question. I shall claim that it is not. Style itself makes its claims, expresses its own sense of what matters. Literary form is not separable from philosophical content, but is, itself, a part of content—an integral part, then, of the search for and the statement of truth.
>
> Martha Nussbaum
> *Love's Knowledge*

Dissatisfied with the discrepancy between form and content in the conventional prose of 20th-century Anglo-American philosophy, "a style remarkably flat and lacking in wonder," Martha Nussbaum turned to the novel. Certain important truths, she argues, require the approach of the narrative artist. Philosophers ought to take fiction—indeed, narrative literature generally—seriously. She takes that a step further when she argues that philosophers themselves ought to seek out forms of writing that are more faithful to their subject matter, citing an article on the subject of love replete with the p's and q's of formal logic as an example of how academic philosophy has gone astray. In *Love's Knowledge*, the book in which she makes these comments, Nussbaum self-consciously applies the principles she argues for to her own writing, mixing in personal narratives among the argumentation like fragrant herbs into an otherwise straightforward stew, near-Dionysian confessions of personal involvement right alongside Apollonian analyses worthy of her blue-blood diplomas. Having described her ideal marriage of philosophical form and content, she takes the responsible plunge: "I have tried to exemplify such a form here."

Meanwhile, in the other camp, Hans-Georg Gadamer in a 1986 interview admits that he had consciously avoided Heidegger's poetic language: "But the poetizing mode of speech used by the later Heidegger, when he spoke of *Geschick* and the like—that bothered me. It made it easy to raise the charge of mythological thinking against him. I said: Here I can show what he means." This is the same Hans-Georg Gadamer who had argued, and was still arguing, that it is that very risk-taking of Heidegger's language that distinguishes him. No one has more persuasively defended the language of Heidegger than Gadamer. Has Gadamer been untrue to his own principles—or is he in the paradoxical situation of the poetry critic who understands the value of a kind of language he himself could never aspire to? Gadamer's solution to the challenge Heidegger posed for him: "We have to learn to see the phenomenon which he meant and then speak on our own. That's why you don't find me using Heideggerian language."

Will the two camps meet in the middle—literature-loving analytic philosophers fleeing from the security of a language too sterile to say anything meaningful and sober hermeneuticists fleeing from the irrationality of poetic mysticism? Will they produce a hybrid prose, part narrative but not too poetic, imbued with just enough passion to get rejected by all the academic journals but not enough to invoke the charge of irrationalism?

I've come at this issue somewhat differently, through a reflection on—and many experiments with—that much aligned and reputedly lesser literary form, the essay. I can't match Nussbaum's pleasing stories about sitting in the tall grass at Bryn Mawr and reading Jane Austen, but I, too, find myself drawing upon my own experiences. I, too, fled from the p's and q's of the American philosophy journals, protesting from my earliest undergraduate days that rigor and clarity are of value only if one has something to be rigorous or clear about—and embracing Aristotle's great insight that the kind of rigor and clarity one seeks depends on the nature of the subject matter.

Searching for the marriage of form and content, I turned to Martin Heidegger's later writings. At first, reading Heidegger reminded me of reading Faulkner—I knew that something important was going on, but I wasn't sure what it was, or how to articulate it.

But, having been moved by Heidegger's language, what do you say? What do you write? The pitfalls of this predicament were brought home to me long before I read Gadamer's solution. In the summer of 1978, while doing research in the library of the University of Trier, I came across an article in an American journal by a "Heideggerian" I had studied Heidegger with as an undergraduate half a dozen years earlier. The words squawked, screeched, clattered. There were no clearings in which the truth might light up, not even a good Black Forest thicket to get lost in. It was, to parallel Nussbaum's comment about Anglo-American analytic philosophy, a style remarkably awkward and lacking in clarity.

The lesson, it seemed to me, was clear: if I was to take my lead from Heidegger, then the last thing I should do would be to ape his language. In other words, Gadamer was right that we have to see what Heidegger was talking about, then find our own words. But finding "my own words" to talk about the things Heidegger talked about in his own words meant for me finding a way of writing that was as consistent with my native language—and the full range of it from formal American English to the regional colloquialisms of my upbringing—as Heidegger's writing was with his. That involved a wide reading of writers from my own homeland, which I recount in several of the chapters in this book, and a reconsideration of the very concept of the essay.

I came to realize that I wanted to be an essayist in the older sense, the original sense, of the essay—in the sense of the French *essayer*, to "attempt." When Montaigne designated his meandering personal and philosophical reflections *Essais*, he meant to indicate the tentative trial-and-error nature of his thought. "If my mind could gain a firm footing," he says, "I would not make attempts [*je ne m'essaierais pas*], I would make decisions; but it is always in apprenticeship and on trial." For that reason, he seems to wander, sometimes aimlessly; but, in fact, it is a controlled wandering. "I love the poetic gait, by leaps and gambols. . . . It is the inattentive reader who loses my subject, not I." Montaigne's subject is his own thoughts, but there is nonetheless a blurring of the lines between thought and story. "I do not teach," he says, "I recount" [*je raconte*]. And because he recounts the course of his own reflections, he recounts, not in the formal language of systematic philosophy, but in the language that is natural to him—"simple, natural speech, the same on paper as in the mouth."

By leaps and gambols, though, the more deeply I thought about the tradition of the essay, the more my thoughts kept turning back to the two philosophers who have most engaged me, Heidegger and Plato. Montaigne makes "attempts" because his mind cannot find a firm footing. I think that something of the same spirit underlies the title of a collection of Heidegger's later essays, even though the scope and subject of his essays are different. Although the magnum opus that Heidegger began before the war was to be a systematic treatise (*Being and Time* represents two of three projected divisions of the first of two projected parts), the insights of that work, and perhaps the darker experiences of the war, led to a different approach. After the war, he abandoned the systematic work and wrote a series of essays and lectures, sometimes cryptically poetic, each striking out in a different direction. He entitled a collection of these essays *Holzwege*, "Woodpaths," because he had come to believe that thinking is not a systematic enterprise, that there is no Cartesian "secure path of reason" that one has simply to follow yellow-brick-road fashion to the truth. Thinking, he came to believe, is more like walking on a path in the woods, as the epigraph to *Holzwege* seems to suggest:

> "Wood" is an old name for forest. In the wood are paths which mostly wind along until they end quite suddenly in an impenetrable thicket.
>
> They are called "woodpaths."
>
> Each goes its peculiar way, but in the same forest. Often it seems as though one were like another. Yet it only seems so.
>
> Woodcutters and forest-dwellers are familiar with these paths. They know what it means to be on a woodpath.

If the woodpaths of thinking "mostly" leave off in a thicket, thinking often requires that you retrace your steps and start out in a different direction. Even though all of the paths of thinking look alike, some of them, Heidegger hints at but doesn't say explicitly here, open into a brightly lit clearing, a *Lichtung*. It's possible, he metaphorically suggests, to become familiar with the paths of thinking, but you can never know with certainty whether you will wind up in a thicket or stumble into a clearing.

I am lumping together vastly disparate philosophical minds, but there is a certain strand of philosophy understood as artful "attempts," as love rather than possession of wisdom, that runs all the way back to Plato's philosophical dialogues. Some interpreters of Plato's dialogues think that Plato had a full-blown systematic doctrine that he directly revealed to his worthy disciples, and that he wrote these cryptic, pedagogical dialogues for the rest of us lesser mortals. The famous "Seventh Letter" is the chief ammunition of the "secret doctrine" interpreters. There's some reason to believe the letter is spurious, but, even if it isn't, it denounces philosophical writing in general, which throws us back into the mystery of the dialogues. A casual read through a couple of the dialogues will convince anyone but the most secondary-source-indoctrinated reader that the dialogues *are* Plato's philosophy—philosophy that is inescapably pedagogical, true, but as full-blown and whole as Plato believed it could be. On a surface reading of the *Republic*, Plato's contribution to the "ancient quarrel between the poets and the philosophers" seems to be a wholesale condemnation of poetry, but the comments about poetry in the *Republic* must be taken within the context of the manifestly poetic works that Plato wrote. His dialogues are philosophical dramas. The answer to the question at the end of the *Symposium*, whether the same man could write both tragedy and comedy, is wonderfully ironic: Plato did. And, I should add, the greatest master of the marriage of literary and philosophical writing that Nussbaum calls for is Plato, even though, strangely, Nussbaum herself never takes seriously the irreducibly literary character of Plato's writing, preferring Aristotle's academic lectures on tragedy to Plato's tragedies and comedies.

As Gadamer so eloquently argues in *Truth and Method*, Plato wrote dialogues because he believed that truth resides in an ever-deepening process of questioning, not in a final answer. Truth resides in the insightful and courageous *attempt*. The process of questioning can't go on without attempts at answers, and, in that sense, philosophy for Plato includes philosophical doctrine. But the answers are never complete and never conclusive, and, in many dialogues, the answers given at the end aren't nearly as good as the ones given in the middle. The understanding of the reader, at least potentially, may ascend until the end, but that is because understanding comes out of the questioning process itself. As much of contemporary scholarship has noted, Plato's philosophy is not doctrinal, but dialogical and exploratory. Plato gives us not the doctrines arrived at, but the attempts, the *essais*.

If the most important truths are like the elusive pronouncements of the oracle at Delphi, philosophy is by necessity driven to the essay, the dialogue, the aphorism. Philosophy is by its very nature driven toward the literary, the poetic—although, I suppose, it never completely arrives there. The essay, then, like the Platonic dialogue, is the marriage of philosophy and poetry. It is a way of writing that is meaningful, truthful, revealing, even when no conclusions are reached.

Looking at the question from the other side, though, the essay is necessarily driven to philosophy—or, rather, as conceived by Montaigne, it is a form that developed from the very process of *thinking the matter through*, or, to borrow Plato's definition of thinking, it is the dialogue of the self with the self. In an essay on the nature of the essay, Joseph Epstein says, "The essay is—or should be—ruminative." It is a chewing and a re-chewing of the matter. Epstein himself doesn't take this claim seriously enough, for he also claims that the essay is ultimately a "modest" literary form. The belief that the essay is a modest literary form—Epstein calls it "piece work"—is a long-standing literary prejudice which derives from the inability to accept the marriage of literature and philosophy that the essay represents.

Rumination is not a popular thing, though. The school-days cliché of the argumentative essay—the thesis-sentence, argument, recapitulation approach—enjoys a greater following, perhaps nowhere more conspicuously than in the academic journal article. And, to be sure, the well controlled argumentative essay gives the reader a sense of security and conclusion; whereas the ruminative essay can be downright irritating. My father read one of my consciously ruminative essays and remarked: "It ricochets off every tree in the forest." And whereas one of my former teachers, indeed a professor of the clarity-is-all school, accused me of making up the stories in a lengthy narrative reflection because otherwise it couldn't have all fit together so well, the editor of *The Georgia Review* responded to the same essay with this piece of bewilderment: "It has some fine moments, but in our opinion it rambles too much."

The essayists I admire take the "poetic gait," the "leaps and gambols," to a sublime extreme. At times their essays seem to have no point, because . . . they have no point. They are *about* something, about important things. But they do not simply make a point, they do not offer commentary; rather, they take us on a journey of reflection and discovery, or, better, through the process of trying to discover.

Essays in this sense of the word risk getting lost in a thicket, and they risk the truthfulness of bursting forth into one of those sunlit Black Forest clearings. The reader risks more as well, for he or she is not at liberty simply to analyze the argument, agree or disagree with the conclusion; a reader who takes the work seriously must think and reflect and ponder right along with the author—must *undergo* something. A reader may go looking for the definitive statement about the human condition or about "being qua being"—and come away with an irreducible, but truthful sense of ambivalence deeply felt and deeply thought or with a reverence for the mystery of being.

Looking more closely at what attracted me to the essayists I admire, from Texas essayist John Graves to Black Forest philosopher Martin Heidegger, I see that the trial-and-error process of working the thoughts and the stories out, the ambivalence, the meandering and questioning, filter right down to the very words and sounds and commas. For these writers, it is not just a matter of taking the reader through the process of discovery, through the process of ruminating; it is a matter of taking the reader, with skill and artistry, through the process of finding the right words. Paradoxically, great essayists give us the perfect words to convey the sense of looking for the perfect words—a sense of the uncertain struggle for just the right sound, just the right word, to make the thing that the words are about step out into the open and show itself.

In *Heidegger's Ways* Gadamer describes Heidegger's struggle with language this way:

> Perhaps it was not to be avoided that this thinker's language often resembles a tormented stammering, for it is a language struggling to awaken from the forgetfulness of Being and to think only that which is worthy of thought. The same man whose words and phrases could be of such visual force and power that they were unparalleled by those of his philosophical contemporaries, whose words allowed us to think of materialized phenomena, whose words made something spiritual tangible—this same man extracts out of the shafts of language the most peculiar lumps, breaks up the extracted stones so that they completely lose their usual outline, and moves around in a world of fragmented word-rocks, searching, checking. These facets, artificially produced in this manner, carry his message. Sometimes he makes a real discovery; then the words spark suddenly, and one sees with one's own eyes what Heidegger is saying. Sometimes a tragic struggle for the right language and a concept with the ability to speak permeates Heidegger's work—in which case anyone wishing to think with him is necessarily drawn into the struggle.

For poetry, one must have already arrived at the right words; in the essay, one must find the right words to convey the sense of finding the right words. The process of discovery, then, is one and the same with the process of finding the right words. When it comes to the deeper questions, ambivalence and questioning and storytelling that lead to significant silence, what I've called meaningful attempts, may well nigh be the only way to get at the truth—and that ambivalence, questioning, that storytelling silence, all come about through the wandering-in-the-woods search for the right words that we call—thanks to Montaigne's unintentional neologism—the essay.

One

A GOOD INTELLECTUAL IS HARD TO FIND

Call me Bubba. Some time ago—never mind how long precisely—having little or no money in my checking account, and nothing particular to interest me in the dog-day glaze of August heat on the high plains of north-central Texas, I thought I would drive about a little and see the mountainous part of the world. It is a way I have of driving off the indigestion and regulating the blood pressure. Whenever I find myself growing lethargic of limb and mind; whenever it is a baked-dry sizzling August in my soul; whenever I find myself involuntarily shopping in K-Marts and Wal-Marts, and bringing up the rear of the drive-in window line at every fast-food joint in town; and especially whenever my fellow committee members at the university, not to mention the fair spirits down at the capital who giveth and taketh away my salary and photocopying privileges, get such an upper hand of me that it requires a strong moral principle to prevent me from deliberately pulling out my mythical .45 and shooting door-nail dead every motorist, student, or high-horse colleague who looks even slightly askance at me—then, I account it high time to get to the mountains as soon as I can.

In the old days, when I was expatriating my life away in the Great Northeast, I would load up a slim volume of Heidegger's densest philosophical essays, my guitar, and my wife (well, actually she got into the car of her own free will) and head for home soil and the greasiest bowl of chili in the greasiest anti-intellectual spoon I could find.

Now, it was not homesickness, but life itself, that brought me to a disillusioned, haplessly frustrated, violence-bent enraged standstill. Five-foot-six motorists who fire the proverbial middle finger at the slightest request for a little intersection give-and-take, assured that their steel armament somehow changes all of the rules of human interaction. Friendships that boil to the surface. Service managers at Toyota dealers who smell of cheap politeness as they twist the jagged blade of your warranty into the deepest crevices of your bank account. Armies of squash bugs that turn weeks of planting and cultivating into fruitless compost. Leaders of the intellectual community talking about things "impacting," people "interfacing" and "prioritizing," and the students I try to lead out of ignorance and glandular reflex behavior as the "products" that universities produce and sell or, even worse, the customers we must cater to.

Cool spring evenings on the back porch, rhapsodic communing with budding pecan trees and sprouting beans . . . now turned to late summer's deadening heat, thoughts of self-worthlessness and the meager words that might or might not survive my mortality . . . . Thoughts of parents growing elderly. A friend who died of cancer in her early thirties. When she had complained once that there was nothing to see in the Texas Panhandle, I had said we all need to experience a bit of nothing from time to time . . . .

There's an emptiness that intensifies the small bit of finitude that we all are, that shatters life's little illusions, that leaves us speechless but enlightened. *Angst* in a certain sense—in Heidegger's—facing one's own mortality. For me, *Angst* in the Texas Panhandle. There's an emptiness, though, that doesn't shatter, but dulls and slows and hovers like the heavy air of a West Texas August. The emptiness of someone else's death, sheer absence. Or the emptiness of life's mere momentum. I know it when I find myself three days in a row walking down the same aisle at Wal-Mart, unable to decide whether or not I should buy a multi-function telephone. The French *ennui*, perhaps. Boredom, lethargy, life reduced to a perpetual but meaningless motion.

I had the need to look over a precipice, a stony, Mother-Nature-made precipice, to look deep into mountain-lake waters of chilling clarity, to watch a summer storm across fifty miles of jagged rocks and scrawny, one-sided junipers engulf an entire mountain range in its dark fury. I had a need to see old friends, to remind myself of where it was that I once intended to go and who I once intended to be, to see their grown children I once held up in the air by the ankles. I had the need to go and go, and climb and climb, up, on up, to get above and out of . . . .

By reason of these things, then, the trip to Wyoming was welcome. When Barbara and Randy called from Omaha to say they had found two log cabins at 8,000 feet just on the edge of the Snowy Range in the Medicine Bow Mountains, Mallory and I started packing, and all of the power and magic of the Rocky Mountains, all of the history and myth of the American West, all of the poetic impulses in my inmost soul, started to operate on me straight away.

"My map shows a dirt road going from here over to Highway 11. Can you tell me where it is?"

The old man was standing at the counter in the crossroads post office that was marked as the town of Woods Landing on my Wyoming map. He eyed me curiously, but not inhospitably, as he chewed over my question.

"It's right at the bottom of that hill there." He pointed in the direction we had been going.

"Can I make it in my pickup?" I asked, nodding towards my obviously new two-wheel-drive small pickup parked just outside the door.

"If you don't make it, don't buy another one."

A city-dwelling New Mexican friend had quipped that people in Wyoming are boring because they don't talk much. Somehow this was the kind of boredom I was ready for, believing, as I do, that people of few words and sinewy character are superior to people who talk incessantly but never have anything to say.

Wana Clayton, the 88-year-old, twice-widowed retired school teacher who owned the two cabins—for privacy's sake, I call her by a slightly altered name—kept referring to our drive out on the main highway from Laramie, and it took several repetitions to convince her that a couple of tenderfoots from Texas could have driven in the back way on the forest service road.

She also explained with the greatest delicacy about the "path." I told her that, although that was not the word we used, I was not entirely unfamiliar with outdoor facilities. Visions of graduate school in Buffalo . . . *Where's your cowboy hat, Tex? Do you have a horse back on the ranch? . . . Y'all? We all don't call it supper . . . Hey, these yokels from Texas have a friend named Hairy—can you believe that?*

A hick in New York, a city-slicker in Wyoming. A refreshing change, though. It's a tiresome routine, either fighting against or playing along with all the cowboy and oil-well myths—sometimes useful, often necessary, but tiresome. Wyoming was the first place I had ever been, including Germany and France, where Texans weren't labeled as backward gun-totin' hicks. And all we had to do to win over Wana was convince her we could drive on a dirt road, negotiate the "path," catch a few trout and cook them over an open fire, and survive a few days in a log cabin without complaining.

It's Coloradans that Wyoming folk complain about, calling them "Greenies," because of their green license plates, and, I suppose, because of their stridently postured ecological love of picturesque greenery, marred, of course, only by the rapidly multiplying mountain-lodge condos owned by Texans. Actually, other than Wana's insistence that we couldn't have driven on a dirt road, people in Wyoming didn't really care one way or another that we were from Texas.

Of course, out where we were, there weren't many people to care. That's why we were there. People, even the most sophisticated, opera-worshiping people of the cultural and intellectual stratospheres, become boring or trying, or they just cease to mean. We ourselves become boring or trying. We dissolve into a bundle of one-dimensional prejudices, and somehow hating Texas and loving New York or loving Texas and hating New York, or loving or hating Wagner or Miles Davis or Willie Nelson, no longer justifies us. We long for purity and emptiness, fresh visions of ourselves and of our half-severed attachments to things natural and unforgivingly what they are.

We didn't talk much as we hiked up the trail, strung out from male adults, Randy with baby in the backpack, to seventeen-year-old Travis now grown far beyond ankle-dangling proportions, to female adults, to seven-year-old Evan bringing up the rear, occasionally shouting out beleaguered requests for a slower pace. We didn't need to be alone, in true Thoreauvian solitude, but we needed to stop from time to time, just at the top of a rise, to look in speechless contemplation upon the next alpine lake, bordered by twenty-foot-deep snow banks, reflecting grey stone and white snow peaks rising threateningly above the tree line. Above 11,000 feet in elevation, we tiptoed over scattered boulders, hopped over endless trickling streams of melting snow, the ground a soft and luscious marsh of lily-like flowers and flawlessly green mountain grasses.

"How deep would the snow be right here in January?" one of us interjected into our theoretical silences. I thought of the 105-degree afternoon that was surely burning its mark into the untheoretical, stupefied gazes of my friends back in Texas. Here the 60-degree breezes curled around the granite ledges and stunted spruce, cooled our sun-warmed faces as the afternoon thundershowers danced in the distance against the brilliant sky.

Thoughts, and questions, come simple in such surroundings. It's not possible to think about committee meetings or how much money you would have made if you'd gone to law school.

I thought about how my Omaha friends seemed settled in, firmly situated in their lives, definitely who and what they were. Then I thought about how they still contemplated giving up careers and moving back to the family farm in Oklahoma. They were here, though, so they wouldn't have to do that. I thought about their kids: one going off to college, a baseball player and a lover of literature, a walking dilemma not unlike his father was; one just starting the second grade, as strong-willed as his older brother is accepting, and absolutely determined, as all kids his age are wont to be, to make sure that we didn't get too carried away with our pantheistic pieties; one brand spanking new baby, sleeping to the rhythms of his father's footsteps.

I thought about what I had thought about when I was the kid tagging along on a hike through the mountains. I thought about where I had ended up in life, or, better, where I was in the process of ending up, about teaching and writing . . . about the purities of a calling and the inescapable entanglements of a job. Was I an academic, a teacher, a professional Texan, a writer, or a slow white guy with a fair jump shot who wished he had had the dilemma my two generations of friends had? I thought about pretense and pomp and all of the things that just fade away in the silence and the deep, pleading breath of thin mountain air. I thought of the flash and clang of words ill-used. Looking at the goddamnedest, jagged rock of a face of a mountain peak, it seemed that words, that my words, if I was going to use them at all, ought to mean something—that they ought to have, at least in the best of moments, that silent feel of good listening and reverent looking. When all is said and done, they ought to just stand there, like the faces of the Snowy Range peaks.

After a couple of hours, we stopped for lunch on a high promontory overlooking a large lake of glistening clarity. Perched on the outmost point of boulders, we looked directly across the still waters at the highest range of treeless peaks. Male egos fantasized about climbing the sheer face of the tallest one, but we sat instead in contemplative bread and fruit partaking.

I was artistically slicing up an overripe peach with a lock-blade hunting knife when two intruders invaded our communion service. True, we had seen a couple of other people on the trail, but they had either passed in reverent silence or stopped to talk briefly about the beauty of it all. These fellows, apparently father and son, had a different look. Both were decked out in all of the latest mountain-climbing fashions from L. L. Bean—monstrous backpacks with sleeping bags and other accessories tied on in the appropriate places, khaki shorts with multiple pockets, suspenders, knee-high 100-percent-wool socks, flannel lumberjack shirts—not an artificial fiber to be seen.

The father stopped to catch his breath next to the rock Randy was sitting on. The son, cheeks as indoor rosy as a Vienna choirboy's, just behind. I kept slicing the peach. I didn't want to talk to these people.

Randy, always more adept than me at talking comfortably with strangers, asked where they were going. They were heading across the pass, intending to camp for about a week. Had to admire them for that. We were just afternoon strollers, by comparison.

"Where are you from?" Randy asked. It's the first question Southerners and Southwesterners always ask.

"Cornell," he answered quickly. I looked up a bit surprised. You're not *from* Cornell, you work there, I thought as I eyeballed him. Then I remembered—folks who hang out at national conferences and symposia, publish findings in "blind refereed" academic journals, and confuse tenure with testosterone always answer the question "Where are you from?" with the name of an ivy-clad university. The school is home, more than home. That, I guess, is why my Italian friend from Rhode Island used to joke about the people who went to "Brown Universe."

Misunderstanding the puzzlement, he explained. "That's a university in upstate New York. I'm a professor there."

"That makes just about all of us professors," Randy remarked. "In fact, we went to graduate school in Buffalo, just down the road from Cornell."

"Oh."

"Ithaca. Nice town," Randy added. "What do you teach?"

"I'm in high-energy physics," the intruder stated in a perfectly unassuming tone.

"I guess you could say I'm in low-energy philosophy."

Touché. I lifted a slice of peach to my mouth with the knife blade. Randy told him what the rest of us taught, and we all nodded politely. Randy had gotten himself into this conversation; he could damn well get himself out of it.

The intruder took his turn. "Where are you people from?"

"We," Randy said as he pointed to Barbara and the kids, "are from Omaha." I looked at Randy's deep-red Oklahoma Sooner baseball cap, and noted to myself that that was the first time I had heard him answer that question without saying something about hailing from Oklahoma "originally." More settled in, with two Nebraska-born kids now, or just not wanting to talk about the subject of homelands with a person who thinks he lives in a university—I wasn't sure.

"These people here are from Stephenville, Texas," he went on. Mallory and I nodded unenthusiastically. The intruder grunted a polite "Um hmm . . ." our direction, then turned back to Randy.

"Omaha. You know I had to come through Omaha to get out here. You just can't get any good food in Omaha."

"Oh?"

"I asked someone I met there where to get good beef, and he recommended Arby's." He laughed knowingly.

"Well, we don't eat out much, actually," Randy answered with marked disinterest, "but Ross's is supposed to be good."

"I did hear there was a good Thai restaurant in St. Louis."

I couldn't keep completely silent. "If you want good Thai food, you should come to Stephenville," I interjected without explanation.

He didn't know what to make of that, so he went on with his culinary lecture. "That's the only thing I don't like about coming out here. You just can't get good food in the West."

No, I told myself, he didn't say you can't get good Tuscan cuisine in Cheyenne, Wyoming, or Hunan in Fredonia, Kansas, or any such reasonably specific generalization—he said No Good Food in The West. By which he no doubt meant everything west of Ithaca, New York—an improvement on the Manhattan view of the world, but not much.

"Have you thought of trying barbecue?" Mallory suggested with carefully measured sarcasm.

I licked the peach juice from the steel blade. Travis tossed a rock out over the precipice. Several seconds later the resonant swallowing sound it made when it hit the water echoed faintly from the mountainsides across the way. I had visions of myself as a character in a Flannery O'Connor story, pondered privately whether anyone would ever find the son-of-a-bitch if we tossed him and his exquisite hiking gear into the indifferent waters below, proving, of course, that Westerners and Southerners and their Texan combination are indeed as uncivilized as academics and artists and opera vultures think they are. And defensive about it, too. Must be the result of eating so much bad food.

Instead I folded the knife as the conversation dwindled more or less politely, and made a mental note to write an essay about this happening. The intruder led his son off to their week in the Western sky, probably wondering what in the hell was wrong with those people. He wasn't, after all, one of the stereotypical obnoxious Northeastern intellectuals. He had tried to be friendly. He was friendly. Why, then, did these people look at him that way? To him, a minor puzzlement, or maybe just a confirmation. To me, an epiphany.

ಌಃ

STUDY QUESTIONS

1. What are your expectations concerning the form in which a philosophical work should be written? Does it makes sense that a philosophical work opens with and is framed by a narration, a story? Can a story be true, not just in that it accurately reflects a series of events that actually happened, but in some philosophical way?

2. The author begins with a parody of the opening passage of Herman Melville's *Moby Dick*. *Moby Dick* opens with "Call me Ishmael," one of the most famous opening lines in American literature; *Learned Ignorance* begins with "Call me Bubba." Is the author just having a bit of fun or is there some significance to connecting his work with Melville's? In *Moby Dick* the narrator goes to sea as a way of "driving off the spleen, and regulating the circulation." The author of *Learned Ignorance* goes to the mountains. What do the sea and the mountains have in common as far as what they represent? How do they differ? What do mountains represent for the author of this book?

3. Nietzsche said that he loved better and mocked his enemies better in winter. The author speaks of "a baked-dry sizzling August in my soul." What does the August heat of Texas represent for the author?

4. The author distinguishes between the French *ennui* and the German *Angst*. What distinction is he making? Does it make sense?

5. What does Wyoming represent for the author? Why didn't he set his work in his home state of Texas? Is there something about getting away from home that helps us to clear our minds, rethink priorities? Does the Wyoming stereotype of Texans as city slickers surprise you?

6. Is the author being fair to the Cornell physics professor? When the physics professor says there is no good food in the West, is he stating a fact, revealing a prejudice, playing to his audience? What is his purpose in making this remark? Why does he think that the people he's talking to would be sympathetic to this statement?

7. The chapter ends, "To me, an epiphany." Based on the story recounted in chapter 1, what epiphany do you expect the author to articulate in chapter 2?

FOR FURTHER READING

Ehrlich, Gretel. *The Solace of Open Spaces.* New York: Penguin, 1986 [1985].

> Ehrlich's account of her experiences in Wyoming, written from the standpoint of someone who has chosen to make her home there. Her writing captures the feel of the land, its customs, and its people.

Trail to South Gap Lake, Snowy Range, Wyoming. Photo by author, 2003.

Two

MIND-FORG'D MANACLES

> That is why the prejudices of the individual, far more than his judgments, constitute the historical reality of his being.
>
> Hans-Georg Gadamer
> *Truth and Method*

> However willingly a person who has a strong opinion may admit the possibility that his opinion may be false, he ought to be moved by the consideration that, however true it may be, if it is not fully, frequently, and fearlessly discussed, it will be held as a dead dogma, not a living truth.
>
> John Stuart Mill
> *On Liberty*

Who cares? you ask. What difference does food in the West make? None, in the end. But ways of looking at the world do. For normal folks, I suppose the encounter would have been a minor irritant, on both sides. Forgive me if I can't resist looking for the universal in the particular, but I saw in this inconsequential interchange in the Medicine Bow Mountains the inner soul and farthest reaches of a powerful world view light up like the afternoon sky.

The well-meaning intruder began with the condescending explanation about Cornell and his "high-energy physics." That is no matter. What matters is that as soon as he knew we were professors he entered, for want of a better word, the intellectual's world, wherein certain basic assumptions are shared and adhered to as surely as the most unreconstructed Southern rednecks adhere to theirs. Why, you might ask, would he badmouth the food in our homeland as if he were making polite conversation? From the perspective of most American intellectuals, I might answer, food in New York, and even in the Northeast generally, is acceptably good, and of course in places like Berkeley and Seattle the Western Easterners, as Larry McMurtry calls them, make sufficiently elevated cuisine; but food elsewhere in the United States is rarely digestible. Since we were professors, we obviously were teaching in Omaha, Nebraska, and Stephenville, Texas, only because we weren't able to get jobs in New York or Boston or Amherst or Ithaca. He wasn't running us down; he was sympathizing with us. Had we really been members of his world—and, of course, at various times and in various ways, we all had had at least one foot in it—we would have no doubt said, "Yeah, the food is bad, but we get by."

How else could a person—not a person trying to be obnoxious, but a friendly person—assume that he could engage in polite conversation by running down the places where we lived, the places, not the universities, we called home? It is just that—sheer assumption—or, to use the more derogatory word, sheer prejudice. Yes, Virginia, intellectuals have prejudices, too.

Had the conversation gone on, had we been cooperative, we would have no doubt been asked to nod in knowing agreement when the intruder commented on the lack of good opera or musicals or bookstores in Nebraska and Texas. He would have surely said something about how tough it would be to put up with racism in the South. Southerners, he would have said with an absolutely straight face to people who had just told him they were Southerners, are so racist. Eventually, he would have commented on how difficult my wife, who had just told him she had grown up in Texas, must find it to try to teach correct English to kids who grow up in Texas. Long before then, I would have said something in incorrect English about him and the horse he rode in on, but you get the idea.

Am I defensively imagining this? If my memory hasn't been totally corrupted by too much barbecue and too many calf fries, I can recall countless episodes, spanning the several decades of my adult life, in which reference to my homeland elicited just such remarks—and usually as polite conversation-making, not as intentional provocation. And, if I may drop some of the anti-Yankee flavor of this argument, let me take an important turn here. These assumptions, notwithstanding that one of them is often knee-jerk New York-ophilia, are not limited to the Northeast or to the prejudices of Northeastern intellectuals against Southerners and Westerners; they are intellectual, not regional, prejudices. They are as unquestioningly rampant at my alma mater, the University of Texas at Austin, as they are at Cornell. And it's not just Northeastern intellectuals who've been so unlucky as to land in Austin, Texas, but Texans and Southerners and Midwesterners and all sorts of people from all sorts of places who share in this one thing, a world view that is made up largely of unexamined intellectual dogma. Yes, there are even Southern intellectuals who learn the tap dance of talking about racism in the South as if nothing has changed in the last forty years and praising the supposed absence of it in the Great Cities of the Great Northeast—even Southerners and Westerners and Midwesterners who kowtow to New York's high culture and regurgitate derisive litanies about Southern and Western and Midwestern boorishness with all the thoughtfulness that their spinal cortexes can muster.

And, in fact, it's not just a prejudice against certain regions of this country that defines the core of intellectual prejudices, although, I admit, that version of intellectual prejudice is particularly galling to me. For American intellectuals the defining value is a rejection of their own rootedness—and the assumption of moral superiority that comes from hovering above the provincial attachments of their unenlightened countrymen. For my generation that rejection manifested itself in an idolatry of New York and the East Coast, and possibly of the West Coast to a lesser degree, and certainly an idolatry of things European, especially French. Nowadays it often manifests itself in a full-blown xenophilia—the more foreign, the better. Of course, this xenophilia often leads to a staunch defense of "indigenous peoples" in foreign lands against the tide of capitalist "globalization," even though it champions a staunch rejection of all rootedness for Americans, at least for white Americans. In many quarters now, the prejudice against the Southern and Western and Midwestern American regions that defined the coming of age for my generation has turned into a full-blown anti-Americanism, and the New York-ophilia and Francophilia and Europhilia of my generation has evolved into a fetishism of the foreign that would have made Gauguin envious. Of course, the mandatory denunciation of Eurocentrism and the heartfelt defense of indigenous peoples don't get in the way of planning that next trip to Paris or London. Generally speaking, that is, the regional prejudices of my generation, contradictions be damned, exist side by side with the more virulent xenophilia of the current intellectual world. And I should hasten to say that although this book is about a way of looking at the world, not about politics, the current form of intellectual prejudice is often stridently political.

And, before you get on your high horse, let me say the issue here is not whether or not these prejudices are borne out by reality. I'll be happy to argue in a moment that many are not; not to mention that many of the ones that are—the paucity of sushi in small Southern towns, for instance—are downright trivial. But I'm talking here about the manner in which they are acquired and adhered to. They are acquired in precisely the same manner as lowbrow prejudices, through the habitual associations and identifications with a particular community. They are values that one simply must have in order to be "cultured," in order to belong to the community of intellectuals. Old-fashioned rednecks—and it is something of an intellectual prejudice to think they still exist—drink beer, hate blacks and Catholics, love Hank Williams and hate opera of the non-Nashville variety, because everyone they grew up with, live with, associate with, and identify with does. These values are their membership card to their community, and their ticket to feeling superior. They are called prejudices, not because they are wrong or backward or uncultured, but because they are acquired and applied without examination and reflection. They are habits, reflex actions, judgments "prior" to examination—in fact, not really judgments at all.

The intellectuals I am talking about reject their childhood prejudices, all of the localized religious and ethnic and regional values that they grew up with, in favor of the more worldly point of view. But, in fact, they simply trade in one set of unreflective prejudices for another—perhaps more sophisticated, sometimes socially, even morally, superior, but nonetheless prejudice. They mouth these new prejudices among their own kind with the same visceral, grunting thoughtlessness that old-fashioned white bigots habitually mouthed the word "nigger" among their own kind. Their prejudices are a membership card, too. That's why prejudice-free intellectuals are free to make sweeping generalizations about whole regions of the country with only the slightest of a basis. Sure, the intruder of my story had eaten a few meals in Omaha and Laramie. Most old-fashioned white bigots had known more than a few blacks and at least a carpetbagger or two. Both are creatures of sheer prejudice. If Mel Brooks were to take on this kind of bigotry, there would be a line in the movie in which someone would say, "My God, the new sheriff is a redneck. I heard him say 'y'all.' And he owns a gun and eats red meat."

But doesn't one expect intellectuals to use their minds and not their spinal reflexes to come to opinions? Doesn't becoming an intellectual mean overcoming prejudice? There's the rub, my dear intellectual readers. One of the most cherished intellectual prejudices is the firm conviction that intellectuals, having overcome some prejudices, are free of all prejudice. That is what is so infuriating. Intellectuals, even of the high-energy-physics variety, are supposedly free of prejudice, when in fact there are hordes of intellectuals who are nothing but carefully cultivated bundles of intellectual bigotry. Everyone knows rednecks are prejudiced, and damn proud of it, as the saying goes. Add, then, hypocrisy to prejudice. And, as another saying goes, intellectuals are people who ought, if they were truly as educated as they would have us believe, to know better.

In "Life Without Principle," Thoreau said it well:

> I hardly know an *intellectual* man, even, who is so broad and truly liberal that you can think aloud in his society. Most with whom you endeavor to talk soon come to a stand against some institution in which they appear to hold stock,—that is, some particular, not universal, way of viewing things. They will continually thrust their own low roof, with its narrow skylight, between you and the sky, when it is the unobstructed heavens you would view. Get out of the way with your cobwebs, wash your windows, I say!

And yet there is even a problem with Thoreau's demand for the purely universal. To be that pure one would have to be Saint Henry (as John Graves, an intellectual backwoodsman from Texas, calls him), almost, as it were, inhuman in one's universality. No one ever looks at things from the purely universal point of view, although we can certainly be more or less universal in our view. No one ever views the unobstructed heavens. There is always, to stick to Thoreau's metaphor, a low roof of some kind or other, and always a window gathering cobwebs through which we must take our view. But my complaint—and perhaps Thoreau accomplishes the same thing by way of the purist's corrective—is that intellectuals fail to recognize that they, too, have their low roof. They think that they view the unobstructed sky, when in fact they are looking through the sooty windows of New York, and from bended knee, to boot.

And I hasten to say that the postmodernist version of the intellectual's transcendence of prejudice, the great revelation that everything is prejudice, that everything is a construct in language based on ideology, offers a new twist on the same hypocrisy. Knowing that everything is prejudice magically elevates the intellectual above the ordinary humans who have these prejudices, for, after all, the revelation that there is no truth, that everything is a construct in language, must be unqualifiedly true, must not itself be nothing more than an ideologically motivated construct designed to promote the material interests of its proponents. The truth is, the current strain of postmodernism is the most dogmatically rigid and the most hypocritical version of cosmopolitan intellectualism to come on the scene in my lifetime. When I look back, entry to the intellectual world for my generation now seems fairly simple; to gain acceptance to the current intellectual community, it is de rigeur that one denounce Eurocentrism, colonialism, American imperialism, capitalist globalization, xenophobia, homophobia, Coca-Cola, Sam Walton, Ernest Hemingway, essentialism, guns, capital punishment, structural racism, racial profiling, the Israeli "occupation" of Palestine, SUVs, Western religions, linguistic violence against women, the binary opposition of good and evil—to name only a few. And of course you still have to denounce small-town Southerners and Midwesterners and Westerners as gun-totin' racists. Never mind the contradictions of denouncing Eurocentrism and Southern small-town rootedness as provincial bigotry while embracing the resurgence of "indigenous" cultures in a "postcolonial" world, no matter how essentialist or binary or bigoted these cultures might be. Never mind the contradiction of treating the binary opposition of good and evil as the greatest evil in the world. The current cosmopolitan intellectual is still a bundle of intellectual bigotry, and still a hypocrite.

Well, if everyone's got it, what then do we make of prejudice? To prejudge, if you will, is human. We are always, intellectuals and rednecks alike, particular in our views, and yet prejudice has a positive function, too: we see what we see, understand what we understand, in virtue of our prejudices, on account of some sort of window, with or without cobwebs, beneath some sort of low roof. To say that everyone's got it is not to say that everything is prejudice; to say that understanding is finite or that it must be from a particular perspective is not to say there is no understanding. To say, as Socrates does in the *Symposium*, that humans inhabit the realm between ignorance and wisdom is not to say that there is no truth.

It is the calling of the intellectual, then—and here I must abandon the ironic use of the term and distinguish between the genuine and the pseudo variety—not to do away with all prejudices, but to examine them ruthlessly, continuously, without end. It is the calling of the genuine intellectual to strive for a kind of transparency on his or her own prejudices and cast them up against the strongest challenges, the finest foes, the hardest questions. Yes, maybe traditional Veal Cordon Bleu is better than grits—although a lot of the faddish "fusion" cuisine does not come close, by the most objective of standards, to, say, barbecued brisket at Angelo's in Fort Worth—but the pseudo-intellectual who simply trades in one set of prejudices for another, and nary an examination of them attempts, is far more worthy of our scorn than the most uncouth cracker who ever lived.

The first principle of the life of the mind, the first prejudice, if you will, that ought to be ingrained into the intellectual's very character, is the principle of self-questioning. Was Socrates, the great self-questioner, an intellectual? I recall that Callicles accuses Socrates of boorishness because of his unrelenting insistence upon questioning any and every opinion, especially those of the great sophists, the pseudo-intellectuals of his day. Grown men, ol' boy (that's with a British, not a Texas, accent), just don't carry on in such a manner. The word that Callicles uses is *agroikia*—it means coarseness or rusticity. An *agroikos* is someone who is unsophisticated, rude, or, more literally, someone from the country. From the point of view of sophistic cultivation, Socrates, ugly of face, ragged of clothes, short on refined manners and polite conversation, was a hick. I'm simplifying a monumental clash in world views here, but not overly so. Was Socrates, then, something of a redneck? No wonder that it has become a popular retort in certain intellectual circles to assert that Socrates has been somewhat "overrated."

City slickers and country rustics aside, I am calling for a revival of the paradoxical distinction between the sophists who were unwise for thinking they were truly wise and the lover of wisdom who was wise because he knew he was not. And, since even thoughtfully earned ideas can degenerate through force of habit and weakness of character into sheer snobbery, vain prejudice, mock superiority, even a Socrates can never rest finally assured that he need never again question himself. Socratic wisdom is self-questioning, ruthlessly on the prowl for sophistic pretense, but ultimately humble, and never self-assured.

And, here's the catch: the intellectual life, the Socratic life, is no leisurely stroll in the park. In the *Meno*, after a good deal of playful mythologizing on the part of Socrates and a rather sophisticated attempt to abandon the process of questioning by Meno, Socrates says:

> Some things I have said of which I am not altogether confident. But that we shall be better and braver and less helpless if we think that we ought to inquire than we should have been if we indulged in the idle fancy that there was no knowing and no use in seeking to know what we do not know—that is a theme upon which I am ready to fight, in word and deed, to the utmost of my power.

Why does it take a fight? Because coming to terms with your own prejudices, coming up against the limits of your own understanding, is a painful, difficult experience—and, taking Socrates as example, it is not a one-time, but a life-time experience.

It was Aristotle, not Plato, who preached that *scholē*, leisure, was essential to philosophy, and who characterized the intellectual virtue of *sophia*, wisdom, without reference to the moral virtue of courage. The Socratic life is "leisurely" in the sense that a life of loving wisdom is valued for its own sake, but remember that Socrates tells the jury in the *Apology* that his philosophical calling did not allow him the *scholē* to take part in public life or to look after his private affairs. Socrates is not a leisurely spokesman for Plato, but a philosophical hero, courageous in the face of ultimate perplexity and ultimately in the face of death. For Socrates philosophy is urgent, essential, but ultimately "aporetic." There is an irreducible *aporia*, an irreducible "difficulty" or "perplexity," and the truth that is available to us, the wisdom that is available to us, if it is to be gotten at at all, will be gotten at through the insightful, but never fully controlled, process of questioning and self-questioning. The intellectual must be intellectually courageous.

The second principle of the life of the mind is the recognition that no one, with the possible exception of Saint Henry, is a creature of universal mind—not the traditional scholar who sees prejudice as an evil to be overcome or the postmodernist who has been liberated from prejudice by declaring that everything, and therefore nothing, is prejudice. It's not just the view that's particular, but the viewer. One of the things the universal mind should recognize is that mortal humans are particular creatures, too. They come from somewhere, they have homes and mothers and fathers; they have desires and fears; they all speak a particular form of a particular language. Recall, if you will, that the great redneck intellectual I am harkening back to was highly and consciously impure in this respect. He even refused to leave his homeland on pain of death by execution, because, as he explained, he could not carry on as a lover of wisdom in another land. I guess, then, that the greatest intellectual hero of Western civilization was not a citizen of the world, but something of a provincial who wasn't smart enough to figure out that a philosopher belongs to his ideas, and not to a piece of rock and soil. No purist, he, except in his dedication to the life of questioning. To solve that old hypothetical puzzle, if Socrates were to come back today and the United States were to adopt a pure democracy similar to Athens's, he would eventually be put to death again, and again intellectuals would be among the chief accusers; but I am sure he would eat chicken-fried steak or Chincoteague oysters or whatever food his homeland served up as long as we let him live.

We are all born into particular pieces of earth and custom, not simply born into "the world." We always find ourselves already having views and habits and values and likes and dislikes and ways of thinking; we never have the opportunity to make ourselves from the ground up out of pure reason. This is what Martin Heidegger meant by his term *Geworfenheit*, "thrown-ness"—that we always are in the position of finding ourselves already thrown into the world with traits and dispositions and a rock-hard past. We can be more or less reasonable, rational, intellectual, thoughtful, insightful, in how we deal with our lot in life at any given moment; we can achieve varying degrees of transparency with respect to our own particularity, what Heidegger called "facticity"; but if we would be truthful with ourselves, we must recognize that we are always already thrown into ineluctable particularities, which we can work with, transform, but never wholly transcend. It makes all the difference in the world how we seize upon the possibilities that are inherent in these particularities, but there is always a fatefulness to life that no amount of self-cultivation can erase. That Heidegger, at least for a crucial period of his life, let his sense of rootedness lead to bigoted nationalism rather than humility in the face of human finitude doesn't mean that we should ignore the insight he had.

The postmodernist perversion of Heidegger's insight, I should also say, seems to embrace it but ultimately flees in the face of it. Heidegger, the Derrideans used to say, went to the edge of the abyss but wasn't willing to look into it. The postmodernist intellectual goes to the edge of the abyss, then jumps into it. It's oh-so-liberating to recognize that all human views are nothing but the expression of the viewers' "situatedness," that no one can get beyond this situatedness to know another age or another person or another culture, that all of us construct our own narratives to further our own interest. Because they are the enlightened ones who know this, postmodernist intellectuals are somehow liberated from it, somehow free to reject their own situatedness, rather than face the more difficult task of finding genuine possibility in it. They recover their innocence by condemning and rejecting their own rootedness. By contrast, if being situated historically and culturally *makes possible* whatever understanding will be available to us, which is Heidegger's position, then we have to come to terms with, we have to appropriate, our own situatedness, our own origins and roots.

Let me offer something of a grand scheme of things intellectual. The path of the intellectual life, as I see it, has three stages, not perfectly uniform, but identifiable nonetheless.

The first is the stage of naive prejudice. We all begin with values that our childhoods give to us, even if they come in large degree from childhood rebellion. Some folks who grow up in intellectual families and environs like to think they have skipped this stage, but they haven't. At best, they've collapsed the first and second stages, not to my mind a happy precocity. By and large, though, the childhood experience is localized, limited, heavy on osmosis, and less than light on true inquiry.

The second stage, the cosmopolitan, is the rejection of the first. We recognize, perhaps through the thoughtful encounter with different values or perhaps through the influence of an intellectual model whose values seem somehow superior, that our childhood values are limited. We reject home and region, sometimes family and childhood friends, local dialect and accent, home cooking, country or rock-and-roll or whatever form of unintellectual music we liked as teenagers or college students; we become worldly, cultured, intellectual. For my generation that meant eating Continental cuisine, talking the Queen's English, and listening to Mozart or Bach or jazz or, at the very least, "folk music." Nowadays, as I've said, the transition to the cosmopolitan stage requires a more extreme rejection of roots. If there's a bit of xenophobia in stage one, stage two requires a xenophilia that is just as unreflective.

And, finally, there is the third stage, the one the pseudo-intellectual never reaches—I would call it the phronetic, from the Aristotelean concept of *phronēsis*, even though Aristotle himself applied the concept only to the practical realm and not to the life of the mind. More to the point, I'm thinking of the way Hans-Georg Gadamer develops Aristotle's concept of *phronēsis*—Gadamer might call this stage the "hermeneutic." It has to do with the recognition of the limits of cosmopolitanism. For those who got into the cosmopolitan stage through the application of Socratic self-examination to their original prejudices, it has to do with the rekindling of that Socratic spirit and its application to newly adopted prejudices. Often it has to do with homecomings, if not physically then spiritually, with coming to terms with one's home, with parents and personal limitations and with mortality. It has to do with accepting one's fatefulness, with "thrown-ness," with "facticity." It has to do with a broader and deeper view of things human, a more difficult one, because the answers are harder to come by.

There are no new clubs with complete sets of prejudices ready-made, just damn hard questions of right and wrong, of noble and ignoble, of beautiful and base, of truth and pretense—and they all rise up out of, and must be answered in terms of, damn particular windows under damn low roofs.

The windows and roofs that Wendell Berry came to terms with were shaped by his childhood in Kentucky. When he decided to leave New York University to move home to Kentucky to write, an elder colleague tried to persuade him, for his own good, that he should stay among the writers and editors and publishers of New York. The conversation made a lasting impression on Berry, and he wrote about it with great insight:

> But what keeps me thinking of that conversation is the feeling that it was a confrontation of two radically different minds, and that it was a confrontation with significant historical overtones.
>
> I do not pretend to know all about the other man's mind, but it was clear that he wished to speak to me as a representative of the literary world—the world he assumed that I aspired to above all others. His argument was based on the belief that once one has attained the metropolis, the literary capital, the worth of one's origins was canceled out; there simply could be nothing *worth* going back to. What lay behind one had ceased to be a part of life, and had become "subject matter." And there was the belief, long honored among American intellectuals and artists and writers, that a place such as I came from could be returned to only at the price of intellectual death; cut off from the cultural springs of the metropolis, the American countryside is Circe and Mammon. Finally, there was the assumption that the life of the metropolis is *the* experience, the *modern* experience, and that the life of the rural towns, the farms, the wilderness places is not only irrelevant to our time, but archaic as well because unknown or unconsidered by the people who really matter—that is, the urban intellectuals.

Intellectuals don't have to go back home, but Wendell Berry has proven that they certainly can. What they do have to do is come to terms with back home and, if they don't follow Berry's path literally, with making a home wherever they are. Forgive me for what will undoubtedly sound like an oxymoron to some ears, but the counter-concept to the cosmopolitan intellectual is the rooted intellectual. The phronetic intellectual is rooted in particular earth, in the finite locations and encumbrances of human life such as it is in its totality. Phronetic intellectuals may not go back home, but they aren't afraid to use the word—and it doesn't refer to a university.

Travel, living abroad, learning languages, reading wide and far—these can be important experiences that provide an opportunity to broaden horizons, horizons that open up the necessary room to reflect, to consider, to gain perspective, to question. One of the things that this perspective helps us to understand is just how crippling human origins—families, places, localized history, languages—

can be. It can also help us to see that the origins that cripple are the same origins that enable; it can also lead to a deeper identity with those origins. But let's be honest: sometimes travel and living abroad lead to snobbery, rather than reflection, and it is nothing but self-serving prejudice to assume that someone who has lived abroad is automatically morally and intellectually superior to someone who has never left home.

For the rootless intellectual there is an ideal—or at least it seems like an ideal—of a life of liberated intellect, including liberation from the embarrassing accidents of birth and childhood, even if that liberation requires an idolatrous worship of the rootedness of other cultures. In this rejection of one's own roots, the world of the intellectual has remained constant—from the itinerant sophists of Socrates' times to the rootless professors of the Modern Language Association and other bastions of contemporary academic orthodoxy. Both the intellectual cosmopolitanism of my generation, which harkens back to the scholarly freedom of Aristotle's *bios thēoretikos*, and the transcending relativism that frees the postmodernist intellectual for self-righteous pseudo-*engagement*, which harkens back to Thrasymachus' and Callicles' deconstruction of conventional morality in favor of a persuasive power that is the only truth that matters—both of these embrace an ideal of liberation.

But if the liberating vision of the intellectual life severs all connections with the common humanity of one's own people, it is nothing more than the latest model of the Glass Bead Game, and the vision it bestows is an abstraction, and worse, an abstraction posing as the concrete whole. Intellect cannot soar without earthly roots, but, more to the point, its soaring, its contact with infinity, must give a greater vision of humanity's finite side, of the encompassing current of everydayness—of family, community, custom, and such—out of which the flashes of artistic and philosophical vision, the moments of courage and character, all rise up. That is just as true for white Southern boys as it is for the villagers in India or Africa trying to preserve their local customs and resist the temptations of Coca-Cola and Big Macs.

Some of my readers will know that I take the term "everydayness" from Heidegger. Many of his detractors—and even some of his defenders—fail to see how inextricably Heidegger understood "authenticity" in relation to everydayness, and not just as an escape from it. Everydayness lulls us into a kind of unthinking intellectual sleepiness, but the answer is not to escape it. A sentence in *Being and Time* that is much overlooked describes everydayness this way: "In it, out of it, and against it, all genuine understanding, interpreting, and communicating, all re-discovering and appropriating anew, are performed." Perhaps the Heidegger of 1933 didn't fully appreciate that sentence; but there it is. I don't think anyone fully understands it even now, but that would lead us far afield.

There's no doubt that intellectual folks, of the philosophical, artistic, or whatever kind, often fail miserably at communal participation, fail to live the good everyday life, often wreck their families, mess up their tax forms, and generally use, abuse, fold, spindle, and mutilate their friends, colleagues, and compatriots. Sometimes intellectuals just aren't capable of being intellectuals and living the good everyday life at the same time—even if that might be an ideal worth holding up to oneself—but they ought to have a vision of it, they ought to toil in their own failure as full human beings, to try to understand why they and all of us always fail in one way or another, how we succeed when we do, and how it all fits together. If their lack of competence at mundane life, if their globe-hopping homelessness, their ethereal unattachment, is motivated by the needs of their vision of humanity's relation to heaven and earth, that is one thing; if it is motivated by the need to feel superior, it is another. Intellectuals may not even find a home, much less go back home; but if their homelessness doesn't at least cast a tragic light on the meaning of home, they are escape artists, not visionaries. I'm thinking now of Hemingway's troubled search for "a clean, well-lighted place," of his inability to settle in one when it did present itself, and of how powerfully we can understand the meaning of belonging, or having a home, through Hemingway's tragically homeless *pathos*.

There's a certain sense in which the intellectual is never simply "at home" anywhere. Intellectuals, Hamlet-like, never simply act, and they never simply belong—in my mind, that makes for a great sadness in some of our greatest writers and a snobbish arrogance in some of our greatest pretenders to greatness. Reflection opens up a space, calls attachments into question, but in that space the sense of hearth and home can light up. Intellectuals reflect and call into question, and they may out-and-out reject certain kinds of belonging, certain kinds of home, for a better kind of belonging; but eventually they must come to let human belonging be, even if their vision may never let them quite be. They may not fully belong, but if they abhor the idea of belonging, the idea of home, they damn well better stay out of the Medicine Bow Mountains.

No, you don't have to move back home. Sometimes there are good reasons to leave and never come back. My parents moved from Louisiana to Texas or home wouldn't be home for me, or it wouldn't be where it is. Human history is a history of migrations; American history is the accelerated version, picking up stakes, setting out to start anew, putting down new roots. My ancestors, as far as I know them, sailed off with good reason from all sorts of misery and oppression, and so did the ancestors of most Americans. And they didn't stop at the Atlantic seaboard either. I wonder, though, if American history isn't so exaggerated in its spirit of frontier freedom that the westward-ho flight has all but obliterated the deeper sense of home, of belonging. This piece of land is sort of home until I mess it up, and then I move on to the next one. Fill it up, use it up—there's so much of it. Maybe we haven't quite learned to make do, to caretake, to truly be at home—intellectuals, cowboys, CEOs, and all.

But after nine years of mind-expanding misery in the Great Northeast, I did go back home, because, as Dave Hickey, a fellow redneck intellectual, put it, "Home, in the twentieth century, is less where the heart is than where you understand the sons-of-bitches." A variation on an old theme, but a good one. Actually, I went back to Texas, not to Houston, but for reasons I've elaborated elsewhere—it's home.

And at times I feel pretty well at home in my everydayness. There are moments on the Brazos River in early spring when the sand bass are running—my very intellect is focused on the sinking jig head, the feel of the bottom as I work it gently in, the barely detectable tap of the sluggishly cold, only half-hungry fish. The sun that warms my back is the same sun I have always known. My fishing buddy—known far and wide simply as Outdoor Man—has never left the state of Texas, but he can find a deep hole full of fish in a ten-mile stretch of river that we haven't fished since last fall . . . second-nature, habit or talent, being at home on a meandering river. In his own way, he is as reflective—and more open-minded—than many of the world-traveled professors I have known.

I can get barbecued beef brisket without driving 1,500 miles, I can slip deep into elongated pronunciations and still be understood, I don't have to use my middle finger as a means of ordinary communication, unless I really want to get into a fight. But it's not, I guess, just that I'm more at home back home—and I certainly am—but that I wish to live out a statement. I wish to live out the apparent contradiction of being a Texan and an intellectual, a hunter and fisherman who studies Heidegger and Plato, a cowboy and a high-minded literary type. I don't intend to apologize, either to anti-intellectual earth-huggers or to anti-earth literati, for my mix of earthly roots, earthy living, and high literary and philosophical purpose. Rooted intellectuals, wherever they're from, shouldn't have to apologize, either to their homefolks for their education or to the members of the intellectual community for their origins or their accents or their sense of belonging.

When I sent off an essay on the subject of cosmopolitan prejudice to a friend who was then working as the book review editor of the *Baltimore Sun*, he wrote back with these remarks: "I like to think that I've put (most of) it behind me; at least, I hope I have; I no longer feel the need to deny my somewhat humble upbringing in Upstate New York (where I used to guzzle quart bottles of beer in the Volunteer Fire Station)." The time for apologies, even for defensiveness, is past, for Southerners and Upstate New Yorkers and for all people who come from places they call home, whether it's Houston or Brooklyn. A bit of offensiveness, however, would still be in order—an apology in the Socratic sense of the word. Think of this book, then, as an *apologia* of the rooted intellectual against a jury of uprooted intellects. And perhaps, indeed, my offensive defense may lead to a good deal of social hemlock—I happily lift my cup. If I exaggerate the truth of the province, it is because the greatest danger of the intellectual life is the temptation of rootless cosmopolitanism. Rooted intellectuals of the world, never apologize, never explain!

STUDY QUESTIONS

1. The author talks about looking for the universal in the particular. What does that mean? Is it possible? This comment is routinely made about literature—does it make sense for philosophy? Is a reflection on intellectual culture that stems from an encounter with one Cornell professor a hasty generalization based on a sample of one—or is there something else going on here?

2. The experience recounted in chapter 1 seems to be, as the author portrays it, primarily about a regional prejudice of the East Coast or Northeast against the West. And yet the author says in chapter 2 that he is talking about intellectual not just regional prejudice. What does that mean? What is his basis for making that claim?

3. According to the author the defining value for American intellectuals is a rejection of their own rootedness. What is positive about rootedness and what is negative? Why does the author think that acknowledging your own rootedness is important?

4. The author refers to the "New York–ophilia" and "Francophilia" that was expected of his generation of intellectuals, but goes on to say that current intellectual culture has embraced a "full-blown xenophilia." What does "xenophilia" mean? How does the author argue that, at its core, this xenophilia is a new form of the same phenomenon he experienced coming of age in the intellectual world? The word "xenophobia" is much more prevalent in contemporary discussions than "xenophilia." Why?

5. The author states that the issue is not whether the prejudices he is discussing are borne out by reality, but whether they are held, however true, in the manner of a prejudice. What makes a prejudice a prejudice? Can there be true prejudices? Is there something negative about holding a true belief in the manner of a prejudice? Or is the truth of the belief, whether it's held as a prejudice or not, the most important thing?

6. The Enlightenment project was, in effect, the eradication of all prejudice, and, in large part, the author's point seems to be an attack on a certain kind of prejudice. And yet he says that prejudice is something that humans can never get rid of: "To pre-judge, if you will, is human." What stance toward prejudice is the author advocating and why? Is there a difference, as the author maintains, between the claim that prejudice cannot be eradicated, that everyone has prejudices and is defined by them, and the claim that everything is prejudice, that, in effect, there is no truth? Does the author succeed in staking out a middle ground be-

tween the Enlightenment rejection of all prejudice and the frightening prospect that all of our beliefs are nothing but prejudices?

7. Is the author rejecting the intellectual life? Does he see himself as an intellectual? Does the distinction he eventually makes between the genuine intellectual and the pseudo-intellectual make sense? Why didn't he make that distinction earlier?

8. The author claims that the distinction he is making between "cosmopolitan pseudo-intellectuals" and "rooted intellectuals" is perennial, that the sophists of Socrates' time were "the pseudo-intellectuals of his day." How does he make the case for that connection? Looking back at Socrates from the standpoint of what we now call Platonism, we associate Socrates with a rejection of the particular and the temporal in favor of the unchanging and eternal forms. On what basis does the author align Socrates with the affirmation of rootedness?

9. The author says, "The intellectual must be intellectually courageous." Do intellectuals need courage? In leading a life of the mind, what is to fear?

10. The author connects Martin Heidegger's concept of "thrown-ness" (*Geworfenheit*)—"that we always are in the position of finding ourselves already thrown into the world with traits and dispositions and a rock-hard past"—with his concept of "rootedness." That suggests that rootedness is a spatial metaphor for something that is as much temporal as spatial. In what sense is rootedness a result of the temporal nature of human existence?

11. The author discusses three stages in an intellectual's life: the stage of naive prejudice, the cosmopolitan stage, and the "phronetic" stage. What distinguishes these stages? What accounts for the transition from one to the next? In the *Nicomachean Ethics* Aristotle talks about three kinds of lives: the hedonistic, political, and contemplative. In the *Republic* Plato has Socrates outline a descending progression of cities and souls: aristocratic, timocratic, oligarchic, democratic, and tyrannical. How do these theoretical frameworks help us understand the kinds of lives we live? Does their theoretical simplicity do justice to the uniqueness of our individual lives?

FOR FURTHER READING

Aristotle. *Nicomachean Ethics*. Translated by Martin Ostwald. Upper Saddle River, NJ: Prentice Hall, 1999 [1962].

> In Book IV Aristotle talks about the concept of *phronēsis*—practical wisdom or good judgment—from which I derive the term "phronetic."

Berry, Wendell. *Recollected Essays 1965-1980*. San Francisco: North Point Press, 1981.

———. *Standing by Words: Essays by Wendell Berry*. San Francisco: North Point Press, 1983.

Heidegger, Martin. "Memorial Address." In *Discourse on Thinking*. Translated by John M. Anderson and E. Hans Freund. New York: Harper, 1969.

Because it was a public address given in his hometown, this is perhaps the most accessible work by Heidegger in print. In it, he attributes the rootlessness of the modern world to the dominance of a technological relation to the world, grounded in what he calls calculative thinking; and he engages in a reflection on the importance of rootedness (*Bodenständigkeit*).

Plato. *Apology*. In *Plato: Complete Works*. Edited by John M. Cooper. Indianapolis: Hackett, 1997.

Socrates' defense of his attachment to his home city of Athens as a gadfly who wakes up his fellow citizens to the care of their souls—and his choice of death over exile.

View of Snowy Range from Mirror Lake area. Photo by author, 2003.

Three

RUNNING AND BEING

> Bold, overhanging, and as it were threatening rocks; clouds piled up in the sky, moving with lightning flashes and thunder peals; volcanoes in all their violence of destruction; hurricanes with their track of devastation; the boundless ocean in a state of tumult; the lofty waterfall of a mighty river, and such like—these exhibit our faculty of resistance as insignificantly small in comparison with their might. But the sight of them is the more attractive, the more fearful it is, provided only that we are in security; and we willingly call these objects sublime, because they raise the energies of the soul above their accustomed height and discover in us a faculty of resistance of a quite different kind, which gives us courage to measure ourselves against the apparent almightiness of nature.
>
> Immanuel Kant
> *Critique of Judgment*

"Have you ever seen so damn much sky?"

"Maybe in West Texas."

We were running cautiously, both more than aware that the air at 8,000 feet was bound to be less generous to the lungs than what we were used to. It was mid-afternoon, and as we approached Wana Clayton's ranch house the afternoon rain showers rumbled off behind our right shoulders, out over the white-tipped mountain peaks in the distance. The Snowy Range peaks were, according to the map, about fifteen miles away, but glitter-sharp to the eye, photographic, *there*. There, right there, beyond the sloping pastures and the half-green, half-brown foothills, permanent, shrine-like. It was impossible not to glance back over our shoulders every few strides.

"Can you imagine what it would be like to grow up here, looking at those mountains every day? It's got to make a difference in how you look at things."

The dirt road climbed up past the house. I looked at my watch. "Must be a half-a-mile already. I don't feel any different yet."

Randy shrugged agreement, then stepped up the pace. The road turned sharply toward the highway and climbed steeply. We were seeing ourselves from the inside out, from solitary heartbeats and private memories and the twinges of old sports injuries; but also from the outside in, looking upon ourselves from the outside's vastness, two silent silhouettes against the slope of so much land and sky, flickering across the hillside. We had run our modest four, five, maybe six miles in Buffalo . . . Omaha . . . Stephenville. Neither of us a fanatical runner, but both of us hopeless jocks manqué—well, he was manqué by choice and I by ability. He a silky, deceptive natural athlete who, in his senior year, gave up college baseball at Oklahoma University and a good shot at the pros to study philosophy; I a hacker, with a little savvy and not much silk—an old friendship ritual that went back to our graduate-school days in Buffalo . . . .

We leaped in stride across the cattle guard and onto the tiny two-lane highway, then turned abruptly back to the left, past the full-size postal service box that Wana Clayton used for her mail.

"I guess they want to make sure they don't have to drive into Laramie for big packages," I mused.

"Guess not."

We were still chugging uphill, climbing, it seemed, one step at a time on up into the mountains. The sun was bright, the air crisp. We breathed deeper, feeling our lungs, expecting to suddenly find ourselves gasping in the thin air. We picked up the pace again, but still cautiously. Now off to our left, the Snowy Range danced in and out of the scattered rain clouds and the pristine sun of a Wyoming summer. If we gasped for air, it was out of uncomplicated awe. An amazing alchemy of space and time, that we'd converged from faraway places like Omaha, Nebraska, and Stephenville, Texas, on this unpretentious but ferociously beautiful expanse of American earth and sky. We ticked off footsteps, inwardly measured heartbeats, fatigue, the feel of hill and air and open expansiveness, the meditative athlete's way of taking a measure of the terrain, of experiencing the newness, of consecrating the experience with sweat and exertion and bodily contemplation.

"I never understood what Sheehan was talking about before. Now, this is running and being."

"Is that being as in the being of beings or as in string beings?"

"You're the one who wrote an article on play and the absurd. If running uphill at 8,000 feet on the first day you've arrived isn't absurd, I don't know what is."

"It's absurd, but we're doing it *as if* it mattered."

"Sixteen minutes—I'd say that's a couple of miles. Do we run all the way to Centennial and call the wives to pick us up or double back now?"

As we made a casual U-turn, a truck pulling a cattle trailer hummed by, the only vehicle we'd seen. The driver nodded. We hit a full stride barreling downhill.

"I'm not exactly fresh as a daisy, but I don't really feel the altitude."

"Not really."

I pushed myself into a three-quarters sprint, and Randy eased alongside. "Let's keep this up to the mailbox."

"How's your knee?" Randy queried.

"I can feel it, but it doesn't really hurt. Hell, we're in the goddamn Medicine Bow Mountains in Wyoming. If I have to take a few days off when I get home, so what."

It had taken me nine years to figure out how to move back to Texas, and I had no intention of ever leaving again, but if I ever did, I could see living out my days here—in a big two-story log house up against a backdrop of fearless mountains, in nippy August days and near-freezing August nights, among solid people who do what they do . . . but not too many of them. What would I write if I lived here . . . if I had grown up here?

Randy and I had shared years of idolizing the Rocky Mountains. It seemed like all of my best friends had had that deep-heart yearning for expansiveness, for high crests and forbidding rocky peaks, not for the serenity of the Appalachians, the deep forested, almost European, greenery of the Eastern mountains—but for the bold and awesome, sometimes even terrible, Western Rockies. Myles used to talk about the Sangre de Cristo range in New Mexico as if it were a religious shrine. A friend had driven Myles's old pickup to the top of the nine-mile trail that winds from 7,000 to 10,000 feet, and Myles had run it like a solitary, self-imposed initiation. I recall a summer as a teenager in Moab, a cabin near the Grand Tetons, a week in the Davis Mountains of West Texas. Magisterial nature, not the soft-spoken European greens. Raw as Americans? A cliché, perhaps. Just another bit of raw material for Western-expansion exploitation? Perhaps. And yet the highest peaks always seem to retain a bit of imposing, impenetrable power and mystery, high above the strip mines and the irrigated deserts and the Wild-West sideshow of the world below.

Here, though, human and mountain live respectfully together. On the tiny forest-service road high up in the mountains you'll see old pickups pulling flatbed trailers loaded down with massive sections of lodgepole pine gathered from dead trees, the only way of heating mountain homes without going broke in the brutal winters. Every summer ranchers run their cattle high up in the alpine meadows of the National Forest, rounding them back up in fall before the big snowfalls. Families pass down government allotments like heirlooms.

As we hurdled the cattle guard and veered off to the right down Wana's ranch road, we were now face to face with the river's panoramic valley sloping up to the jagged skyline of sparkling snow and stone.

"I feel a little light-headed, how about you?"

"A little."

We kicked up small puffs of dust as we soared over the rise and floated down the hill, looking, seeing, not quite thinking, but considering, taking the measure, tucking away images for future Proustian reveries.

"That's what Kant meant by the sublime in nature," I said as I swept my left hand across the skyline.

STUDY QUESTIONS

1. The author quotes Kant's famous passage about the experience of the "sublime" as an epigraph to this chapter, and he ends the chapter by having the narrator remark, "That's what Kant meant by the sublime in nature," referring to the experience of the landscape that the narrator and his friend Randy undergo during their run in the mountains. What does Kant mean by the sublime? Does the author's experience recounted in this chapter line up with Kant's account of the sublime?

2. Michael Polanyi talks about "tacit knowledge," knowing in a way that cannot necessarily be articulated. In recent years a number of philosophers have explored the idea of emotions as a way of knowing the world. For example, Robert Solomon wrote a book called *True to Our Feelings: What Our Emotions Are Really Telling Us*. In this chapter the author seems to be suggesting that we know the world, at least in part, through our bodily experience of it. Is that consistent with the theoretical perspective that the author adopts in this book?

3. The first three chapters reveal the author's plan for the structure of the book—to alternate between short narrative chapters set in Wyoming and discursive chapters of a more overtly philosophical nature. Once the author has used the initial story of chapter 1 as a springboard for his philosophical reflections, why does he continue to bring back the Wyoming mountains in such a central way? Why does he intersperse his philosophical reflections with narrative episodes set in Wyoming?

FOR FURTHER READING

Feezell, Randolph M. "Play and the Absurd." In *Sport, Play, and Ethical Reflection*. Urbana: University of Illinois Press, 2006.

Four

THE QUEEN'S ENGLISH,
OR THAT AWFUL ENGLISH LANGUAGE

>This is the age of cloacal nihilism; English is dead; we destroy our mother tongue, our sacred heritage, and call Calaban's brutal jargon the American language.
>
>Edward Dahlberg
>*The Sorrows of Priapus*

>"This one's for you, Queenie."
>
>Louis Armstrong to Queen Elizabeth

Permit me, then, to take on a few of the prejudices of the cosmopolitan stage of the intellectual life and try to suggest, through a bit of disrespectful examination, some of their limitations—if you will, to recount some of the reasons for my disillusionment with cosmopolitanism and pseudo-intellectualism. Getting to the third stage, the phronetic, requires that you pass through the second one, the cosmopolitan. The danger, of course—and I no doubt succumb to it from time to time—is that you can get so fed up with "fusion" cuisine and people who say "It is I" (and, if they ain't too smart, "between you and I") and high-energy damn Yankees who expect you to nod approvingly when they badmouth the food, music, language, and gene pool of your homeland that you just revert back to the good ol' loves and hatreds of stage one. In a sense, stage three initially, and probably permanently, involves a bit of bouncing back and forth between stages one and two. Permit me, then, to bounce back and forth and in the process explain how some of the pseudo-intellectual prejudices are just that—prejudice.

To borrow a phrase, or half a phrase, from Mark Twain, let me start with that awful English language. In order to become an intellectual, a cosmopolitan, I spent years trying to master it, not as one would master a second language but in order to replace the provincial tongue that my childhood had given to me. I practiced short *e*'s, saying *get* instead of my native *git*. I religiously pronounced the final *g* of "ing." I expunged "ain't" from my vocabulary, and, once transported up north, I abandoned "y'all" in favor of "you guys," although I bristled at ignorant Yankees trying to parody Southern English by using "y'all" as a singular. Even as an undergraduate at the University of Texas, I was ashamed of my native accent, thanks in part to my professors' cosmopolitan citizenship, Northern origins, or plain old resentment at being stuck in Texas—and thanks in part to my own headlong dive into the life of the worldly intellectual. As a testimony to the enduring nature of this bigotry, thirty-five years later my nephew found himself being made fun of for his speech by some of his classmates at Rice University, never mind that he was speaking the native tongue of the city that Rice is smack in the middle of.

There's no doubt that strong regional accents of any kind can get a person into serious humiliation at the hands of a worldly intellectual. Even a strong Brooklyn accent is not acceptable, but the long dominance of Northeastern cities and universities in the nation's intellectual life has resulted in a tendency to regard Southern accents as the very epitome of ignorant boorishness in language. Angelo, my Italian friend from Rhode Island, once said to me in his construction-worker Rhode Island accent, that he couldn't imagine living in the South because those people just sound so dumb when they talk. I pointed out that his accent, to my ears, sounded like a parody of Brando's godfather. He was speaking from the honest perspective of his provincial ears, but it was the weight of intellectual prejudice that gave him the license to make such a comment to a Southerner, and the presumption to believe that I would agree. It is the weight of intellectual prejudice that permits the intellectual to insist that Gloucester, Massachusetts, be pronounced as the locals pronounce it—not "Glue-chester" or even as "ouster" with a *g* and an *l* on the front, but "Gloss-ter"—and then turn right around and ridicule the native of Louisiana because he says "Looz-ee-anna" and the Missourian who says "Miz-zoo-ruh." After all, intellectuals like to hang out in Glosster, or at least they like to act as authorities on the pronunciation of its name; whereas they wouldn't get caught dead in Looz-ee-anna or Miz-zoo-ruh.

As a Texan in Buffalo, New York, I felt some identification with Goethe as I read in his autobiography this passage about the learned lads and ladies of Leipzig making fun of his Frankfurt accent and dialect:

> The Upper-German, and perhaps chiefly he who lives by the Rhine and Main (for great rivers, like the seacoast, always have something animating about them), expresses himself much in similes and allusions, and makes use of proverbial sayings with a native common-sense aptness. In both cases he is often blunt: but, when one sees the drift of the expression, it is always appropriate; only something, to be sure, may often slip in, which proves offensive to a more delicate ear.
>
> Every province loves its own dialect; for it is, properly speaking, the element in which the soul draws its breath. But every one knows with what obstinacy the Misnian dialect has contrived to domineer over the rest, and even, for a long time, to exclude them. We have suffered for many years under this pedantic tyranny, and only by reiterated struggles have all provinces again established themselves in their ancient rights.

What a lively young man had to endure from this continual tutoring, may be easily inferred by any one who reflects that modes of thought, imagination, feeling, native character, must be sacrificed with the pronunciation which one at last consents to alter. And this intolerable demand was made by men and women of education, whose convictions I could not adopt, whose injustice I thought I felt, though I was unable to make it plain to myself.

Later on I was more severely challenged by reading Heidegger's defense of Johann Peter Hebel's *Alemannisch*, the local dialect of southwestern Germany. I realized, too, as I dabbled in the German language and wandered in the German forests, that Heidegger's own philosophical writings, especially the later, more poetic ones, reflect the earthy dialect of Messkirch, his birthplace, and Todtnauberg, the village sixty miles away where he did much of his work.

When did I begin to reclaim my native speech? When I began to get serious about writing, when I became serious about words, when I aspired to the loftiest of language—then, by a kind of natural necessity, I began to reclaim the earthiness, the embedded folk traditions, the humor, the rhythms, of my grossly incorrect mother tongue. I did it, in part, by reading the loftiest of literary works from my home province—John Graves's *Goodbye to a River* and *Hard Scrabble*, William Humphrey's *Home from the Hill* and *The Ordways*, Larry McMurtry's *Horseman, Pass By* and *In a Narrow Grave*. I wanted to write like these fine wordsmiths, but their very loftiness was rooted, artistically, craftily, humorously, but deeply, in the rich vernacular of their, and my, homeland. Since Texas represents the epitome of provincialism on the scale of intellectual prejudice, this was something of a struggle for them. But you'll find no apologies for regional language in these fine writers. John Graves, as highly schooled in learned letters as he is rooted in his region, recalls in an interview how a copy editor at Knopf rewrote the entire manuscript of *Goodbye to a River*, changing all of his idiosyncratic commas and deliberate touches of the colloquial; as he put it, "she was helping out that poor old illiterate down in Texas." The book is a work of art, high art, but it is rich in the rambling, storytelling vernacular of Texas, just as the works of Philip Roth echo the language of New York and Ivan Doig's his childhood Montana.

If my fellow Texas writers didn't convince me to rethink the idea of correct English, then there was Faulkner. I couldn't find "yessum" in Webster's, but there it was in *Absalom, Absalom!* clear as day. Of course, I didn't need to find it in Webster's, because I found it in my childhood memories. In Faulkner I saw the language of my Southern family roots—with a few Southwestern and generational modifications, the language I grew up in—burst forth into the flashes and deep shadows of great artistic vision. I felt no temptation to write my graduate school papers in Dilsey's black dialect or Benji's broken stream of Southern consciousness; but I felt a great need to rethink the correctness of correct English.

Mark Twain prefaces *Huckleberry Finn* with this "Explanatory":

> In this book a number of dialects are used, to wit: the Missouri negro dialect; the extremest form of the backwoods South-Western dialect; the ordinary "Pike-County" dialect; and four modified varieties of this last. The shadings have not been done in a haphazard fashion, or by guess-work; but pains-takingly, and with the trustworthy guidance and support of personal familiarity with these several forms of speech.
>
> I make this explanation for the reason that without it many readers would suppose that all these characters were trying to talk alike and not succeeding.

Twain is playfully thumbing his nose at high literary society, but he's dead serious, too. What do we do with poor Huck, then, dismiss him for bad grammar? Of course, you object, Twain is using "poetic license." Huck is just a fictional narrator, an ironic one at that. Twain certainly doesn't mean for all of us to talk like Huck. No, but he is willing to let Huck talk the way he would have talked, willing to tune his ear to his native dialect rather than bemoan it. There's something peculiar about the high-flown intellectual who recognizes the courage of Huck's decision to suffer the Everlasting Fire of Hell rather than betray his friend Jim back into slavery, but assumes that any real-live human being who sounds like Huck must be morally depraved as well as mentally retarded. The language of high literature, like the language of the human lives it is about, is a complex creature.

In fact, a veritable plethora of great writers in the English language would have to be summarily dismissed as boorish, city gutterish, and just plain incorrect if we held puritanically to the canons of a perfectly rigid Queen's English. If we take British English as the standard, which Queen, which century, do we set up as the standard? Chaucer's, Shakespeare's, or Princess Di's? That is, in fact, just the point. The "Queen's English" is a nineteenth- and twentieth-century artifice of upper-class snobbery, a defensive barrier thrown up against the democratic tide of the times. Most of the greatest practitioners of the English language, ironically the very ones that many of the language crusaders idolize, didn't write it or speak it. From Chaucer to Shakespeare, from Joyce to Seamus Heaney, from Melville to Twain to Faulkner—the great artists of the language are rich in the vernacular and damn near indifferent to "correct" English.

Many American intellectuals, I must admit, have championed the distinctiveness and the democratizing impurities of American English from the very beginning. But for every anti-British Mencken and Twain, there are two professors and three community-leading doctors and lawyers who just can't seem to remember that Valley Forge ever took place. Language snobbery is alive and well in America.

Even when language snobbery doesn't kowtow to British English, it condescends to the regional aberrations, especially the Southern ones. Again, sheer prejudice. Cleanth Brooks, as linguistically proper a Yale professor as a Yale professor can be, took on some of the prejudice against Southern English in a series of lectures which appeared in book form as *The Language of the American*

South. Southern English, he argues, is not a corruption of proper English, but a preservation of older British forms. For example, the Southern habit of dropping the *g* in pronouncing "ing," as Brooks demonstrates with the rhyme schemes of Wordsworth, Coleridge, Byron, Shelley, and Keats, is more conservative and historically faithful, not less.

And yet historical veracity isn't everything. Brooks's well-aimed rebuttal aside, there are new developments that the experience of a new continent has added to American English, Northern and Southern and otherwise. What do we do with those? Even if Americans do depart from British English, we need not say they've gone astray. Even if they have wandered, they may have wandered upon something very fine and rich. As for Southern English, if we judge by the literature it has produced, then, yes, indeed, we have wandered upon, or preserved and wandered upon, something very rich. As for American English overall, that is, American English in its many historical and regional odysseys, if we judge by the literature, then, yes, God save the colonists.

And of course the terrains of linguistic prejudice have gotten considerably more complex since my coming of age. Whereas my generation of American intellectuals could reject its roots by abandoning regional American English, especially the Southern version, and embracing the Queen's English, "postcolonial" intellectuals nowadays must champion "indigenous languages" in the former European colonies and condemn the Queen's English as a language of imperialism in order to receive their membership cards. Logic be damned, the same professors who applaud the resurgence of indigenous languages in Africa and India, who assign slave narratives and women's diaries in literature classes, endlessly pronounce on high that the white Southerners they teach are barely literate because they say "I'm fixin' to."

There are many varieties of English, in different countries and within each country. It takes not just rules of correct English, but thought and insight and wisdom, to see them in their rightful places. Nations, maybe even regions of nations, need rules of *their* standard English, for there can't be communal identities, commerce, political debate, and such without a high level of language standardization; but the standards must be taught as general rules that require reasonableness and insight in their application. And reasonableness requires the acknowledgment that there is a time and a place for standard English, and a time to talk with the homefolks, and a time to risk the irregular, the poetic, the intuitively right. Reasonableness requires the recognition that language is a dynamic historical creature, not a static thing that can be categorized and canonized once and for all.

To be sure, abandoning the sheer prejudice of the cosmopolitan's correct English always presents the danger of lapsing into a willy-nilly linguistic relativism in which anything goes, in which, say, gangsta rap or Bubba's redneck slang is proffered as the equal of Shakespeare's English—or even a deliberate scientific relativism in which value-free descriptions render all languages equal. Somehow, though, rejecting prescription in favor of description always seems to be a cover for reintroducing the same old prejudices against the offending dialects and accents. But dropping the artificially rigid barriers of the pseudo-intellectual's English simply means that we do indeed have to judge, to think and to judge, instead of spasmodically shouting dogma. Not in all respects, but surely in most, Shakespeare's English is superior to Ebonics and Bubbonics—that's a reasonable judgment that is easily made. And maybe our schools ought to do a better job of reversing the currents of resentful separatism that run through the latest street and country lingos, especially designed to befuddle the appropriate outsiders. But, like it or not, the local dialects exist, and, separatist or not, they are parts of American English. They infuse the whole with their rhythms and metaphors, and our aspiring urban and rural Shakespeares reflect them in their lofty versifications, just as Will reflected the language of Elizabethan craftsmen and shopkeepers, and Frost the language of New England farmers, and Faulkner the rural and plantation dialects, black and white, of Mississippi.

Pedagogically we ought to be rigid as hell on the subject of correct English; but philosophically we ought to be Socratic, phronetic, wise in the limits of our wisdom. Precisely when we care about greater and lesser language, the concept of correct English becomes problematic, and language becomes enigmatic; only when we care exclusively about technical precision and proficiency, or about social superiority, is the "correctness" of language as simple as some would have it.

Robert MacNeil, a Canadian-American broadcast journalist of impeccably correct speech, offers some eloquent testimony on the transition from a cosmopolitan to a phronetic understanding of that awful English language. He begins his *New York Times Book Review* essay "It Is Not I but Me, and I Say: Leave American English Alone!" with this candid characterization of the cosmopolitan stage:

> For a long time I have known that the English language was "going to hell." I think I shared that belief as an article of faith, part of today's intellectual climate, with many people. We accepted it uncritically. To be pessimistic about what was happening to the language was a cultural marker. Everyone you knew believed there was a crisis of literacy.

After spending three years working on a television series on the English language, he began to question that belief:

> I have now learned that the English language has been "going to hell" for hundreds of years—without any help from this generation. It has been a wonderfully liberating experience, giving me a very different perspective on language. For me and my collaborators, the research and filming were an exciting re-education. We have come away with enormously increased respect for the vigor of language, its resilience, its capacity to thrive on ceaseless change, and with awe for what the Anglo-American scholar Logan Pearsall Smith called "the Genius of the language."

"Re-education" means the rethinking of intellectual prejudice, and the recognition that intellectuals, too, have "articles of faith," as it were, articles of faith with the stamp of reason on them. MacNeil's confession is a classic case of seeing through the sham and vanity of the cosmopolitan stage. Legitimizing change and slang and variety opens many dangerous doors, and MacNeil doesn't claim to have worked out all of the difficulties that this new openness introduces. But thinking never does make things easier—it makes them more difficult and us more truthful.

It makes it difficult for me to find the proper mix of formality and locality in my writing. The possibilities are infinite, and, quite frankly, the decisions are downright frightening. But such is the task of genuine writing. There are no creative-writing-school formulas by which a Faulkner weaves his remarkable fabric of high poetic and earthy vernacular, by which a John Graves rings artistically and regionally true. There are basic principles, to be sure, but in the end there is the writer's phronetic insight, the well-tuned ear, the feel for words and meanings. I stumble along, here a proper "whom," there a defiant "ain't," as the meaning I'm groping toward unfolds itself.

Quite frankly, I even find it difficult to speak. In Germany there's a stronger split between educated *Hochdeutsch* and the local dialects; for a small-town person, learning standard German is almost like learning a foreign language. The professor Heidegger spoke *Hochdeutsch* in the classroom—albeit with a noticeable regional accent—and *Alemannisch* in the village of Todtnauberg. But in America the process of language education tends to gradually obliterate the local speech, rather than supplement it with a different manner of speaking. It's difficult to keep them separate, because they aren't two different things.

I find myself slipping in and out of regional and formal speech, depending on the circumstances; but there's no clean dividing line. I grew up pronouncing Louisiana, the state my parents grew up in and I was born in, the way the folks who live there say it; in college I switched to the "standard" pronunciation. Now I go back and forth, sometimes in the same conversation. As a teacher I make considerable effort to stick to the English of the academy, but it doesn't bother me that I never quite do; and, on occasion, I consciously sound like an unadulterated hick. I grade essays and papers according to unforgiving rules of standard English, but I remind my students that formality is an ideal possibility, never a full actuality, and that other possibilities of language come to the fore when the purpose is not argumentative or communicative, but poetic. If I'm fishing with Outdoor Man on Palo Pinto Lake, I might lapse into a slang-ridden local dialect that would drive an English teacher to drink—and not for poetic purposes, but for purposes of hopelessly adolescent male camaraderie; and, to tell the truth, sometimes I have no idea how to talk about fishing and lures and such in formal English.

I never say "It's I"—if the French can say "C'est moi," we can say, with our own emphatic pronoun, "It's me." I use "y'all" as the plural of you, because there ain't no second-person plural pronoun in English, we need one, and "y'all" is a perfectly good contraction of "you" and "all." It makes perfectly good sense, more sense than "you guys," which renders the sex of women peculiarly nonexistent—and, my dear friend Angelo, it sounds a lot better, at least to my warped Southwestern ears, than "youse." When a friend of mine, an English professor from South Carolina, was driving through Harlem with his wife, a prep-school English teacher from New Jersey, a young black man came up to the car at an intersection, espied the look of disorientation on their pale faces, and asked, "Y'all lost?" Sticklers for correct English, neither of them would have been caught dead using the expression "y'all." Nonetheless, the South Carolinian not only understood, but suddenly felt at ease, almost at home; the New Jerseyite didn't feel at home, but she understood. The Southerner asked directions politely; neither one of them corrected the man's English.

୬୭୧୪

STUDY QUESTIONS

1. Education in America typically involves a process of mastering formal English: one of the most conspicuous signs of a highly educated person is the use of "proper English." Does it surprise you that the author says that he started to reclaim his native speech, his local dialect, when he became serious about writing?

2. Local dialects are often used by characters in fictional works of literature. Although it was something of a shock to polite society at the time, it certainly makes sense for Mark Twain to have his unlettered character Huck Finn speak the local dialect of his province and time. Does the use of local dialects in philosophical writing make sense? The characters in Plato's dialogues speak as the Greeks of that time spoke, but should we be concerned, as the author suggests, with the influence of local dialect in a philosophical writer like Heidegger?

3. In spite of his plea for respecting and using local dialects, the author claims that a certain degree of language standardization is necessary. Why? Can you have it both ways? Also, in discussing his approach to education he says: "Pedagogically we ought to be rigid as hell on the subject of correct English; but philosophically we ought to be Socratic, phronetic, wise in the limits of our wisdom." What does this mean? Is it consistent?

4. How does the author use Robert MacNeil's "re-education" concerning the English language as a model for the transition from the cosmopolitan to the phronetic stages of the intellectual's life?

5. The author says that "language is a dynamic historical creature." In what sense is language "historical"? Does that mean that everything is constantly changing, that there are no lasting rules? Or does it mean something else?

FOR FURTHER READING

Brooks, Cleanth. *The Language of the American South*. Athens: The University of Georgia Press, 1985.

Graves, John. *Goodbye to a River*. New York: Knopf, 1979 [1960].

> A fine example of high-minded literature that draws on the conversational vernacular of Texas.

McCrum, Robert, Robert MacNeil, and William Cran. *The Story of English*. New York: Penguin, 1986.

> Based on the PBS series on the English language.

Wine bottles near Centennial, Wyoming. Photo by author, 1986.

Five

WINE OF WYOMING

> ". . . C'est bon, la bière. C'est très bon pour la santé."
> "It's good," I said. "It and wine too."
> "You're like Fontan. But there was a thing here that I never saw. I don't think you've ever seen it either. There were Americans came here and they put whiskey in the beer."
> "No," I said.
> "Oui. My God, yes, that's true. Et aussi une femme qui a vomis sur la table!"
> "Comment?"
> "C'est vrai. Elle a vomis sur la table. Et après elle a vomis dans ses shoes. And afterward they come back and say they want to come again and have another party the next Saturday, and I say no, my God, no! When they came I locked the door."
>
> Ernest Hemingway
> "Wine of Wyoming"

Late afternoon set in with a five-minute shower. When a hovering sun flashed through patches of blue, we all emerged from our cabins with the same idea in mind.

"I brought a little wine," I said as I opened the box. I sat on the tailgate of the pickup and handed the bottles to Randy, who put them on the rough-timber table outside of our cabin.

"Remember that one?"

"Chateau Monbousquet. I sure do."

"It's not a 1970 like the ones we used to get in Buffalo, but '75 ain't half bad either."

Randy cradled the bottle in both hands, then placed it on the table.

"This one's from Weatherford, about 60 miles north of Stephenville."

"A Texas wine?"

"Not great, but good. We drink a lot of it."

"A Texas wine, no shit?"

"Come on, Feezell, don't you remember my story about Orth drinking all the wines from the vineyards right outside of Trier? If Orth drinks wines from Trier, then why shouldn't I drink wines from Weatherford?"

"All right, all right."

"Well, I guess I shouldn't be lecturing you about wine—you and Barb gave us our first set of wine glasses that first year in Buffalo."

"Yeah, but we've been at a disadvantage. We've got three kids to put through college, and I figure sooner or later one of them will insist on Harvard or Yale, so we have to confine our high-class wine to special occasions."

"Well, damn it, this is a special occasion as far as I'm concerned. Look at this Chateau St. *Gene* or *John* . . . or *J'on* . . . or however you say it. I don't know how they pronounce J-E-A-N in California. Brewster brought a bottle over once in Buffalo. Pretty good firewater."

Randy and I lined up the six or seven bottles that I pulled from the box, Travis rounded the corner with two bottles under one arm and a half-gallon jug under the other. Evan stumbled along a few steps behind with a bottle in each hand.

"Goddamn."

"Put 'em on the table, Trav, Ev. Barb and I had this Chardonnay for my birthday. And for old times' sake—"

Randy sat the jug at the end of the line of bottles.

"Carlo Rossi, I can't believe it." I thought of how we'd sit around for half an afternoon and all of an evening talking basketball and Heidegger and sloshing down the Carlo Rossi. Somehow I'd get myself home, and get up the next morning and sail right into a seminar on Edmund Husserl's phenomenology, and scratch, bite, and claw at my fellow graduate students like graduate students are supposed to do. We were younger then.

"You never know, we might run out."

From one end of the large table to the other, about twelve feet of table, the bottles stood, like so many of Wallace Stevens's jars in Tennessee. We placed a whole bunch of wine bottles in Wyoming, and round they were, upon a table. It made the slovenly wilderness surround that table . . . .

"It's almost a political statement," Randy said, "wine from France and Germany and California and Texas sitting right here in the Medicine Bow Mountains."

We made up some chicken and some squash brought from the Feezell garden back home on the hot plate in the Feezells' cabin. A light drizzle kept us inside for the meal, so we huddled around the small Formica table and wolfed down the make-shift grub along with our two bottles of California Chardonnay.

We conjured up sharp memories of particular bottles of wine we'd had on particular occasions, of conversations and old friends, Premier Liquors in Buffalo . . . Randy bringing out the Schnapps one winter night after we'd run out of wine . . . . I told the story of Mallory and me going off to Germany with just enough knowledge of wine to think that the only good wine was dry, but not a stitch of knowledge about late-harvest Rieslings in Germany, about sipping sweet wines and talking into the wee Teutonic hours. We'd go into the *Weinstuben* and insist on a "very dry" wine—the waitress would say, "Oh, you want a *diabetischer* wine." We'd look at each other, shrug our shoulders, and say, "I guess so."

The rain gradually died out, and as the daylight faded all of us larger folks moved out to the table in front of our cabin where the rest of the wine still stood, now damp from the light shower. I opened a German *Auslese*, and picked up the story of our apprenticeship in German oenophilia.

"Finally, this geology professor at the University of Trier invited us over for dinner—Herr Professor Negendank. He served a dry Alsatian wine with dinner, and we went on and on about how much we liked dry wine, and how ignorant Texans like to drink that cheap sweet stuff. After dinner he disappeared into the cellar and emerged with a middle-Mosel *Kabinett*. We snotted off about how it was pleasant, but a little too sweet. Every half hour or so he'd disappear again and come back with a slightly sweeter wine. At about five the next morning we were sipping on a *Trockenbeerenauslese* and arguing philosophy. He was all excited about American Positivism and I was praising German Idealism. I remember telling him in my half-assed German that I could reduce the whole concept of positivism to blatant self-contradiction, but it lost something in the translation and even more under the influence. Anyway, that's how I learned what German wines are all about."

As the sun set in Wyoming, four of us sipping on the *Auslese* made for relative coherence and lucidity. But the fatal stroke had already been prepared. Randy had slipped the jug wine into the cooler. It didn't need much chilling, though—the temperature dropped sharply, and we struggled with the damp firewood to get a good fire going. We propped our feet up on the edge of the table, rolled the chilled wine against the backs of our tongues, and warmed our hands and faces against the fire. The fire made a circle of warm light in the darkness. The gurgling roar of the river just below the silhouetted trees was like a soothing lullaby.

That's about all I remember, though. I rolled out of bed the next morning alone. Everyone else had been up for a couple of hours. My head feels fine, I thought, but the cabin floor seems uneven. It even moved as I walked softly toward the screen door. I made it to the big table outside, plopped down on the bench, and watched the world swim by.

Mallory came up from the river and looked accusingly my way. "I'm dizzy," I announced. "Now I know what the effects of 8,000 feet of altitude are. A four-mile run was nothing." I struggled up and, stumbling across the shifting ground, back into the cabin and back into bed. I propped myself up against the headboard and breathed deeply, eyes closed, hands folded corpse-like across my chest. Every half hour or so I'd try to move, the world would swirl, and I would collapse back into my meditative pose. Travis and Evan came by and peered in the screen door, as if they were watching an animal at the city zoo.

About noon I finally made it up and retraced my earlier path to the table outside. Randy, Travis, and Evan were off somewhere. Mallory and Barbara were talking quietly, probably about the insatiable childishness of the male sex of the human species.

"Overdid it, did you?" Mallory asked declaratively.

"Uh."

STUDY QUESTIONS

1. For the author and his friend Randy, drinking wine seems to function as a kind of ritual of friendship. And particular wines seem to mark particular events in their memories. Do friendships require rituals, markers of the passage of time?

2. The author explains how he learned to appreciate the sweet late-harvest Rieslings while spending a summer in Germany during graduate school. Was the author's preference for dry wines an intellectual prejudice? Are matters of taste relative to cultures, geographical regions, historical periods, individuals? What is the author's position on this issue?

3. What is the author's defense for drinking wine from Texas even though he acknowledges that it's not great wine? He mentions a German named Orth "drinking all the wines from the vineyards right outside of Trier," but he neglects to say that the wines from the Middle Mosel are considered some of the best in the world. Is an attachment to the wine, food, or other aspects of your local culture, even when they are in some perceivable way inferior to other options, an unreasonable provincialism? Is it possible to judge wine in some absolute sense, to say that a wine is one of the "best in the world"?

FOR FURTHER READING

Johnson, Hugh, and Jancis Robinson. *The World Atlas of Wine*. London: Mitchell Beazley, 2001 [1971].

Six

WIT AND THE ART OF CONVERSATION

> Both Brahmin wit and yarn humor have had a long history in the United States and have suggested two aspects of the American mind and character, one related to urban life and formal learning, the other to rural life and homespun learning. The classic centers of these somewhat antipodal styles were New England for wit and the Old Southwest for yarn humor . . . .
>
> Charles Neider
Introduction to The Comic Mark Twain Reader

> The art of questioning is that of being able to go on asking questions, i.e., the art of thinking. It is called 'dialectic,' for it is the art of conducting a real conversation.
>
> Hans-Georg Gadamer
Truth and Method

After a particularly highbrow social gathering during our graduate school days, my friend Angelo remarked, "Have you ever noticed how the conversations at these parties aren't *about* anything?"

That remark would probably be true of just about any kind of social gathering, but this society was not just any old society, but a society of intellectuals—professors, graduate students in philosophy and literature, writers, university hangers-on. They who knew so much—how could they say so little, you ask? They who used so many words, how could they not say something?

The truth of the matter is: they weren't trying to say anything. They were using all of the powers of their intellects, all of the years of learning and discoursing on learning, all of their energies *not* to say anything, but, mind you, to say nothing wittily. Or, rather, it was wit which enabled them to speak and say nothing—wit, not in the sense of having your wits about you, but wit as in "He's very witty" or "He's a consummate wit."

The word is old and rich, a fine old English and Germanic noun which originally meant "mind" or "understanding." It comes from the Middle English verb *witen*, to know—*wizzen* in Old High German and *wissen* in modern German. Originally, the noun had nothing to do with the clever use of words, but with intelligence, good sense, ingenuity, or mental quickness in a general sense. It came to connote cleverness in expression, but expression in service of ideas. Locke explained wit as "the assemblage of Ideas, and putting those together with quickness and variety." A certain quickness and aptness of expression suggests that the expression is apt *for* something, in reference to something. But therein lies the possibility of separating aptness of expression from what the expression aptly expresses—wit becomes sheer wit. In *The Autocrat of the Breakfast-Table* Oliver Wendell Holmes saw through it well: "We get beautiful effects from wit,—all the prismatic colours,—but never the object as it is in fair daylight." Pushed to its abstracted extreme, it doesn't give the object at all.

The chief virtue of intellectual conversation, then, is wit in the sense of sheer wit, wit in its distilled abstraction. Without wit, the intellectual is lost. It's a matter of survival, and advancement—a habit learned by necessity through countless dinner parties. To wit: At a cocktail party hosted by the widow of the late dean of St. John's College in Annapolis, you and your wife mingle unmaliciously with the guests, trying to carry on an earnest, good-natured conversation—human being to human being, so to speak. Frau Klein introduces you to a group of "tutors" from St. John's College. She mentions with a straight man's grin that your wife is a "professor" at the Naval Academy. One of the tutors looks around knowingly to his comrades and asks your wife, "Oh, what do you profess?" A veteran, she responds: "English. What do you toot?" When in Rome . . . .

Living in a highly intensified, if somewhat eccentric microcosm of the intellectual world, nurtured on the Great Books Program and several generations of educational inbreeding and self-congratulatory intellect stroking, the tutors were convinced that no one else in the world could possibly discuss those books with them, especially a witless naif from the Naval Academy. Rather than actually talking about teaching at the two institutions, the tutor chose to deflect the conversation and gain the upper hand with wit. He lost the battle, but I guess he thinks he won the war; for my wife and I soon left the battlefield, and I imagine he and his fellow tutors went on exchanging witty put-downs of the rubes from the Naval Academy. At a later gathering when the same fellow discovered that my wife was "tutoring" some of the better English majors in classical Greek, and that her education was as solid in "their" Great Books as theirs, his mouth hung aporetically open for a few seconds before he retorted, as half-hearted wit and half-spontaneous remarking, "I didn't know there were English majors at the Naval Academy." There were many things he didn't know, and many he didn't know he didn't know. For all the schooling in Socratic wisdom, his wit was the best defense he had against facing the limits of his understanding. Wit is the intellectual's best defense against *aporia*—for it prevents the conversation from addressing anything important enough to elicit the difficulty of not knowing, while all the time giving the conversation the firm ring of ultimate importance.

Wit is by nature cosmopolitan. Wit enables the speaker to rise above everything, to judge everything and belong to nothing, to win the argument without really taking a position, to gain the upper hand in a conversation without really admitting the competition is under way. Like the snobbishness of the Queen's English, wit is all the more powerful because it has no content. In the battle of wits, the object is not the forthcoming of truth, but dominance, humiliation, and the mutual reinforcement—quite entertaining and pleasurable within the proper society—of a social superiority.

True, highbrow intellectual wit requires, and displays, a good deal of esoteric knowledge, but it is not the knowledge which counts but a kind of virtuoso intellectual prowess. There might well be a flash of insight in a certain kind of wit—and certainly one meaning of the full-fledged word implies that—but the end of sheer wit is not insight, but display. Why wasn't Angelo's party conversation about anything? Why was the conversation with the St. John's tutors not about the Great Books, or, better, about what the Great Books are about? Because the participants weren't trying to talk about something—they were trying to demonstrate to each other how witty they were, and, in the end, how superior they were to a lowly Naval Academy "professor." However faulty the postmodernist claim that all words are about nothing beyond themselves, that there is no object other that what we construct in language, it is an apt description of what witty intellectuals have been doing since the sophists of Plato's time dazzled their audiences with rhetorical cosmetics.

I care about conversation, and its denigration by the dominance of wit, as a talker; but I care about it as a writer, too. I became particularly concerned with wit and the art of conversation because I locate myself as a writer within the venerable tradition of the "familiar" essay. Since Montaigne championed "simple, natural speech, the same on paper as in the mouth," the nature of human conversation has been a literary as well as an existential problem. Graduate-school days now long gone—what with all of us with careers and kids and life's adult tribulations to take care of—I don't get to sit around talking for hours on end, not even with pseudo-intellectuals, but I do, by calling and by profession, sit around reading and writing for hours on end. As an essayist, I've gone in search of "conversational" English, and I've found wit rearing its decorous head there too.

William Hazlitt, Ye Old Godfather of the "familiar" English-language essay, championed "conversational" English over the stiffness and, as he put it, the "pedantic and oratorial flourishes" of Samuel Johnson and Charles Lamb. That was a major turning point in the English-language essay; but, ironically, Hazlitt's conversational English was the so-called "literary-colloquial English"—the conversation of poets and critics, of coffeehouses and innovative journals. Rambunctious and uninhibited and personal as it was, it was not truly the English of conversation, but of "conversationalists." Conversationalists don't have conversations. They display their powers, pit their powers against the powers of other conversationalists. Hazlitt's admiring description of Coleridge's ability to hold forth to large parties of ladies and gentlemen at great length reminds me of the opening of Plato's *Gorgias*, of Callicles' admiring description of Gorgias' ability to declaim lengthily and elegantly to large audiences and to answer any and all questions. Socrates asks if Gorgias might be willing just to talk with them, and suggests that he deliver the rest of his performance at some other time. For all his study of philosophy, I'm not sure Hazlitt understood the difference between Socratic dialogue and sophistic display. He describes Coleridge's "powers of conversation" this way: "In digressing, in dilating, in passing from subject to subject, he appeared to me to float in air, to slide on ice." In my book, Hazlitt's conversational essays are too much air and ice, not enough earth and stone—even on his celebrated walks in the country.

Disarming, charming wit; scornful, spiteful wit; clever, admiring wit; much ado about exposing pretense and sham—these are the values of a powerful tradition of the essay, from Samuel Johnson and Addison and Hazlitt and Mencken right down to Joseph Epstein, "America's premier essayist" according to George Will. At their best, the essays of these writers are certainly "conversational"; but too often they wittily opinionate rather than truly think the matter through. Even when the London salon becomes the Chicago suburb or the Baltimore saloon, the demeanor of this kind of essay is too urbane; the blood is middle-class redder than that of the to-the-manor-born country or city aristocrats, but still too blue; the language is spirited and caustic, but often too witty for its own good. Too seldom do these essays truly *attempt*, in the sense of *essayer*—and therein is my aversion to the witty iconoclasts, British and American.

I'd like to trace another line. I'm looking for conversational language, but I guess I'm more inclined toward country front-porch talking; or even a marketplace Socratic encounter, sometimes clever and comic and often cagey and caustic as hell, but never merely witty; or even a Montaigne or a Descartes alone with his own thoughts in his own dark study; or a Heidegger in his Spartan hut, peering in mournful silence over the serene valley of Todtnauberg, in a lifetime conversation with his philosophical predecessors. When Heidegger wrote about Hölderlin's line, "Seit wir ein Gespräch sind" ("since we have been a conversation"), he wasn't thinking about good conversationalists in a London coffeehouse.

I'm looking, too, for the essayistic English that is American, even Texan— "literary-colloquial," yes, but reflecting the simple talk, the handed-down expressions and phrasings, the sounds, of the common language of my homeland. I find it in Mark Twain more so than in Thoreau and company, although I guess you could say Thoreau wrote the unadorned conversational English of *his* community. I find it in Norman Maclean's sparse but poetic tale of the Montana of his youth; in the more personal essays of fellow Texan Larry King; in John Graves's rambling ruminations about a river and a patch of land a couple of stones' throw down the road from me.

If I may wax philosophic momentarily, genuine conversation matters in writing because conversation matters in life. It more than matters *in* life; it is, as the line from Hölderlin that Heidegger devoted so much thought to proclaims, what life truly is all about. Conversation is what we are. It is not an art, by which we display intellectual prowess, entertain ourselves, pass the time, survive cocktail parties, get tenure; it is of our very being. Translated, Hölderlin's lines run something like this:

Much has man experienced.
Of the heavenly ones many named,
Since we have been a conversation
And able to hear from one another.

Aristotle defined the human species as the "animal having language" (*zōon echein logon*), but language is itself most fully language in the give-and-take of conversation, of talking the matter over, even of talking the matter over with oneself. *Logos* is *dialogos*. Or, as Hans-Georg Gadamer puts it in German, "Sprache ist nur im Gespräch"—"language *is* only in dialogue."

The question is not whether we engage in dialogue, for even in the greatest silence of the self with itself, there is the give and take of the conversation. If mystics truly achieve the ineffable level at which dialogue is completely suspended, all power to them; but they have simply taken a break from their humanity. There is no nirvana of human dialogue, escaping from it or somehow elevating it to perfection. It is the human task—a task for which there is no speech-class formula—to engage in that dialogue revealingly, with a sense of justice and measure.

In a sense, my attack on wit is itself too formulaic. For wit is indeed an inescapable *aspect* of conversation. I mean to attack wit as an absolute value, as a virtue in abstraction from the greater goods of conversation. In conversation in the broadest sense, humans work out their differences; weigh what is justly due to each; bond themselves together into marriages, friendships, families, communities; express grief and joy; find meaning; talk about what is. Sheer wit is a perversion of genuine dialogue—it is sophistic display, manipulative monologue (of one or of many), intellectual titillation. And it is one of the chief means by which cosmopolitan intellectuals signify to each other their membership in the society of cosmopolitan intellectuals.

In a genuine intellectual conversation, the talk ought well to be talk about what is. Socrates says in the *Gorgias* that a truthful dialogue is one in which "one person discusses with another desiring to know that thing itself which the speech [*logos*] is about." Truthful dialogue requires true listening, a kind of openness to the other's claim, a willingness to let your own point of view be challenged by the other's, even to make the other's position stronger. Gadamer explains that one of the German words for "thing," *Sache*, really means the thing "at issue," the "issue": "It is originally the thing which is thrown down in the middle between the contending parties, because about it, it's still to be decided and it's not yet decided." Genuine dialogue accepts that the thing, the issue, is *not yet decided*, even if the participants may feel very strongly about it. Genuine dialogue creates an open space "in the middle," between the speakers, in which the thing which the dialogue is about may appear.

Of course, as Plato's dialogues illustrate, talk about *what is* will not necessarily, or even preferably, take the form of a humorless, straightforward exercise in sincerity and mutual respect. The sort of serious playfulness that casts a light on the comic nature of life itself is a necessary ingredient in the best of conversations, and even not-so-serious but good-natured leg-pulling playfulness. Hammerton remarked, "There is more 'heart' in humor, and more 'head' in wit." In humor there's more humanity, too.

Sometimes, though, the fellow speaker cannot help but be an opponent; sometimes the dialogue by all rights must be a damn bloody battle. But in the best of intellectual competition, it is the thing itself which the competition is about that requires a downright uncivil Socrates. And, because the thing itself in intellectual conversation is or ought to be the sort of thing Socrates asked about—courage, love, justice, virtue, knowledge—the thing itself has something to do with the persons we will be, not as contestants in a duel of wit or of philosophical argumentation, but as humans for whom it is better to be better than to be worse, and for whom talking about things is a necessary element in being better.

Truthful conversation may well need a good bit of storytelling—the ironic Socratic mythologizing; the satiric or ironically self-effacing, homespun Twainian yarn; the poetic indirection of a story well told. But Socrates' *muthologiē* are about something; good stories are, and good satire. You might say Twainian yarn-spinning satire is the Southwestern version of wit, and I certainly would be willing to suggest that virtuoso yarn-spinning can fall into the same ball park, but satire, yarn-spinning and otherwise, isn't really wit.

Truthful conversation might even need a kind of wit that reveals in a flash of well-worded insight, but I'm inclined to call that an aphorism, not wit. Truth, evasive as it is, may well evade the simple statement, may well require the aphoristic, the poetic, the narrative, the caustically satiric. But the intellectual who forgets that his aphorisms ought to be about something, and about important somethings, is living a life of intellect abstracted from life, words abstracted from what they are about. The line between pure wit and clever words in the service of worthy ends is never obvious; but it can be drawn, and it is a line which distinguishes the true intellectual from the counterfeit one, the cosmopolitan intellectual from the phronetic one. The anti-intellectual talk of using "language skills" for "communicating" is no solution either. When it comes to human dialogue in the deeper sense, we aren't talking about skills but ways of being. And ways of being can be encouraged, envisioned, inspired, but never mechanically reproduced.

The graduate-school days of witty combat, and even of not-so-witty battles of logical argumentation, of technically rational but humanly perverse arguments and counterarguments, were, I guess, not a bad way to cut the thinker's teeth, learn the depth of human egoism, cultivate necessary tools of survival and strength of character to survive among the highly cultured and lowly behaved. But, in the end, I don't want to soar combatively, wittily, argumentatively above the things that truly matter, risking ego but not self, establishing intellectual superiority but skirting all of the deeper issues. I want the kind of involvement with the things that the intellect of the intellectual ought to have to do with, the kind of involvement that Heidegger calls for in *What is Philosophy?*:

When we ask, "What is philosophy?" then we are speaking *about* philosophy. By asking in this way we are obviously taking a stand above and, therefore, outside of philosophy. But the aim of our question is to enter *into* philosophy, to tarry in it, to conduct ourselves in its manner, that is, to "philosophize." The path of our discussion must, therefore, not only have a clear direction, but this direction must at the same time give us the guarantee that we are moving within philosophy and not outside of it and around it.

Or the kind of homespun involvement that Wendell Berry describes in "The Making of a Marginal Farm":

In coming home and settling on this place, I began to *live* in my subject, and to learn that living in one's subject is not at all the same as "having" a subject. To live in the place that is one's subject is to pass through the surface. The simplifications of distance and mere observation are thus destroyed. The obsessively regarded reflection is broken and dissolved. One sees that the mirror was a blinder; one can now begin to see where one is. One's relation to one's subject ceases to be merely emotional or aesthetical, or even merely critical, and becomes problematical, practical, and responsible as well. Because it must. It is like marrying your sweetheart.

The intellectual life ought to be a life in which the intellect is fully involved—if only in wisdom-loving inquiry, in aphoristic *essais*, in rambunctious Twainian humor, in hopelessly flawed human dialogue—in the things that truly matter, and thus to live, tragically and comically, close to those things.

I enjoy the logomachy of the cosmopolitan intellect, and I can rise to its venom if need be; but I guess I'm more inclined these days to calmer talks, just talking. These days I'm inclined towards conversations that take place on long walks in the country, on screen porches in hot climates, over dinner in the home of a friend, on my back porch on Sunday morning with my wife, in a blue-collar or redneck bar, in a coffee shop, or in the silence of the soul's dialogue with itself. These days I like to talk to people who don't like to talk, at least until they decide you're worth their time and until they get properly loosened up.

೫೦೦೩

STUDY QUESTIONS

1. In this chapter the author gives an etymology of the English word "wit." Is this relevant, philosophically significant? Martin Heidegger, a philosopher the author repeatedly refers to, dwells extensively on the root meanings of ancient Greek philosophical terms. Is the inquiry into the origins of our words and concepts philosophically necessary or beneficial, or is it a kind of linguistic antiquarianism?

2. Central to the author's argument in this chapter is the notion that words should be *about* something, and that there are ways of talking and writing which are not about anything. The traditional concept of truth as "correspondence" of mind and thing or of word and thing (*adaequatio rei et intellectus*) suggests that words are about things by "corresponding" to them in some way. What is the author's concept of the way words relate to reality?

3. The author says that wit is a form of self-protection—against what?

4. Does the distinction between wit and humor that the author endorses hold up? What is the difference? What do you make of the distinction between "Brahmin wit" and the "yarn humor" of the Southwest that the first epigraph to this chapter refers to?

5. The author says that wit is cosmopolitan. How does he make that connection and is it a legitimate one?

6. In one sense the author aligns himself and his writing with the tradition of the "familiar" English-language essay which features "conversational" English. On the other hand, the author is also critical of that tradition, claiming that its language "was not truly the English of conversation, but of 'conversationalists.'" Should we write exactly the way we talk or the people around us talk? In what sense should good writing be conversational? In what sense is the writing in this book conversational?

7. The author, playing off of a line in one of Friedrich Hölderlin's poems, says: "Conversation is what we are." Clearly, he does not mean that we are literally talking all of the time. What is he trying to get at with this formulation? Aristotle says that someone who lives outside of human society is either a beast or a god. In what sense are we "conversational" beings? In what sense is language inherently social? Contrast this view to the concept of humans as atomistic individuals.

8. At the end of the chapter the author quotes Heidegger's demand that we think about the nature of philosophy in order to enter into philosophy and Wendell Berry's defense of living in his subject as opposed to having a subject. How does this approach conflict with the ordinary concept of objectivity, which requires that we observe an object from the outside in order to avoid personal involvement with it? How does the author's condemnation of "mere wit" fit together with this plea for personal involvement in the subject of inquiry?

FOR FURTHER READING

Epstein, Joseph. "Piece Work: Writing the Essay." In *Plausible Prejudices: Essays on American Writing.* New York: Norton, 1985.

Heidegger, Martin. *What is Philosophy?* Translated by William Kluback and Jean T. Wilde. New Haven: College and University Press, 1956.

Plato. *Gorgias.* In *Plato: Complete Works.* Edited by John M. Cooper. Indianapolis: Hackett, 1997.

> Plato's indictment of Gorgias' sophistic rhetoric, which he contrasts, not to rhetoric-free language, but to the philosophical rhetoric of Socrates. One of the chief characteristic of sophistic language, Socrates brings out, is that it is, like pure wit, not *about* anything.

Little Laramie River near Centennial, Wyoming. Photo by author, 1985.

Seven

THE FISH

> I stared and stared
> and victory filled up
> the little rented boat,
> from the pool of bilge
> where oil had spread a rainbow
> around the rusted engine
> to the bailer rusted orange,
> the sun-cracked thwarts,
> the oarlocks on their strings,
> the gunnels—until everything
> was rainbow, rainbow, rainbow!
> And I let the fish go.
>
> Elizabeth Bishop
from "The Fish"

Mallory was sitting in an old wooden chair that she'd carried down to the gravel point that jutted precariously out into the bend in the river. From the back door of the cabin I could see her just below the trees, the peaceful pools of the small cut-off going off behind her to the left and the roaring rapids of the main river swirling past her to the right. She was reading Norman Maclean's *A River Runs Through It*, which she'd put off reading for several months because she knew we'd be going to the mountains—Wyoming, not Montana where Maclean's book is set, but well-matched nonetheless. It's a common practice to select an appropriate piece of music to set the mood for reading a particular book, or writing one, but driving a thousand miles to find the right setting to read a book is probably extravagant.

Evan was patiently and gleefully casting a spinner bait into the shallow rapids. After much hounding from him, I had broken down and shown him how to use my spare rod, and he had occupied himself for over an hour casting and reeling, occasionally screaming for help when the lure would hang up in the rocks. He was deep in concentration, the motion becoming more fluid with each cast, bearing, not surprisingly, a strong resemblance to the abbreviated overhand throw of a shortstop. Even though Randy and Barbara had grown up on farms, they hadn't gone in for much fishing, and no hunting, so I felt like the backwoods uncle taking the city kid on his first outing.

Release the button just as you cast. That's it. Don't let the lure sink all the way to the bottom or it'll get hung up. Make sure no one's behind you. Watch out for Mallory. Move over here a few steps. Wrist, relax your wrist. That's it . . . .

Travis wasn't interested. He had wandered off to climb the boulder-strewn cliff-side just above the cabins. Barbara had taken the baby back for a nap, and Randy and I, confident that Evan was proficient enough not to hook Mallory or himself in the eye, walked over to the Feezells' cabin where Randy had a six-pack of beer on ice. Just as we got there, a shrill scream burst from the river bottom and echoed from the cliff behind us.

"What in the hell is that?"

We ran back down toward the river, figuring to find Evan with a hook embedded in his forehead. We met him running up from the river carrying the rod; and dangling from the end of the rod was a tiny brook trout, four or five inches at most.

"I caught a fish, I caught a fish," he screamed in near hysteria.

"I'll be damned."

"I caught a fish, a fish—" he screamed excitedly, but now with a bit of apprehension.

"I wasn't sure I could get it off the hook to throw it back," Mallory said. Liberated to the hilt, but not quite ready to forgo the last vestige of male chivalry, my taking her fish off the hook, she was helpless. "I don't think he realizes it will die."

Randy saw what was coming, too. "Evan, if you catch 'em, you've got to keep 'em and eat 'em."

Evan squirmed.

"If you're careful, you can put them back without hurting them," I reassured. "It's probably too small to keep anyway."

"Is it going to die?" Evan asked with an anguished look on his face.

"Well, I don't know. It's been out of the water for a long time. Let me see what I can do."

I removed the small, motionless trout from the hook. It left a visible hole in the side of his mouth. I brought him to the edge of the stream and knelt down at the water's edge. I moved the tiny sliver of a fish back and forth in the still waters behind the point, and finally took him around to the other side and held him head-first into the edge of the current. The clear, chilling waters rushed over him, into him, through him. Evan hovered over my shoulder, as if he'd done something terribly wrong that only an act of the gods could set right. I was no god, just a low-budget fisherman who kept any of his fish that were conceivably big enough to eat and tossed the others immediately back.

The fish moved weakly. I opened my hands, expecting him to swim off, but he rolled over and sank limply to the rock bottom. I moved him through the water again, against the rippling current. Within a few feet of my hands, no doubt dozens of other trout darted in streaks of colored lightning at some hapless smaller creature.

Evan was near tears. My fingers were numb. The tiny fish wiggled, wriggled, wiggled and wriggled again. I opened my fingers, his tail fluttered momentarily, and he vanished into the crystal clear, but impenetrable rapids. I wasn't sure if he would survive that much handling and that long out of the water.

"It's hard to say—he'll probably be all right," I said somewhat pensively. Evan looked out over the river.

☙❧

STUDY QUESTIONS

1. This chapter opens with the author's wife reading Norman Maclean's *A River Runs Through It* which, as the author explains, she had put off reading in order to have the right setting for reading it. In one sense, good books transport us from where we are to another place and time; but they also complement and resonate with our surroundings. Does a life lived well involve a conscious orchestration of literary, aesthetic, and philosophical experiences? Throughout this book the author repeatedly refers to his reading of literature. What is the relationship between reading about mountains and being in them, reading about what it means to be human and living a human life?

2. What is the significance of the story about Evan catching his first fish and realizing that it's going to die? We've been exposed to the beauty of the mountains and the rivers so far, but this chapter introduces a new element in our encounter with the natural cycles. Based on the themes that have been established thus far and the titles of the upcoming chapters, how do you expect this chapter to foreshadow some of the themes that will come up in later chapters?

FOR FURTHER READING

Maclean, Norman. *A River Runs Through It, and Other Stories*. Chicago: The University of Chicago Press, 1976.

> A classic of American literature, sometimes devalued because of its "regionalism" and its "naturalism." The finest writing about fly fishing ever, but fly fishing as the thread that ties together a family and a family with the beauty and mystery of nature. One of the greatest opening passages and one of the greatest closing passages in all of American literature.

Longhorns in bluebonnets near Glen Rose, Texas. Photo by Kathryn Jones, 2006 (used with permission).

Eight

"A MINOR REGIONAL NOVELIST"

> Certainly the secret of being a poet, Irish or otherwise, lies in the summoning of the energies of words. But my quest for definition, while it may lead backward, is conducted in this living speech of the landscape I was born into. If you like, I began as a poet when my roots were crossed with my reading. I think of the personal and Irish pieties as vowels, and the literary awarenesses nourished on English as consonants. My hope is that the poems will be vocables adequate to my whole experience.
>
> Seamus Heaney
> "Belfast"

> The writer operates at a peculiar crossroads where time and place and eternity somehow meet. His problem is to find that location.
>
> Flannery O'Connor
> "The Regional Writer," *Mystery and Manners*

A number of years ago, Larry McMurtry came to speak at the mid-size state university in Texas where I teach. The very next day the national press announced that he had won a Pulitzer prize for his trail-drive epic, *Lonesome Dove*. The members of our symposium committee were distraught that the announcement hadn't come a day earlier. Then he could have been contacted at the Stephenville Holiday Inn instead of the one in Uvalde, and the name of our humble little town would have appeared in every paper in the country.

Was this the same Larry McMurtry who had penned this well-founded skepticism in 1968:

> As a regionalist, and a regionalist from an unpopular region, I find the problem of how to get heard rather a fascinating one. I haven't found it especially depressing, but then I wouldn't have gone in for writing if I hadn't liked talking to myself. I quite recognize that there have always been literary capitals and literary provinces, and that those who choose for whatever reason to abide in the provinces need not expect a modish recognition.

The same McMurtry who had sarcastically said that all a Texas writer needed to do to get *The New York Review of Books* to beat a path to his door is explain the assassination of Kennedy and make it possible for President Johnson to be impeached?

Fact of the matter is, even in the summer of 1987 a friend of mine, a major critic of Southwestern and Western literature, wrote the following sentence in an overview of all of the reviews of McMurtry's *Texasville*: "I doubt if I will live to see the day when *The New York Review of Books* takes note of a Texas writer." The next day—really, the very next day—the latest issue arrived in the mail with a lengthy review essay on *Lonesome Dove*, *Texasville*, and the reissue of *The Last Picture Show*. Luckily, my friend's review of the reviews had not gone into print, and in the final version he replaced his *faux pas* with a sagacious remark about a David Levine caricature in *The New York Review of Books* showing that McMurtry really had made it.

Never mind that the reviewer was a New Yorker living in Santa Fe; that he screwed up the geography of McMurtry's Archer County (he has McMurtry from Wichita Falls, when in fact he was born there but grew up around Archer City, and he has the fictitious Thalia based on the real Thalia, which was the source of the name only, instead of Archer City); that he mentioned two successful movies made from McMurtry's novels, the two that share the same names as the novels, and somehow neglects *Hud*, based on McMurtry's first novel, *Horseman, Pass By*; that he completely missed the ironic, critical perspective on the heroes of *Lonesome Dove*; that he therefore wimpily concerned himself with the fact that these heroes aren't *sympathique* because they are too violent; that even though he saw in the *Texasville* characters "endurance" and "vitality," he played to his New York, his intellectual, audience's need to give thanks that they are not from the Thalias of this world, or, if they are, that they have escaped.

But never mind all of that. McMurtry had made it into the most intellectual of intellectual review publications, into the Glass Bead Game of the book world. Despite the reviewer's shortfalls, he did compare McMurtry's literary windows on the small-town world favorably with Thomas Hardy's anti-provincial tomes. He even suggested that Eastern critics had mistaken McMurtry for a writer of cowboy melodramas because of his Western settings, and that even though "comparison with classic American writers is probably premature," he concluded that Wichita Falls (which should of course read Archer City) has indeed "produced an artist." And the creator of Hud had received not only modish recognition, but recognition from the highest brow in New York's publishing world.

Back in the early 70s McMurtry had sported a T-shirt emblazoned with the words of a reviewer: A MINOR REGIONAL NOVELIST. Had he now become a major regional novelist? Or was he no longer regional? He had certainly gained a national reputation, even in some intellectual circles. But *Lonesome Dove* and *Texasville* teeter on a thin line between literary high-mindedness and good popular fiction, and the *New York Review of Books* treatment teetered between a serious positive review and self-satisfying confirmation that life in the provinces is just as bad as we thought it would be. "Zero culture" was the reviewer's summation. But McMurtry shows us the zero culture well. . . . Did the folks at the New School for Social Research run out in droves to buy their copies after reading the review? I doubt it. Still, to the extent that he had "made it," McMurtry was no longer a regional novelist, major, minor, or otherwise. McMurtry had taken offense at the regionalist moniker because, in certain circles, it is a tool of condescension, sometimes hardly conscious, but nonetheless a tacit snub. Ironically, it was *Lonesome Dove*, a return to his regional roots after several, shall we say, "transient" offerings of lesser quality, that exploded the regionalist label for McMurtry. What McMurtry has done with that national recognition since *Lonesome Dove* is a matter of some disagreement, but the story of *Lonesome Dove* still makes my point.

Norman Maclean tells a story about a publisher, presumably in New York, returning his autobiographical stories set in his boyhood Montana with this complaint: "These stories have trees in them." Maclean, a professor emeritus from the University of Chicago, had his own circle of intellectual connections, though, and the University of Chicago Press published his book. It is a masterpiece. New York can't take all the blame, though—a Chicago editor suggested that Carolyn Osborn's short stories shouldn't be set in Texas because that made them seem "provincial." Osborn spent her early childhood in Tennessee, and has been living in Texas since 1946 when she was twelve. Asking her to set her stories elsewhere would be like asking Faulkner not to set his stories in Mississippi. Luckily, she won the argument. The battle goes on: I remember reading in *Newsweek* about a mystery writer from Chicago who had some difficulty selling her first manuscript because New York publishers were afraid that a Midwestern setting would seem "alien" to readers. To what readers?

There is a recurring contradiction between the world of the intellectual and the world of the writer, or at least the world of a good number of the very best writers. Some intellectuals, true intellectuals, belong to a place, have a sense of local origins; some writers inhabit the ether of pure intellect, or at least they worship globe-hopping to the exclusion of home-soil remembrance. But the reverse is more common. Intellectuals, the people who read, judge, and engage in conversation about books, believe that leading an intellectual life, which of course includes reading books by people like Faulkner and Frost, will free the intellectual from the uncivilized customs and prejudices of local identities. Although the writers and thinkers I have in mind never belong to their places with all the innocence of a child or an uneducated local, they recognize in themselves and in the human condition the power of the home place. There are writers who are intellectuals and who play out the prejudices of the intellectual life with great wit and artistry—Henry James, T. S. Eliot, and a host of other Americans who wanted to be European—but the great traditions, American, European, classical, Biblical, are not cosmopolitan, but stubbornly aboriginal. Intellectuals stuck in the cosmopolitan stage tend toward cosmopolitan writers, but sometimes they engage in the bald-faced contradiction of thinking they have become worldly by reading writers who thrive on the spirit of localized place.

Do they believe the message of Faulkner is that one should not be from Mississippi? Or that if one is, one should hightail it the hell out? Faulkner scholars tend to be Southerners who know where they're from, but I've known quite a few who have religiously refused to apply Faulkner's insights about his homeland, his loving it and hating it, to themselves. In my own quest for cosmopolitan citizenship, I started reading Martin Heidegger's poetic evocations of Black Forest roots without the slightest notion that in order to emulate Heidegger's thinking I would have to come to terms with Texas, not the Black Forest—or perhaps Texas and the Black Forest. Of course, I had to go to the very hillside, stand next to Heidegger's hut above the village of Todtnauberg, to realize that I was as rooted in my Gulf Coast, my frontier myths, my Louisiana parents, as he was in his bucolic Black Forest. Was Heidegger a regional philosopher? Was Kant? Was Plato?

Eudora Welty wrote a great deal about the regional identifications of the writer:

> It seems plain that the art that speaks more clearly, explicitly, directly and passionately from its place of origin will remain the longest understood. It is through place that we put out roots, wherever birth, chance, fate or our traveling selves set us down; but where those roots reach toward—whether in America, England or Timbuktu—is the deep and running vein, eternal and consistent and everywhere purely itself, that feeds and is fed by the human understanding.

But she knew the confusion and the condescension of the term regional too:

> When I speak of writing from where you have put down roots, it may be said that what I urge is "regional" writing. "Regional," I think, is a careless term, as well as a condescending one, because what it does is fail to differentiate between the localized raw material of life and its outcome as art. "Regional" is an outsider's term; it has no meaning for the insider who is doing the writing, because as far as he knows he is simply writing about life. Jane Austen, Emily Brontë, Thomas Hardy, Cervantes, Turgenev, the authors of the books of the Old Testament, all confined themselves to regions, great or small—but are they regional? Then who from the start of time has not been so?

John Graves wrote in *Goodbye to a River*, "And one river, seen right, may well be all rivers that flow to the sea." To call a writer with such a universalizing project a regional writer is true in one sense and dangerously misleading in another. The very category cries out for some serious rethinking.

Perhaps Southern American writers, perhaps Western American writers, make more of the rooted aspect of the human, live it out, write it out self-consciously, hold onto it as it threatens to slip away into modernity's homogeneity. It's not all there is, but it's essential. There's pure imagination too, soaring, infinite, pure possibility. It is, we might say, the interaction of native memory and unattached imagination that enables a person to pick up stakes and set out for new territories, for a new home where at least the children will have different roots. But whether a person stays, or returns, or sets out and never comes back, human self-understanding has to deal with the finitude, the fatedness, of individual lives. No matter how intellectual we become, even if we move from place to place military-brat-style, we grow up in, live in, particular places. The voices of those places talk all around us and inside of us and make us who we are, and the winds and the lay of land and the fall of the snow, or the rain, or the shimmering summer rays.

The writers who dig the deepest into Eudora Welty's vein of humanity call up their places and voices, whether from Manhattan or Texas. If I turn to the very literature that I voraciously soaked up precisely at the age when I was intent upon losing my provincial origins, I find writers who were as Greek or German or English or Italian or Irish as I am Texan. Let me add to Welty's list.

Was Homer a regionalist? Was he provincial? Was Odysseus, whom history has rewritten into the great adventurer, the lover of travel? Not Homer's Odysseus—he rejected the Phaeacians' life of painless high culture abstracted from human fatefulness and Circe's offer of eternal bliss for the mortality of home. We become more "worldly" in the encounter with Homer's *Odyssey* not because Homer was a worldly intellectual who preached against provincialism; in Homer's story we encounter a homesick wanderer. We encounter not the world, but another province that puts our province to the test, holds it up to a challenging light. Homer's story is epic because it ends up revealing something universal about human life, about the injustice of war, about courage and cunning, about the sacredness of hearth and home, about the unadventuresome relation of fathers and sons and husband and wife. The Greeks were great sailors, colonizers, warriors; but, remember, they called anyone who did not speak Greek the *barbaroi*.

Italy's greatest contribution to "world" literature, Dante Alighieri, wrote about good and evil, salvation and damnation, virtue and vice, and everything in between, which is why my high school English teacher in Houston, Texas, some seven centuries later expected me to read him in order to transcend my provincial view on the world. Dante the pilgrim may well be the ultimate world traveler, who journeys to heaven and hell and back; but Dante's poetry is populated with the places and people and stories of his localized experiences. Dante belongs to the world, but it doesn't take long in central and northern Italy to see how much Dante belonged and still belongs there. Every hilltop village seems to have at least one plaque with a quotation from Dante that refers to that village. In the fortress at Gradara, just off the Adriatic coast, you'll be shown the very room, legend has it, where the murder of Francesca da Rimini and Paolo Malatesta, recounted by Dante in the fifth canto of the *Inferno*, took place. That story speaks across countless cultures and centuries, but, in Welty's terms, he got it from and crafted it out of the "localized raw materials" of his life. And even his language is local: Dante wrote his universal poetry in his native Tuscan dialect. It's hard for us to think of the Italian of *La divina commedia* as a local dialect, since it sounds like an earlier version of standardized modern Italian. But that's because his poetry, written in his native dialect, had a major influence on the development of modern Italian. Was Dante a regional writer?

Shakespeare dealt with universal themes as well, but his Elizabethan eyes and ears found the local sounds and the customs, the street-vendor turns of phrase, by means of which he crafted his universal tales. Even when he played off of foreign sagas, from Denmark or ancient Rome, the characters sound unabashedly Elizabethan. The actors of Shakespeare's day played Hamlet in Elizabethan English get-up, and Julius Caesar looks upon an anachronistic clock. Was Shakespeare a provincial? A regionalist? J. Frank Dobie, Texas folklorist and the originator of a course on Life and Literature of the Southwest at the University of Texas at Austin in the 1920s, once remarked that Shakespeare was his kind of regionalist.

And, since we are retracing the literature that made me worldly, take the damnable Irish. Yeats was obsessed with a national literature:

> Irish poets, learn your trade,
> Sing whatever is well made,
> Scorn the sort now growing up
> All out of shape from toe to top,
> Their unremembering hearts and heads
> Base-born products of base beds.
> Sing the peasantry, and then
> Hard-riding country gentlemen,
> The holiness of monks, and after
> Porter-drinkers' randy laughter;
> Sing the lords and the ladies gay
> That were beaten into the clay
> Through seven heroic centuries;
> Cast your mind on other days
> That we in coming days may be
> Still the indomitable Irishry.

These days I read Seamus Heaney's less apocalyptic, but more faithfully Irish and, if you will, truthfully warm-eyed lyricism. But, I ask you, should Yeats be demoted as a poet because he wrote of Irish poets and not just of poets pure and true? Ireland of his time was a hopelessly superstitious, proudly uncultured, quintessentially provincial sort of province. Provinces, of course, are usually provinces in relation to capitals, empires, civilizations. England was of course the empire of empires, and Ireland the province of provinces. But, oh, what a music in the tongue, these Celtic-rhythmed English speakers. It's no accident that my fellow provincial, the world-traveled John Graves, quoted this line from

Yeats in his elegy to a Texas river: "Have not all races had their first unity from a mythology, that marries them to rock and hill?"

Even the expatriate Irishman par excellence remembered where he hailed from. In a very fine poem called "Gravities," Seamus Heaney reminds us that

> Blinding in Paris, for his party piece
> Joyce named the shops along O'Connell Street....

I am reminded of Frank O'Connor in Annapolis, Maryland. He spent a number of his later years in Annapolis before returning to Ireland. Ironically, I learned the lesson of the writer's relation to his homeland most powerfully from the stories of this very foreign foreigner, perhaps because I got to know his son Myles through highly un-literary circumstances. Many years after Frank O'Connor's death, I was walking along State Circle in Annapolis with Myles, musing, I suspect, about my own expatriation there, certainly not as world-historically significant as Frank O'Connor's but just as befuddling. We stopped at the beginning of Maryland Avenue, which heads off past antique shops, art galleries, the Little Campus where his father was known to partake of the Creature from time to time, and down to the Naval Academy grounds. Myles pointed to the sidewalk outside of Johnson's clothing store, where he had recently spent the few hundred dollars he had to buy a fine suit, so, as he put it, he would have something to be buried in.

"One afternoon, when I was about sixteen," he said as he gazed upon the light pole at the corner of Maryland Avenue, "I was walking along with my new American girlfriend. As we rounded the corner, right there, we ran into my father, dressed in his Irish tweeds and tasseled tam. I was embarrassed by him, by his foreignness, by his accent and his clothes. Of course, my girlfriend loved him. He wrote a story about it."

I had a clear image of the whole episode, and every time I passed that corner from then on I could see the look on Myles's face as clear as if I had been there. Sometime later when I finally got my hands on the story, I discovered nothing of the Annapolis I knew. Frank O'Connor had set the story in his childhood Cork. Like Faulkner and his South, O'Connor loved and hated his boyhood Cork, but it was, whether he was in Dublin or New York or Annapolis or London, the very stuff of which his stories were made.

Once O'Connor criticized Joyce by saying that when he left Dublin he lost track of his "submerged population" and ended up turning to his own subjectivity: "This is something that is always liable to happen to the provincial storyteller when you put him into a cosmopolitan atmosphere," he wrote. O'Connor was not satisfied with the names of the shops along O'Connell Street. I think Joyce's novels are certainly an exploration of his own subjectivity, but I would suggest that they reflect the power of Joyce's submerged population, of his Irish-ness, differently but just as much as O'Connor does his. I am attracted more to O'Connor, to the so-called "provincial realism" of his stories, because I am looking for deeply rooted writers, living out my protest against cosmopolitanism; but Joyce is rooted in his way, too.

But even forgetting Joyce, what do we do with Frank O'Connor? A major regional short-story writer? He learned his trade at the feet of Yeats; explored the most fundamental and universal traits of human relations with timeless vision; published dozens of stories in that mouthpiece of American cosmopolitanism, *The New Yorker*; lived in several different countries; served on the Board of Directors of the Abbey Theater in Dublin; lectured at Harvard and Stanford—but set virtually every story he wrote in his native Cork, built his worldly status from the poverty and turmoil of his provincial origins. He railed against the provincialism of Cork, even of Ireland; when in Annapolis, he wrote to Irish friends of the provincialism of Annapolis; but he showed in his stories the inextricable ties between the provincial and the human. In his heart and in his writing, he never left home.

And if I turn to the other great European love of my younger days, German literature, which I read religiously in my college days in order to become worldly, to escape my cowboy provincialism? I could easily ask about Hölderlin's many poems on homecoming, following along in Heidegger's interpretive footsteps. But look even at Goethe, whose *Faust* earned him a place in the pantheon of "world literature." Read his autobiography, not just the passage I've already cited on his provincial accent, but the whole story of his provincial origins. Hölderlin a provincial? God help us, Goethe a provincial?

In the American literature that has reached the status of global significance, the story is the same. Look at the power of particular time and place in Hawthorne and Melville. Twain's return to his Mississippi River boyhood for his tales of shared humanity is renowned. And—I can't seem to escape him—there's Faulkner's Yoknapatawpha County, a fictional place as true and real as the true and real place it was based on. Even the French read Faulkner—I'm not quite sure how, but I know why. We can surely find less of a "submerged population" in Wallace Stevens than, say, in Robert Frost, but there's a good deal of region even in Stevens. In Frost it's dominant. Chicago echoed from the pages of Saul Bellow, even as the Swedish ink dried on the document proclaiming him as international as Kipling, Yeats, Hesse, and Albert Camus.

How do you get from the regional raw material of life to the outcome that is art, so that cosmopolitan intellectuals will cease to call you regional and admit you to the canon of high art? You do indeed have to dig down through the merely regional to the human vein, the wellsprings—no easy task. The merely regional would no doubt be an artistic, and a moral, failure. But there is no such thing as the purely universal. The condescension toward literature that reflects its author's region—intentional or not—offers no help in the matter. If it is artistic failure that earns a novelist the cosmopolitan's label of regionalism, then that would seem to imply that artistic success would consist of art that does not reflect the author's region, art that has no hint of provincial origins, or, lord forbid, provincial residence. The greatest literature, in my book, is provincial *and* universal, and the latter by way of the visionary use of the former. And even the notion of raw material for artistic use, perhaps an accurate description of the actual creative process, paints a one-sided, much too condescending picture. The people of one's home are not just raw material; there's a certain sense in which the artistic outcome is "for" the people of one's homeland, even if they don't read it or don't understand it if they do. Flannery O'Connor goes so far as to say (and why shouldn't she go that far): "I wouldn't want to suggest that the Georgia writer has the unanimous, collective ear of his community, but only that his true audience, the audience he checks himself by, is at home." And in the same essay: "For no matter how favorable all the critics in New York City may be, they are an unreliable lot, as incapable now as on the day they were born of interpreting Southern literature to the world." Flannery O'Connor's stories are worthy of being interpreted to the world because, no matter how much her vision transcended the people of her homeland, she never forgot that she was one of them.

I learned these lessons largely from great writers of other provinces in part because I started adult life in a frenzied attempt to escape my province—and in part because my own province admittedly wasn't exactly teeming with great writers to teach me where I was from, or least with writers who had received the stamp of greatness. And I wasn't willing to learn from anyone who hadn't received that stamp. Katherine Anne Porter had, but in order to do it she had covered her Texas tracks pretty well. Of course, if I'd read "Noon Wine" or "The Old Order" I would have seen it then. And some other very fine, if not great writers—several of whose books may yet vie with history for the status of literary greatness—could have told me then, except that I was headlong into the flight to the life of the intellectual, and my professors at the University of Texas, generally speaking, were eager to send their prize students off to the hallowed halls of truly cosmopolitan graduate schools with nary a trace of their Texas origins left.

So I came back to my native ground by learning about rootedness from the classics of European and American literature, and by confronting the contradiction between admiring the rootedness of writers from other cultures and rejecting my own. Only then was I able to come back to writers from my own province; only then did I realize that to find that human vein that Eudora Welty talks about I would have to dig down deep enough in my own provincial soil. It's a journey I had to make, though. There's a great intensity that comes from the tension between reputedly humble origins and high intellectual or artistic aspiration, from the going away from and the eventual coming to terms with the inescapable stamp of origins. It comes from the power of troubling ambivalence, a working out but never fully getting it worked out of art and life, mind and home.

Nowadays as I watch my own students coming of intellectual age, much has changed, but I think they confront the same contradiction, only intensified and more virulently politicized. Certainly, the very idea of a literary canon has long been under attack, and although it's still expected that one will be familiar with the dead white males I was required to read, they are often thought of in current intellectual circles as nothing more than an expression of the imperialist, capitalist, Eurocentric, phallocentric culture than spawned them. But the phenomenon I am describing has simply taken on a more exaggerated form. Whereas I had to demonstrate a rejection of my Southern and Texan roots in order to be admitted into the exclusive club of worldly intellectuals, this generation must rail against the entirety of American capitalist values, indeed against the entirety of Western civilization. In one sense, for American and European intellectuals, the rejection of one's own roots is still a rite of passage; only it's become more encompassing, and the quasi-moral and self-righteously politicized slant on it more strident.

But the contradiction is still there, and it's more overt. My generation became worldly, escaped its provincialism, by embracing European writers rooted in their own soils; students now escape their province by embracing "indigenous" writers from Africa and India, by embracing a literary xenophilia complete with a canon every bit as rigid as the one I came up on. It should follow without saying, based on what I've said so far, that I support genuinely indigenous writing wherever it's from, but how is it that I should applaud the indigenous character of Arundhati Roy's *The God of Small Things* and condemn my own rootedness? I, too, am indigenous. If Arundhati Roy should be applauded for coming to terms with her own culture and place, then why shouldn't I? In today's climate, then, the phronetic intellectual should realize that studying indigenous writing from foreign cultures does broaden our perspective and take us beyond the perspective of our own province, but, in the end, it should bring us back to reflect on our own rootedness.

Of course, there is a political and quasi-moral dimension I have neglected here. "Indigenous" culture in current parlance means a culture that has been the victim of Western imperialism and colonialism. "Indigenous" or "post-colonial" writing means writing in former colonies that reveals the injustices of European and American—and now we must add, I suppose, Israeli—colonialism. Of course, writers from the imperialist Western cultures can score intellectual points, too, so long as they are condemning that culture, or can be construed to be condemning that culture. Indigenous cultures are good when they are resisting the tide of capitalist globalization in Africa, but presumably the indigenous culture of north-central Texas where I live is nothing more than an expression of the "hegemony" of Wal-Mart and Coca-Cola.

To my mind, this way of thinking represents a thoughtless reductionism that can only survive in the absence of genuine criticism and reflection, but that would take us far afield; in fact, it would take another book. Suffice it to say that young American intellectuals, especially from the South or West or Midwest, must still reject their own literary roots and embrace the rootedness of writings from foreign cultures in order to receive their intellectual walking papers, and that a phronetic reflection on that contradiction still can and should, but often doesn't, lead to a spiritual homecoming. To the extent that the emphasis on indigenous writing and indigenous cultures might get all of us to see that localized human roots—limiting, debilitating, enabling, and all that they are—lead to that one enduring vein of humanity, that is a "political" consequence of literature and literary study I embrace. To the extent that the emphasis on indigenous writing might get all of us to see that we share the predicament of having to deal with the particularities that life, history, culture, and geography have dealt us, that would be a good thing. Somehow, I think, it's going the opposite direction.

ಸಂಚಿ

STUDY QUESTIONS

1. The author indicates that in application to literature the term "regional" is a term of condemnation. Is that true in other areas? Is the term "regional cuisine" negative? "Regional university"? What is negative about literature, or anything else, being regional? What is wrong with literature, or anything else, being "merely regional"?

2. The author quotes Eudora Welty advocating deeply rooted art, but those roots, she claims reach down to "the deep and running vein, eternal and consistent and everywhere purely itself, that feeds and is fed by the human understanding." How does this relate to the earlier remark in chapter 2 about looking for the universal in the particular? Is there something about the human understanding, about humanity, that is always and everywhere the same? And, if so, does it make sense to say that we can understand it only by embracing our particular experiences? Is this a contradiction? A paradox?

3. Why doesn't anyone ever refer to Homer or Sophocles or Dante or Shakespeare as a "regionalist"? Does the author's claim that most great literature is strongly rooted in a local culture hold up?

4. Why does the author take issue with Eudora Welty's distinction "between the localized raw material of life and its outcome as art"? How should writers view their relationship to the people they write about? Are the "characters" in this book "raw material"? In his acknowledgments the author quotes Joan Didion's famous remark that "Writers are always selling somebody out." Contrast that remark with the remark that the author quotes from Flannery O'Connor that the writer's "true audience, the audience he checks himself by, is at home." And Wendell Berry's comment, quoted in chapter 6, about living in his subject rather than having a subject. What moral obligations does a writer have to the people he or she writes about?

5. The author claims that he came to appreciate his own native ground "by learning about rootedness from the classics of European and American literature, and by confronting the contradiction between admiring the rootedness of writers from other cultures and rejecting my own." Reading these writers from other cultures presumably had also played a role in the author's passage from the first stage, the stage of naive prejudice, to the second, the cosmopolitan stage. How

does reading writers from other cultures present a challenge to the assumptions and prejudices we grow up with? Does reading a writer rooted in another culture and place have a broadening influence? Is the author right, though, that reading writers rooted in other cultures and places can lead us back to our own roots? Why doesn't the author's return to his own roots amount to a regression from the cosmopolitan stage to the first stage of naive prejudice? What does this recognition, that the great classics of European and American literature are firmly rooted in their native soil, imply for a reflective person trying to live a wise and just life?

6. The author is critical of what he calls a xenophilial approach to the question of a literary canon, claiming that contemporary intellectual culture tends to embrace "indigenous writing" from former European colonies and condemn the traditional European literary canon. Is a literary canon, as some contemporary literary intellectuals claim, simply a matter of who has the power to enforce it? Do the writers of the traditional European literary canon always express the values and promote the interests of the dominant forces in that culture or do they sometimes cast a critical light upon them? Is there such a thing as literary merit? If so, is it timeless or is it relative to the needs and concerns of each particular age? And if some works are timeless, is that a matter of transcending time, of standing outside of time, or is it the result of a continuing process of renewal? Is the concept of a "classic" legitimate? If so, what makes a classic a classic? Does it make sense, at the author argues, to read the literary and philosophical works of one's own culture even if they have not earned a spot in the canon of "world literature"?

FOR FURTHER READING

Clifford, Craig. *In the Deep Heart's Core: Reflections on Life, Letters, and Texas*. Texas A&M University Press, 1985.

Clifford, Craig and William T. Pilkington, eds. *Range Wars: Heated Debates, Sober Reflections, and Other Assessments of Texas Writing*. Dallas: Southern Methodist University Press, 1989.

Knox, Bernard. *The Oldest Dead White European Males: And Other Reflections on the Classics*. New York: Norton, 1993.

An argument for the enduring relevance of the ancient Greeks.

McMurtry, Larry. *Horseman, Pass By*. New York: Penguin, 1979 [1961].

———. *Lonesome Dove*. New York: Simon and Schuster, 1985.

———. *In a Narrow Grave: Essays on Texas*. Austin: Encino Press, 1968.

> McMurtry is of course best known as a novelist, but he is also a fine essayist. "Take My Saddle from the Wall: A Valediction," a reflection on the McMurtry clan, is a masterpiece of writing that finds the universally human in the peculiarities of particular roots.

O'Connor, Flannery. *Mystery and Manners: Occasional Prose*. Edited by Sally and Robert Fitzgerald. New York: Farrar, Straus and Giroux, 1984 [1969].

Welty, Eudora. *The Eye of the Story: Selected Essays and Reviews*. New York: Vintage, 1979.

———. *One Writer's Beginnings*. Cambridge: Harvard University Press, 1984.

Ranch near Centennial, Wyoming. Photo by author, 1985.

Nine

WANA

"You came in on the forest-service road? It's pretty rough. A few years ago there were three women who were renting rooms here in the house. They were kind of peculiar, and they weren't really seeing anything or doing anything. I was a bit younger then, and I decided to take them on a day-long drive, about a hundred miles all total. Well, we packed up sandwiches and headed out at sunrise. Everything was just fine until we got to the forest-service road, the one you came in on. I told them this was the prettiest scenery of the day, but when I glanced at them, there they were with their hands over their heads, scared to death we'd bounce off a rock in the road and go right over the edge. *Oh my God, oh my God*, they were whispering. They never looked up once 'til we got back to the paved road."

She covered her head with a slightly exaggerated dramatic flair.

"That was the funniest thing I've ever seen, three grown women afraid to open their eyes for twenty miles of the prettiest countryside in America."

"I was a little worried at times, but I always pick the back roads."

"Did you come in on the forest-service road?"

"Yes, ma'am. I always take the back roads."

"You know people come out here and sometimes they're real disappointed. It's pretty rough."

"Wana" was her first name. Of course, we called her by her properly prefixed, second married name when we addressed her, but we couldn't resist referring to her among ourselves as Wana. Not out of disrespect by any means, but because the name had the same spunky, matter-of-fact character that she had. A woman named Wana would live in Wyoming and drive three introverted city-slicked spinsters over a dirt-and-rock road along the edge of a sheer drop-off canyon.

Her name was even spelled like it ought to be spelled in Wyoming. When Barbara had called to give Mallory the information about the cabins, Mallory, well-schooled in Tex-Mex, wrote down "Juana" without a second thought. How else would you spell it? When we drove up to the big mailbox at the entrance to the ranch, we saw the W-A-N-A clearly printed on the side of it, looked at each other, and simultaneously said, "Wana. Oh."

"What's it like in the winter?" I asked her. I noticed that her cookstove was half electric and half wood stove, and there were wood stoves for heat in other parts of the house. I figured there must be times when the power lines are out for days.

"It's cold, but we get by. That's why you see all those people up in the mountains cutting wood."

She glanced out of the screen door.

"My second husband was killed in a snow storm in '62, right over there on that hill. Tractor turned over on him."

She certainly hadn't hightailed it into town. Her son and a grandson and their families lived on the place and helped her run it. When we met her grandson's wife, she was carrying around a brand-new baby. Would that next generation stay on the ranch? Stay in Wyoming? She told us about the University of Wyoming giving special breaks to children of its alumni, because so many Wyomingites were going out of state to college.

Wana had taught school for 35 years in Laramie—retired in the 60s. She had been retired longer than I had been working. It was easy to picture her in front of a classroom full of boys and girls with good solid, straightforward names like her own. I imagine there weren't discipline problems, and I imagine she would throw in a good yarn or two when interest and enthusiasm needed a bit of a boost. She could tell a good story.

I could also imagine her over the years, taking in tourists every summer, in the ranch house and in the cabins. The ones in the house she fed at the big dining-room table every night, and I can imagine the stories swapped there. She told us about the traveling salesman, who would walk out the ten miles from Centennial in the dead of winter, his overcoat pockets filled with watches and assorted gadgets.

"He came through a couple of times a year, for maybe ten or twelve years. He'd stay for a few days. Unusual man. He carried a jar of this health food—now what do you call it? Wheat germ—that's it. Every morning he'd sprinkle a bunch of this wheat germ on his oatmeal. Everyone thought he did it for health reasons, but one time when he was here I ran out of oatmeal. I told him I'd try to figure out something else that he could put his wheat germ in, and he admitted, after all those years, that he was putting the wheat germ in the oatmeal because he didn't like oatmeal. Isn't that something?"

"I'll be—"

"My son and grandson want me to quit taking in boarders. Think I should start taking it easy. I don't advertise anymore. For several years now, I've only taken return guests who already know about me, or a few who find out like you did. It's not that hard, though. My son and grandson cut wood for the cabins and keep the path mowed—you know, the path to the outdoor plumbing. I cook and clean up for the guests in the house, but my grandson's wife helps out. It's kind of a family affair."

Barbara had called up the Laramie Chamber of Commerce and asked for information about cabins in the mountains. The woman she talked to was going to mail her the usual package of shiny brochures, but Barbara asked if she knew of anything a little off the beaten path. The woman hesitated, then asked if we would be interested in some really rustic cabins. She knew this retired school teacher, a real interesting person, a character. She wasn't sure whether she was still renting them out, but we could try. At that time, all we had come up with was a two-bedroom condo in central Colorado—tennis courts, sauna, wall-to-wall New Yorkers and Houstonians. Rustic, hell yes—give me that phone number. . . .

"The family that stayed in the back cabin just before you came was from Wisconsin. They used it as a base and traveled all over the state. I've had people from all over the country. No one from Texas, though. Now I hope the cabins aren't too rough for you. I always try to explain to people so they know what they're getting into."

"No, ma'am. Just what we were looking for."

"Did you stop at the university on your way through Laramie?"

"Well, yes, we did," Randy said.

"We came in the back way, on the forest-service road," I chimed in.

"We're proud of it." She talked for a while about some of the professors she'd known. "I don't know if he's still around. He might be retired. Built up that department single-handedly—now he was a strange one. It's a handsome campus."

"I did stop by the philosophy department," Randy explained. "We both teach philosophy," he said looking toward me. "Also looked over the baseball field. They've got a respectable division-one program. I played a little college baseball, and Travis is getting ready to." Travis nodded. "It's a nice campus. It's sort of a habit with me—whenever I get to a town that has a university, that's the first place I go. Looks like they've got a pretty good honors program—"

"It's too bad, you know—a lot of our kids are going to college out of state." Wana turned her attention back to us. "Now you'll have to stop by on the way out," she scolded. We said we'd definitely go out through Laramie and stop by. She was satisfied.

We walked out onto the porch. She surveyed her domain.

"I've got three miles of river you can fish on. My place goes from that pasture there over to that one," she explained with the sweep of her hand. The air was crisp, the sky as big as Texas. Her land sloped up against the main range of the Medicine Bow Mountains, and the peaks of the Snowy Range were the centerpiece of the goddamnedest front-porch view I've ever seen.

ೞಃ

STUDY QUESTIONS

1. The great college basketball coach John Wooden once said that he wanted his players to have character, not be characters. Wana certainly is *a* character, but the author clearly thinks that she *has* character as well. What does the author admire about Wana's character? Although she is a retired school teacher, the author does not appear to think of her as an intellectual, either of the pseudo or genuine variety. Aristotle says that the highest form of human life is the con-

templative life, but he hastens to explain that that life is only available to a few. Most humans, he says, actually live a hedonistic life, but most should strive to live what he calls a "political life," which is a life for the sake of moral virtue, what we might call a life for the sake of good character. What can you tell from the author's account of Wana in this chapter about her character?

2. How does Wana serve as a foil for the pseudo-intellectuals the author is condemning? How does Wana's story about the three women she takes on a tour of the countryside mirror the conflict between the genuine and pseudo-intellectuals that the author is trying to articulate? How does her life and the life of her children and grandchildren provide a sharp contrast to the cosmopolitan life that the author criticizes? Is she provincial? Are her children and grandchildren living on her ranch provincial? If you were a professor at the University of Wyoming and you were teaching her grandchildren or great grandchildren, would you advise them to transfer to a university in another state? To leave the family ranch and move to a city?

FOR FURTHER READING

Webb, Walter Prescott. *The Great Plains*. Lincoln: University of Nebraska Press, 1981 [1931].

> A seminal exploration of the effect of the land and climate of the American West on the people who settled it.

Bass Performance Hall, Fort Worth, Texas. Photo by author, 2006.

Kimbell Art Museum, Fort Worth, Texas. Photo by author, 2006.

Ten

CULTURE VULTURES

> Well, then, the works themselves stand and hang in collections and exhibitions. But are they here in themselves as the works they themselves are, or are they not rather here as objects of the art industry? Works are made available for public and private art appreciation. Official agencies assume the care and maintenance of works. Connoisseurs and critics busy themselves with them. Art dealers supply the market. Art-historical study makes the works the objects of a science. Yet in all this busy activity do we encounter the work itself?
>
> Martin Heidegger
> "The Origin of the Work of Art"

I recall a friend in Maryland who was a living lesson on the limits of another well-worn high-tone prejudice. He was a Southern gentleman, Vanderbilt-educated, cultivated and cultured in manner, speech, and values to the nth degree. He was flawlessly knowledgeable about English literature, a Milton scholar by trade, and broadly read in many other major literary traditions. He had a weakness for Tammy Wynette and other reminders of his Southern origins, but he justified country music as an American equivalent of opera, and he had certainly made a valiant effort to become learned in classical music. To my surprise, he always deferred with great humility to his father-in-law, a clothing store magnate in New Jersey, who had turned his hard-earned leisure and money to a generous patronage of the performing arts, in particular a gifted concert pianist. My friend once remarked to me that he felt so inadequate around his father-in-law because he was so "cultured." Puzzled, I asked why. Earnestly, he replied, "Because he knows so much about classical music."

The very concept of being cultured needs rethinking, but even if we accept for the moment that "being cultured" is a human virtue worthy of inclusion in Aristotle's *Nicomachean Ethics*, my Milton scholar was selling himself short because he had learned, uncritically, one of the reflex dances of the intellectual world. Being well-read in Milton and company can also become a sword of snobbish superiority, but in his case it was a labor of humble love. But knowing, even teaching, Milton is a quiet, lonely sort of enterprise. The performing arts are public, showy, great occasions for pomp and tux and limelight patronage. The clothier's pianist presumably loved music or excellence or ruthless competition, not just showiness, and maybe the cultured clothier himself was truly as interested in the beauty of good music as he was in the elevated social status that his art dollars could buy. But the prejudice is clear. Operas, concerts, Broadway musicals, and art museums are chunks of high culture that call for gown and garb and, afterwards, much gab about having been there. I'm talking about the intersection of high society and the intellectual world here, but the point is the same. Am I more cultured if I can hum the "O patria mia" aria from *Aida* or if I know how the classical influences got the upper hand of Milton's Christianity? Am I not cultured if I have no taste for Italian operas (save the theme song to *The Lone Ranger*) and scant knowledge of Mozart's, but unassailable mastery of Lefty Frizzell's honky-tonk two-steps and a long and hard-earned knowledge of Plato's dialogues? One could argue, idealistically, that the truly cultured person would know all of these things, but that is another matter.

It's the great need to talk about being cul-chud, not the love of art or the deep faith in art's edifying effect, that leads to never-ending migrations of intellectual aspirants from unlikely backwaters to the capital of cul-chuh. If I go to a local play in Stephenville, Texas, I can't get much mileage out of talking about that at the next meeting of the American Philosophical Association—I can't even get much mileage out of it among my university colleagues in Stephenville, or at the next charity fund raiser run by the local doctors and lawyers. Now, if I go to New York and see a play on Broadway, that's something to talk about. Well, he may wear cowboy boots, but he went to a play on Broadway . . . .

When I mentioned to my friend Adrian, a local doctor, that we might spend several weeks in Wyoming, he insisted that we save our money for a trip to New York. He and his wife had just returned from several days of museums and Broadway plays. It was wonderful, they proclaimed. My wife, whose parents fled New York in a New York minute a couple of years before she was born, reminded our culture-vulturing friends that they had earlier admitted that at least one of them had fallen asleep during every play they'd gone to. And, what's more to the point, that they never go to the local theater in Fort Worth, which, if not great, is very good, and only occasionally to Stephenville plays which, if not great, are at times very good too.

There's no doubt that actors and critics, maybe even playwrights, who've devoted their entire lives to drama might well ought to pack up their bags and bite, kick, and scratch their way into New York. I wish it wasn't that way, but it is. But I'm talking here about pseudo-intellectual reflex, the professors and doctors and artsy-fartsy cul-chuh vul-chuhs of all walks of life, who flock to New York like buzzards to dead armadillos on a West Texas two-lane, who ooh and aah anytime fellow vul-chuhs say that they've been to a play on, off, or in the general vicinity of Broadway. Because I believe that good drama is a vital ritual of cultural self-renewal and self-evaluation, I usually ask if the play was good. That usually gets that old familiar stare, that unforgiving look that says I've broken some rule of civilized chit-chat.

For my comic and tragic rituals, I prefer local and regional theater—seeing my students measuring themselves against the words of great playwrights or driving into Fort Worth to see a struggling company put on a fine production in a makeshift theater. I find there the willingness to do a classic, and less concern with trendy vanities. I also find a working up and a working out of local identities. In Stephenville and Fort Worth I see plays by Texas authors who tell me who I am—if not always with great artistic accomplishment, still with competence—just as much as Sophocles and Aristophanes told the Athenians who they were. Perhaps some day, I'll make my way back to New York. I don't even mean to say that New York isn't the testing ground of the best drama in the country. But I argue for local theater here to counteract the intellectual prejudice that seems to suggest that you haven't been to a play, to The Theatre, unless you've been to New York. Often a play in Stephenville or Fort Worth or Dallas can be very good, and sometimes a play in New York can be a veritable disgrace; but you can't build up your intellectual credentials by talking about one of John Templin's productions at the Sage and Silo Theater in Fort Worth, no matter how good it is. I'm not saying (although I know myself well enough to know that I would like to) that high culture is better in Stephenville than New York, or that life in New York, like food in the West, just isn't any good. I am saying that cultural life in the cultural provinces can be just as rich as, can in individual cases be richer than, life in the cultural capital; and that one of the basic intellectual prejudices blinds the mind of the intellectual to that possibility. Even my colleague Don Zelman, who regularly acts in local plays, responded to one of my dissertations on the importance of local theater and the headaches of trips to New York by saying, "Yeah, but, come on, the plays, the museums, the culture in New York really is better." Yes, yes, yes . . . .

Now don't get me wrong. I did my time in The Metropolis. Living in Buffalo and Annapolis, I made several pilgrimages a year to New York, visiting my cousin, the white sheep of the family, in Connecticut. He's a patent lawyer who lives for art. His high-rise condo was an art gallery. My wife helped him edit the biographical text in a catalogue of the work of Theresa Bernstein, a fine American expressionist. When we first met her she was a spry, crusty 90-year-old Bohemian still living winters in her studio apartment on West 74th Street. In the old days she and her husband, William Meyerowitz, spent summers in a big house in Gloucester, Massachusetts. He advanced the technique of color etchings, and his expressionism shows his Russian origins—stately, classical, hints of Chagall's colors, European even in his portrayal of the Gloucester fishermen he so loved. Theresa, originally from Philadelphia, took the German and Norwegian expressionism she saw in Munich and Berlin during visits between 1911 and 1914 and introduced the vibrancy of American humor, colors and lines dancing to the rhythms of Duke Ellington and Louis Armstrong. My cousin has launched a one-man lifelong crusade to convince the world that she is one of the greatest American artists of the 20th century, and I understand and admire him for what he has done. I was charmed and beguiled by my visit to Theresa and Bill's studio—as a writer, I drifted off into romantic thoughts of what it would have been like to walk into Gertrude Stein's flat in Paris, or into a Parisian cafe to find Hemingway scribbling away at the tip of another submerged iceberg of a story.

    I feel the attraction of artistic and literary capitals, and I like to meet artists and writers and dancers and actors who are single-mindedly devoted to their arts.

OK, I even like to talk about meeting them, write about meeting them. I even liked the tour of the humanely small Frick Collection, at least when my cousin, a genteel Southern boy, spared us the subway ride and drove us into Manhattan cussing and gesturing at taxi drivers and pedestrians like a veritable Roman. After several years of visiting the Metropolitan and coming away with a weeklong headache perpetrated by an overload of aesthetic experience, I finally learned to pick one wing and take my time. On one occasion, I let my friends rush on ahead, and I spent a half hour looking at one Greek vase depicting a well-endowed satyr chasing a fair maiden. I walked in a slow circle around the vase, trying to imagine how a flesh-and-blood human being worked with his ten-fingered hands on this very vase over two thousand years ago, and thinking about how trite the truth-is-beauty and beauty-is-truth equation seemed in the face of history's millennial weight. Of course, I later heard that a number of the vases turned out to be forgeries—another piece of culture bites the dust.

One of the best experiences I've ever had in a museum was in Buffalo, that Midwestern butt of endless culture-vulture jokes. Wasn't there a line in a Broadway hit about suicide in Buffalo being redundant? The Albright-Knox houses another humanely small, intelligently laid-out, finely chosen collection. (Well, let's pretend the pop and op art wing doesn't exist.) Hans-Georg Gadamer, with whom my main graduate-school professor had studied in Germany, was a visiting lecturer, and I was bestowed the honor of chauffeuring him about town. We walked into the museum at about 4:30, a half hour before closing time. The guard insisted that the museum was about to close, hinting strongly that we shouldn't bother to come in. In good Germanic fashion, Gadamer pointed out that the museum closed at five and that we would therefore leave at five, then walked up to the first row of paintings, deliberately, unperturbed, as if the guard didn't exist.

"I never look at more than a few paintings. One must consider them, discuss them, in order to see them," he explained.

He would walk past a couple of paintings or drawings with a nod, then settle on one and look it over for several minutes. We looked mostly at European impressionism and expressionism. At about ten 'til five he pulled up in front of a Franz Marc painting—*The Wolves*. Gadamer spoke of Marc as of an old friend. He explained how the red color of one of the three wolves is repeated in the flank of the victim—was it a deer, a wounded wolf? I don't remember for sure, but I do remember how he explained that the repetition of the red gave the sensation that the three wolves, led by the red one, are moving inevitably toward their prey. We stood mesmerized, like the frozen, fated prey.

Years later, after we'd moved back to Texas from Annapolis, a friend in Annapolis asked me on the phone, "My God, how can you stand it in Texas? I couldn't live without driving up to New York to the museums." You, I told him, drove through four hours of Eastern seaboard and fought through crowds of every damn culture vulture from every inch of the country to see the Courtauld Collection when it was in New York; I drove through sixty miles of pleasant countryside, cruise control engaged and Terry Allen's "A Truckload of Art" blaring from the tape player, parked in the lot right by the front door of the Kimbell in Fort Worth. Admittedly it was a weekday; on a weekend I might have ended up walking a good fifty steps from the side street. Safely inside, I stood in front of Cézanne's *Lac d'Annecy* and soaked up the deep mood of blues and blackgreens. Sure, occasionally a baggy-clothed art major from TCU blocked my line of vision, but I felt satisfaction in that too. My wife, who's been in museums all over the world and grew up with a house full of art, collapsed into the pure joy of a twelve-year-old before Degas's *Two Dancers on the Stage.* "I grew up with a poster of that painting in my bedroom. I can't believe it—I'm looking at the real thing." Van Gogh's *Peach Blossom in the Crau* shimmered in my mind's eye—a perfect balance between the violent unbalance of his madness and the serenity of a countryside, of farm houses and peach trees in bloom, in which everything is in its place.

"Well, actually," my friend admitted, "I couldn't get up to New York."

Anytime I please, I can drive into Fort Worth on a sunny Sunday afternoon, maybe take in a bit of the Van Cliburn piano competition at Bass Hall; drive by Kay Kimbell's old house where Mr. Cliburn himself now lives, and wave at the poor misguided soul out mowing his grass and wondering why he foregoes the cultural mecca to live back home in the wasteland of Texas; take in a few Russells and Remingtons at the Sid Richardson downtown, and a few more at the Amon Carter in the museum district; maybe a quick tour of the new Modern Art Museum across the street, designed by Tadao Ando; and then head on to the Kimbell in a fit of cultural deprivation to take a quick gander at the provincial cowtown collection of Rembrandt, Velázquez, Goya, Monet, Cézanne, El Greco, La Tour, Van Dyck, Rubens, Manet, Matisse, Titian, Picasso, and Caravaggio that Louis Kahn's edifice keeps the rain off of. The old charge about cultural Neanderthals driving Cadillacs with longhorn hood ornaments trying to buy culture with big bucks is a half-truth at best. Yes, Fort Worth got culture the same way New York did—it bought it.

There's something to the relation of visual art and community, too. We have two Theresa Bernstein etchings and one by her husband as well, but we also take great satisfaction in the art of my wife's family friend, Houston artist Bob Fowler, whose art from time to time sells very well, some in Houston and some out of a gallery in New York. He's lived his entire life in Texas. I take greater satisfaction from the art of my wife's childhood friend and my friend since college, Margaret Rochelle, especially the pencil drawing that hangs in my office and appears on the cover of my first book. A painting by Mark Davis, a colleague and friend, hangs in our living room. And several by Bob Wade, a fine artist who shows in Dallas and lives down the road in Dublin, Texas. His studio is a small building in his small-town backyard, not a studio apartment on West 74th Street in New York, but out of it come remarkable paintings that reflect the landscapes and lives that he knows just as Theresa Bernstein's paintings reflected the village of Gloucester and the musicians of the Cotton Club.

Maybe artists need direct contact with the art world, even more so than writers who can get all the contact they need from reading—and a few lecture tours here and there. But then there was Andrew Wyeth, too. The vultures couldn't get him to come into New York for all the money and adoration in the world. It's pretty obvious that some folks in the art world have held that against him. All in all, artists do what they have to do, not out of pretense but out of inexplicable artistic necessity, or because of marriage or economics or many other perfectly normal reasons. My complaint is not so much with artists as with intellectuals who build up credentials with loudly proclaimed consumption of art. Let's let artists do what they do, and let intellectuals quit worrying about using art to feel superior to common humanity. Let them *be* superior in the ways they are superior, but let them quit talking about it.

Theresa Bernstein lived a life of art in New York City, but she cared little for intellectual pretense, and preferred to see her paintings in more ordinary hands. In 1933 she wrote in *The Gloucester Daily Times* of her attempt to reach the "average man":

> The artist has already given his time and effort and tried to lead him gently along the path to beauty where it might become the vital necessity to the average man that it is to the creator. Art and the community have to come closer together if the art of today is to be given the same chance with the art of the past. If the average man, who is the prospective art patron of today, will provide himself with a few paintings, etchings and sculptures during his life-time, he will have contributed a propeller to the culture of his own age and given himself the chance to enjoy art.

Theresa was as much a salesman as an artist, but there's truth in what she says, and it runs against all of the grain of the culture vulture's boastful superiority.

"Another breed of intellectual prejudice," a friend wrote to me, "is a sort of perverse rarefying of one's alleged tastes till one does not like just classical music, but only *obscure* classical music. A friend of mind used to have a roommate whose record collection consisted only of, you know, undiscovered black blues singers and virtually unknown études by Polish composers who died young and whom only specialists had heard of, and Afro-Brazilian dance music but only of a particular tribe in the darkest heart of the jungle near Brasilia, and . . . well, you get the picture. Plain old Merle Haggard and Mozart and the Stones just weren't swank enough for this guy."

The musical obscuranti, I like to call them. Their little game, obscurantism, is a game intellectuals love to play. Literary critics do it, too. If you can find a composer that someone else doesn't know, you must be culturally superior to that person. "You mean you're not familiar with—"

It reminds me of the uses and abuses some cosmopolitans make of "folk music." I recall a friend who pronounced his distaste for country music when he heard an old Hank Williams tune on my stereo. "I listen to *folk* music," he announced with much ado. "The music of which folks?" I asked to no avail.

Back in our graduate school days Russell and Gail Hatton from West Virginia played banjo, guitar, and dulcimer, and sang Scotch-Irish and English ballads that echoed off the West Virginia hills all the way back to the Old Country. And there are many people who study, play, listen to, love folk-musical traditions from many different locales who do so out of genuine and legitimate interest in a deeper understanding of different traditions, and thus, in the process, of their own. But I liked Russell and Gail's assessment of the snooty intellectual identification with folk music: they called that kind of music P-H-O-L-K.

I've always found it remarkable that pseudo-intellectuals always listen to the music of other folks, never to the music of their own folk. Somehow it makes them superior to their own folk, listening to the unlettered oral traditions of the Appalachians or Ireland or Zimbabwe. When I invited a new colleague to go to a free concert by Guy Clark in the city park here, she declined because, as she put it, she doesn't listen to country music. She prefers, she said, traditional English folk music. P-H-O-L-K I thought silently to myself.

The folk traditions of my folks and of my place are Cajun and Southern American, and the folk traditions of my homeland are Western and bluesy and country. Country music has indeed become so commercialized that much of it has degenerated into hopelessly homogenized pap; but young singers rise up out of deep traditional roots and poetic creativity and get their folk music on the same stations with the pap, and, even if they don't get much air time on the popular radio stations, they're playing all over Texas in places like the Stephenville city park. Country music, especially the Texas version of it, is the music of my folk, the musical lifeblood of common culture. Folk music is not just the music that doesn't make money; otherwise, most of the folks of the folk music movement of the late 50s and early 60s would be disqualified right along with Willie Nelson. Folk music is the music of a folk, and what makes it attractive is that it represents a rich traditional way of life, a sense of place and communal identity. It is crafted out of the local language, playing upon it, sometimes against it—at its best, it turns local language into poetry. When I played Guy Clark's "Rita Ballou" for an Italian friend who is fluent in standard English, it took twenty minutes to explain the first verse:

> She could dance that slow Uvalde,
> Shuffle to some cowboy hustle,
> How she made them trophy buckles shine, shine, shine.
> Wild-eyed and Mexican silvered,
> Trickin' dumb ol' cousin Willard,
> Into thinking he's got her this time.

Of course plain old mainstream classical music is often used to pump up cultural egos, to demonstrate ethereal worldliness, membership in the city of the cultured intellect, freedom from the backwardness of one's provincial origins. It's easy to forget that classical music, as high as it reaches, is classical because it speaks beyond the place and time, not because it has nothing to do with them. Bach's music echoes the Lutheran hymnal that he grew up on. Tchaikovsky went to school to the Germans and French, but his music is Russian, in complex rhythmic ways, in themes, and melodies, in ways that reach back into long folk traditions.

The power of "classical" music is that it rises up out of a place and time and, without obliterating its origins, reaches for universal beauty, pure form. Bach's rootedness in the life of his church, in a world at once mundane and sacred, precludes the notion of pure art, of purely formal relations of sound; but even Mozart, so much the pure artist of pure form, the artist with whom Hesse associated the idea of a Glass Bead Game of pure intellect—even Mozart would never be mistaken for an Italian, or a Russian, or 19th-century German, or 20th-century American. If Wagner expressed one side of the German spirit, Mozart, even as he soared above us all, expressed another. When we say someone composes opera in the "grand Italian style," we may indeed be thinking of stylistic elements that we could look up in some great musical catalogue in the sky; but the style is "Italian" because Italians, bringing in all of the flavor and gesticulation of their Italian-ness, have composed in that way, because we can somehow detect an affinity, a sameness, between the music and the people.

Like Flannery O'Connor's rooted writers who, from their point of view, simply write what they know, composers may see themselves as composers of beautiful music in the purest sense of the word; but like O'Connor's writers, they reflect their place in untold ways, unwittingly, in different degrees and ways, but unmistakably. Whereas Wagner took musical nationalism to a perverse extreme, Verdi, urged by a friend to push for an equally nationalistic "Italian music," replied:

> And you are, I repeat, a pretentious bigwig with your Italian music. No, no, there is no Italian music, nor German, nor Turkish . . . but there is MUSIC! Don't harass me with these definitions. I write as I please and as I feel.

Nationalism was a kind of intellectual snobbery in the 19th century, and crass nationalism or back-patting provincialism that stifles the creative spirit should always be abhorred—it's pretty clear what Verdi is reacting to. But is there any question that Verdi's music is Italian? If Wagner's music is self-consciously, pompously Germanic, Verdi's is organically, uncannily, perhaps unintentionally, but vibrantly Italian. It's important not because it's Italian, but because it's great music; but that it's great music doesn't mean it has no connection to where its composer came from. Local origin may not mean as much for classical music as it does for folk music, but classical music is full of folk themes and melodies. Local origin may not mean as much for classical music as it does for great literature, for classical music, at least certain forms of it, tends much more in the direction of pure form; but it's still there. The intellectual who believes that he can rise above his origins by way of classical music doesn't fully understand the nature of the music he proffers as the badge of unattached intellect.

Another sure sign of high culture is frequent viewing of what we in Texas like to call fur'n films, and the ability to pronounce "Bergman" with a vaguely European accent. Now, I don't mean to imply that I don't watch foreign films. To be sure, the encounter with deeply probing, seriously artistic films from other cultures is challenging, broadening, thought-provoking, prejudice-challenging. I certainly went to school to Bergman and Fellini and Lina Wertmüller. And I could reel off a list of foreign films I've watched in the past few years that dig down to that universal vein of humanity: the German-Italian *Mostly Martha* (*Bella Martha*), the French *Amélie*, the Georgian-French *A Chef in Love (1001 Retsept Iz Menyu Vlyublyonnogo Povara, Les Mille et Une Recettes du Cuisinier Amoureux*), the relentlessly Italian *The Last Kiss* (*L'Ultimo Bacio*), to name a few. But the great need to talk about watching only foreign films, the assumption that foreign films are generically, categorically, more worthy of the intellectual's consideration than a homely, crass, commercialized Hollywood movie—yet another prejudice of the culture vulturing pseudo-intellectual. In the end, fur'n films are as unreflectively mandatory for the would-be intellectual as the love of *High Noon* is for a young boy growing up in Texas.

Looking back, though, I now know there was more to *High Noon* than met my toy gun-totin' childhood eye. My father told me that *High Noon* was the best movie ever made. Of course, as a kid, I agreed. Years later, off at college at the University of Texas in Austin, I was beyond cowboys and gunfighters, aspiring to be a poet or philosopher, when, to my great surprise, John Silber, a devout Kantian, devoted an entire lecture to *High Noon* as an artistic illustration of Kant's theory of moral duty. He contrasted Will Kane's sense of duty with the vagabond hedonism of Captain America in *Easy Rider*—keep in mind, this was 1970. I was persuaded by my philosophy professor of the essential rightness of Will Kane's single-minded commitment to duty, but, let's face it, the best looking college girls, even in Texas, were chasing after Captain America imitators, not Will Kane party-poopers. I had a serious conflict of heroes.

A few years later, during graduate school, I spent a summer in Germany. There I encountered a professor of Slavic languages, a Herr Professor Gerigk, who was obsessed with American Westerns, and especially *High Noon*. He was looking for an antidote to the German sense of duty, which, he argued, made it so easy for Hitler to gain power. In the Western American ethos, he saw a rejection of universal law, of Kantian duty, a focus on the individual as a creator of law and order. The frontier, he argued, was a place of chaos, and Will Kane was a law-bringer, or, even better, a law-creator, instead of a law-obeyer. He is the perfect antidote to the overbearing sense of duty that governs the German mentality.

Well, I think that the truth is somewhere between Professors Silber and Gerigk. When I delivered a paper sorting out these opposing interpretations at The Western Literature Association's annual meeting, the most knowledgeable and enthusiastic questioner in the audience was a Frenchman. My dissertation director, who was studying in Germany when the movie came out, informed me when he discovered that I was from Texas that his philosophy professors at the University of Heidelberg had discussed *High Noon* in their seminars. Americans become cosmopolitan by watching European women go mad with introverted moodiness and Europeans become cosmopolitan by watching Gary Cooper gun down the bad guys? Yes, in a sense, but that should tell you that art and the intellectual life are not quite so simple.

In the normal process of intellectual life, foreign films are a rite of passage, a way to jar the habits of the homeland about a bit, a way of deepening an understanding of deepest humanity. But it's silly to think they are *as a class* intrinsically better than American films. Perhaps on average they are because Hollywood makes 500 pieces of utter trash for every reasonably good movie, but Hollywood makes a hell of a lot of movies. And we don't watch movies on average; we watch them individually. American intellectuals need to come back to their own culture as well, to see and think about Hollywood movies that tell them who they are: classics from the golden age like *The Searchers*, *On the Waterfront*, and *The Misfits*; counter-culture reassessments of the classical American mythos like *Five Easy Pieces*, *One Flew Over the Cuckoo's Nest*, and *The Deer Hunter*; dead-serious surprises like *Schindler's List* from the man who directed *Jaws* and the Indiana Jones adventures; "entertainment" pieces that appeal to "mass audiences" and somehow, at the same time, get right in the middle of who we are if we don't turn our noses up at them, like *Moonstruck*, *Grand Canyon*, and *My Cousin Vinny*—not to mention great American independent films like the Coen brothers' *Raising Arizona* and *Fargo*. Why? Because American intellectuals need to deepen their understanding of their own culture as well as broaden their understanding of other cultures, and because some of these movies are, in the most universal sense, as good as anything ever made.

On the subject of things fur'n, I might make at least a brief mention of fur'n talk. The study of foreign languages, whether or not you'll ever have a practical use for them, is an indispensable part of a liberal education. Language and thought are deeply interrelated, and the study of another language is the study of another way of looking at the world. It's not just that you learn to speak French, but that in speaking French, even if badly, you think a little bit French, you look at the world a little bit like the French do, you recognize that there are other possibilities. Foreign languages give perspective, breadth. They help you understand your own language for the first time. For some scholarly purposes, you just can't substitute a translation for reading the original text; but for deeper intellectual purposes, for thinking, the encounter with other languages makes language into an issue, gives a kind of transparency that can be gotten at in no other way.

These are noble purposes for foreign language study. But it doesn't always work that way. I recall arguing with my fellow graduate students in philosophy about the importance of foreign language study, not just as a research tool, but also as an educational, philosophical necessity—as a means for learning to think. I insisted that two foreign languages should be required for the doctorate. A friend, fluent in several languages, pointed out that one of our professors knew nine languages, but couldn't think his way out of a wet paper bag. There are no guarantees. The study of languages offers an opportunity for learning to think, but it doesn't assure that thinking will result.

Much too often foreign languages are nothing more than one more outward sign of cultural superiority, a badge of a good education even when the education failed miserably to liberate that Socratic spirit that a liberal education ought to liberate. I still think that a PhD in philosophy ought to require several languages—at the very least a good familiarity if not a down-pat knowledge. But I'm on the lookout for the fellow who flaunts his foreign languages the way people flaunt their season tickets to the opera. Foreign languages can become just one more piece of carrion for the buzzards of culture.

Now most intellectuals don't get the opportunity to speak at great length in foreign languages, except in foreign countries where any street vendor will recognize *them* as foreign as soon as they speak; but they do find great opportunity to insert foreign words into their speech and writing. Here, again, there is no easy test to distinguish between the legitimate, thought-provoking use of foreign words and showy, intellectual snobbery. I can't teach Plato without covering the blackboard with words like *aporia, phronēsis, aretē*. I can't write about Plato without using some of his words. Maybe I'm just trying to give the impression that I am a master at classical Greek, when in fact I have at best a good philosophical vocabulary and a very rusty rudimentary knowledge of the rest of the language. No doubt a little showing off is a necessary element in teaching, but I think I have good reason for suggesting that something rich and powerful was going on in Plato's Greek and that our English equivalents for some of these words lose something of that power—or perhaps they retain it, but only in a concealed way. (This approach also allows the students the opportunity to describe what goes on in my classes as all Greek to them, but that is another subject.) I can't write about anything important without looking into the Greek and Latin and Germanic roots that lie beneath the surface of our English words, that give them historical resonance. Thinking about the words we think with and thinking about where they come from is an intellectual necessity—I don't mean to throw out thoughtfulness about languages with the language-snobbery bathwater.

I recall one friend, though, who grew up in Texas, but was so determined to prove his cultured erudition that he insisted upon referring to the town which provides the setting for Larry King's *Best Little Whorehouse in Texas* as *Lah Grawn-juh*. Whatever the origin of the name, every self-respecting Texan, and now, thanks to Larry King, everyone else in the country, knows that the town of La Grange is pronounced *Luh Grainge*. I recall David Rodriguez and me sitting with a culture-vulturing friend in Scholz's Beer Garden in Austin. The culture-vulturing friend kept referring to the Rio Grawn-day River. Aside from the fact that she was saying the "Big River River," her obvious pretense ruffled David's feathers. David, a Mexican-American songwriter from Houston, refers in one of his songs to "the river that the gringos have always called the Rio *Grand*," but faced with cosmopolitan intellectual pretense, he couldn't help himself. "It's called the Rio *Grand*. This is Texas, isn't it?" Bilingualism in Texas is another thorny moral issue—in fact, I would argue that every Southwesterner ought to be able to speak Southwestern Spanish. Luckily, though, I have an excuse here to stick with a pretty simple topic, the use of foreign pronunciation of perfectly Americanized American names to demonstrate intellectual or cultural or moral superiority.

Another example. When my wife served a wedge of French brie after dinner one night, another friend, fluent as an American can be in French, repeatedly referred to the cheese with its full-fledged, phlegm-clearing *r*, unannounced, right in the middle of a perfectly normal conversation in the American English language. "Would you pass the brrrrr-ee?" Give me a brrrr-eak! It's an English word now, so why do we need a French *r*? Even in reference to foreign place names, I really don't think we need to parade our French or German or what have you. A reasonable, Anglicized facsimile will do. Surely, we don't need the deep purring sound of the German *burg* when we pronounce the Texas town of Freyburg (which, incidentally, retains the older spelling of the first syllable). For that matter, do we really need it for the German town of Freiburg when we are engaged in an English conversation in America? Do we need a crisp German short-*e* when we speak of a summer in Heidelberg? In German you'd be hard-pressed to make yourself understood with an Americanized collapse of the *berg* and *burg* endings, but do you think the Europeans pronounce our cities and towns exactly as we do when they are speaking their own languages in their own countries? Why should they?

Fair is fair. So let's keep the guttural r-r-r-r in France, in French poetry recited in French in my wife's French classes, and out of my dining room. If you have a great knowledge and love of things French or German or Italian or whatever, and you're sitting in my dining room, tell me what you know and share whatever insights you've gleaned from what you know, but tell me in English, or at the very least Tex-Mex. If you want to organize a session to practice speaking German, I could gladly use a lot of practice, or if you want to help me learn Italian, I need all the help I can get; if you want to discuss the origins of the word "culture" or help me read Homer in Greek, I'm ready and rarin' to go; but if you want to signify your membership in the great tribe of cosmopolitan intellectuals, mercy, but no mercy, if you know what I mean.

The whole notion of being cultured, of high culture and the like, too often functions as an unexamined article of intellectual faith. I would suggest that too many highfalutin folks assume that they know what they mean when they use these words. I recall a professor who was fanatically opposed to the sociologist's use of "culture" to apply to different cultures, as opposed to culture in the sense of a qualitative ideal. Now, I'll admit, he had thought long and hard about cultural relativism and about Weber's fact-value distinction and about human excellence; but this qualitative approach to culture often amounts to nothing more than a more philosophically sophisticated version of intellectual snobbery. How many people who talk incessantly about "being cultured," about small Southern towns and big Western cowtowns having "no culture," about New York or London or Paris as "centers of culture" and "cultural capitals"—how many have asked themselves what it is that makes culture culture, and why we all ought to be trying to get some of it?

There's a broader meaning to the word. In a certain sense, the modern world understands all of human activity as culture—culture as opposed to nature. Forgive my insistence upon using fur'n words, but "culture" comes from one, and even though we don't need to talk about *cultura* in the same breath with *brrrrr-ee*, we ought to think about it if we're going to make such a big deal of it. *Cultura* is the Latin word for cultivation—it comes from the verb *colere*, meaning to "cultivate," but cultivate in the sense of tilling the soil. The original meaning of culture was agri-culture. I don't know if my colleagues in the Ag Department would be happy to know they are really working in the Department of Culture, but I'm fairly certain that the folks who proclaim an urban monopoly on cul-chuh would not like the idea. Culture is the result of a tilling of the soil, a caring for, a nurturing—a meeting ground of civilization and nature, of human and earth.

Culture in the sense of something an individual can get some of easily loses its relation, even the metaphorical one, to the tilling of the soil that involves a people and a land. In the Phaeacians Homer gave us one of the great treatments of culture cut off from the harshness of nature's seasons and whimsical violence. After ten years of trying to get home, Odysseus lands upon the isle of the Phaeacians, a people who had long ago fled to the island of Scheria "far from bread-earning men," and far from the Cyclopes, "presumptuous men who used to injure them, and were more powerful in strength," to live a life of high culture and poetic leisure. They have no dealings with other humans, no friends and no enemies. Theirs is a closed society. They intermarry, and although they are hospitable to Odysseus and eventually are persuaded by Odysseus' moving story to risk destruction by taking him home, they are suspicious of strangers. Their lives are free of toil and, although they are mortal like other humans, they are not subject to the seasons, they fight no wars, they suffer no hardships. They lead a godlike existence of civilization freed from the toils of nature and strife. But through their encounter with Odysseus we discover—and perhaps they do themselves—that they are also freed from the fatefulness of mortal life. Their existence is ultimately without meaning.

The Greeks spoke of the conflict between *nomos* and *phusis*, culture and earth, custom and nature, law and physics—the Phaeacians were pure culture, the Cyclopes pure nature, but both races were descended from Poseidon, the nature god par excellence. Plato knew as well that an absolute bifurcation of culture and nature was a sophistic trick of one kind or another. The brute savage of nature, whether noble or vicious, sees *nomos* as mere culture, as sheer artifice; the ethereal culture-vulture sees nature as brutish, unthinking, unrefined. The phronetic intellectual must think *nomos* and *phusis* in relation to one another. To move from the cosmopolitan to the phronetic understanding of culture, we must cultivate the soil in which our artistic and intellectual plants will grow, the soil of the earth and the soil of our own natures; but we must respect, attune ourselves to, pay reverent heed to that soil as well—let it be what it is even as we cultivate it. As caretakers of the creation, we can get awfully hubristic about our "dominion" as soon as God leaves the picture, and there's no one to remind us that we are caretakers, not owners. The boundless cultivation of unrefined "raw material" is a concept of culture just as misguided as the one that sees culture as a fleeing from nature. Heidegger saw the prevalence of the concept of culture in the modern world, not as a last-ditch struggle of the humanities against the onslaught of modern science, but just the opposite—as a manifestation of our technological relation to nature, of our dominance over the earth.

There's a richness in the Latin *cultura*, *colere*, but there's a great danger, too. The culture vulture overlooks both sides; the true intellectual ought to cultivate a spirit of Socratic questioning on the very concept of culture. It is one of the most questionable, one of the most unthought words in the intellectual's vocabulary. Here, I've only begun to question it, but let me suggest that a serious inquiry would eventually lead us back through the Roman *cultura* and its transformation of the Greek *paideia*, back into the Greek *nomos* and *phusis*, and into the question-worthiness of Homer's "grain-giving earth" and "grain-earning men." Was it a pre-rational, primitive consciousness that caused him to refer to humans as "the mortals who eat bread upon the earth"? One of the words Homer used for earth was *chthōn*—the phronetic intellectual, as opposed to the culture-vulturing variety, could also be called the autochthonous intellectual. This is not a matter of mere etymology, for words really matter here. It is not a matter of philosophical or historical or literary scholarship, but of our very being.

At the very least, I hope I've shown that the culture vulture's air of superiority deserves some further examination. When self-cultivation means taking account of one's deepest capabilities and making the best of them that education and dedication and integrity can enable, it is a fine ideal. When it means forgetting one's origins, making oneself, as if from thin air, into the fantastical creation of high culture; when it means losing a sense of earthy beginnings and an earthly end, and believing that one can really and truly escape those beginnings and that end; when it means losing track of shared humanity; when it means feeling superior instead of being excellent—then it is not a virtue, but a sham. The greatest artists have been very much in touch with earthly origins and common humanity, and more than one of them has called up images of the plant with the deepest roots rising to the highest reaches of the unobstructed heavens. That Homeric sense of the earth recurs in the artistic mind century after century—why is it such anathema to the intellectual world that claims intellectual ownership of the works which artists produce?

Let me end with a statement from Pablo Casals, whose artistry rose rather spectacularly into the heavens. Like Verdi, he played Music, not Spanish music; and he lived much of his life in exile from his native Catalonia. But he played Bach's cello suites with a Romantic—dare I say Spanish?—flair that irritated more than a few pure Germanic spirits and pseudo-Germanic purists. Casals knew where he was from and who he was. How many culture vultures whose knowledge of Bach's cello suites gives them that self-assured sense of cosmopolitan superiority, whose casual cocktail reference to Casals's rendition of them scores them cultural brownie points, would speak of their own relations to their homelands in the way Casals spoke of his in his autobiography?

> That splendid Catalan poet, Joan Maragall, once wrote, "To take flight to Heaven, we must stand on the firm soil of our native land." Catalonia is my native land. I had been gone for almost three years, and it was a joy for me to be back.
> During my lifetime, I have traveled in many lands, and I have found beauty everywhere. But the beauty of Catalonia nourished me since infancy. And when I close my eyes, I see the ocean at San Salvador and the seaside village of Sitges with the little fishing boats on the sand, the vineyards and olive groves and pomegranate trees of the province of Tarragona, the River Llobregat and the peaks of Montserrat. Catalonia is the land of my birth, and I love her as a mother. . . .
> I am, of course, a Spanish citizen. Though I have lived in exile for more than thirty years, I still carry a Spanish passport. I could not dream of parting with it. An official at the Spanish consulate at Perpignan once asked me why I did not relinquish my passport if I chose not to return to Spain. I replied, "Why should I give it up? Let Franco give up his. And then I shall return." But first and foremost I am a Catalan. Since I have felt this way for almost a century, I do not expect to change.

STUDY QUESTIONS

1. What traits do you associate with the concept of a "cultured person"? What kind of knowledge and what kind of experiences are required for someone to be "cultured"? Does the author's story about his friend in Maryland, a Milton scholar, who thought of himself as less cultured than his father-in-law, a patron of classical music, ring true? Do we tend to value the showier arts like opera and theater more than the quieter solitary ones like a knowledge of literature and philosophy? If so, why? Should a knowledge of philosophy count as much as a knowledge of classical music?

2. Is the ideal of being cultured a legitimate ideal? Socrates said the unexamined life is not worth living—should we say that a life without culture is not worth living? The author decries culture snobbery as one element in the pseudo-intellectual world view. Is he condemning the ideal of being cultured as such or is he arguing for a different concept of being cultured?

3. Is there a relation between "a culture" and "being cultured"? What makes a culture a culture? Is there a relation between the normative sense of culture, as something we admire and aspire to, and the sociological or anthropological sense

of culture, as a way of referring to the customs, norms, and perspectives of groups of people?

5. The author refers to good drama as "a vital ritual of cultural self-renewal and self-evaluation." What does he mean by that? Was Sophocles' *Antigone*, a play which depicts a conflict between civil authority and moral obligation, a ritual of self-renewal and self-evaluation for the Athenians of that time? Was Aristophanes' *Lysistrata*, an anti-war play performed in Athens during the Peloponnesian War, the war between Athens and Sparta? Can you think of American plays that perform this function for American culture?

5. The author talks about the importance of owning art by local artists. In the epigraph to this chapter he quotes Heidegger's comment about collections and exhibitions turning artworks into "objects of the art industry," and he quotes a newspaper article by the American expressionist Theresa Bernstein in which she urges the "average man" to own artworks. Where do artworks properly belong? In what context is an artwork allowed to be itself? Does placing them in museums turn them into something other than artworks? Does the use of artworks as decorative elements in an office or in someone's living room diminish their aesthetic value, prevent them from functioning fully as art? Should art be solely for "art's sake," or is it an essential part of art to be integrated into the culture it arises in?

6. The author says that "folk music" is the "music of a folk." In one sense, that would be true of all popular music, which does not seem to be the author's point. What, in his view, makes music truly "of a folk"? What music would qualify? He mentions country music as the music of his folk? Is rap a kind of folk music?

7. The author says that the music of the great classical composers is "rooted" in their cultures and places. Do the operas by Rossini, Donizetti, Bellini, Puccini, and Verdi sound Italian? Do Mozart's operas sound German? The author also points to the use of folk traditions in the music of various classical composers. What is the relation between the original folk music and the classical music it becomes a part of? Are the folk elements "raw material"?

8. The author says that foreign language study is part of a liberal education. What does he mean here by "liberal education"? In a "global economy" knowing more than one language is obviously an advantage. But the traditional concept of a liberal education focuses not on practicality, at least not in a direct way, but on preparation for citizenship and pursuit of the truth for its own sake. How would foreign language study serve those ends? The author goes on to say that foreign language study helps you to "understand your own language for the first time." How can studying a foreign language give you a perspective on your native language?

9. The author connects his discussion of culture to the Greek distinction between *phusis*, nature, and *nomos*, custom. He argues that cosmopolitan intellectuals have opted for custom and culture separated from nature, and that "the phronetic intellectual must think *nomos* and *phusis* in relation to one another." How does this relate to the author's defense of an intellectual life that is rooted?

FOR FURTHER READING

Casals, Pablo. *Joys and Sorrows: His Own Story as Told to Albert E. Kahn*. New York: Simon and Schuster, 1970.

Heidegger: "Origin of the Work of Art." *Basic Writings*. Edited by David Farrell Krell. New York: HarperCollins, 1993.

Heidegger's great essay on art as a fundamental form of truth.

Centennial, Wyoming. Photo by author, 2003.

Eleven

CENTENNIAL

> "Make it a corned beef on rye,"
> She'd sing with a gleam in her eye.
> The headlights were burning,
> The big wheels were turning,
> Her sweetheart would come by and by.
>
> Kinky Friedman
> from "Highway Cafe"

The sign said: "CENTENNIAL. POP. 100. ELEV. 8076." The town looked more like an encampment, the scattered array of hodgepodge buildings strung out along the beginning of the highway's steep climb up to the pass. A motel of pieced-together odds and ends on the left. A couple of ser sta gros, as John Graves calls them. Ser sta gros with fishing gear to boot.

A beat-up black-and-white was perched on the left side of the highway, with all the appearance of just daring one of those out-of-state tourists, or even one of those whooping-it-up University of Wyoming students, to ignore the town speed limit. The first time I saw it, I slowed instinctively down, even though I was already creeping along at about twenty miles per hour, gazing up at the mountains ahead. Just like Texas, I thought—every small town in the state a speed trap. I remembered the judge in some town between Austin and Houston asking for a check made out to his name. Somehow that ticket never showed up on my driving record.

In several trips over several days, though, I noticed the car hadn't moved. Something was fishy. Instead of glancing innocently away, I looked more carefully. The two figures in the front seat, fully decked-out in police uniforms, were dummies, and the car, on closer inspection, was a battered wreck. It worked, though. I later saw a newspaper article pinned up in the Chuck Wagon Cafe with some remarkable statistics on how many people slowed down when they saw it. From wooden Indians to wooden policemen. . . .

The Chuck Wagon Cafe was no bigger than a trailer house. I've always bragged about stopping at greasy-spoon cafes as I've gallivanted across the country—in this case, I had no say in the matter. The Chuck Wagon Cafe was just about all there was.

Most of the customers were locals. I could tell by the way they looked at us as if to say we weren't. But not inhospitably, curiously perhaps. The proprietor was a tall big-boned woman who cooked, kept coffee cups filled, and directed a couple of tall big-boned kids, presumably hers, to clean off the counter, wash out a couple of glasses, refill a sugar container.

"Buffalo burgers?" I asked her.

"Yeah. Pretty good stuff."

"Where do you get the buffalo?"

"Oh, there's a fellow up in Idaho. Drove a truck up and hauled a load back myself."

"Seems fitting for Wyoming and all. I'll have one, with cheese. Does it come with lettuce and tomato?"

"Unless you don't want it."

"No, give me the works."

Out the front window, we could see the motorists hit their brakes as they saw the mock-police unit. A light, wet snow had turned to a light drizzle, and the potholes in the gravel roadsides were still half full of water. The drizzly grey of the sky reflected from the wet pavement.

"Imagine, snow in August. I'd like to hole up right here for about a year. You don't have to worry about traffic jams."

"There's your burger."

It looked like a normal old-fashioned hamburger to me. The meat might have had a more distinctive taste, but probably not.

"You ever think about moving to a city?"

"I think about it some. But not much."

"You from around here?"

"No. I'm from Idaho. Came here eighteen years ago. Never thought I'd stay more than a year. I like mountains, I guess."

"You don't miss going to a picture show, or going to a fancy restaurant?"

"I think about it, but I don't miss it. Never have lived in a city to miss it."

I thought about her life. Would her kids go off to Cornell and come back to the Medicine Bow Mountains well-dressed hikers? Not likely. Would they go to the University of Wyoming in Laramie? Would they go to college at all? Would they finish high school? Were they missing out on something? Yes. Did they get something in return. Yes. How did it all balance out? I didn't know, and probably she and her kids didn't know. But there they were, and there I was.

I finished the buffalo burger and ordered a cup of coffee. I listened to the locals talk about the weather. Forty-two last night in town. Thirty-two up at Smith's place. Might be an early fall this year . . . . The coffee was hot, the cream straight from a cow, the bustle behind the counter rhythmic and relaxing. It could have been Jake and Dorothy's in Stephenville, except for the scenery out the window and the August temperatures that the regular customers were contemplating.

On the way to the post office, we walked past the police car and inspected the dummies at close range. "It's hard to believe we couldn't tell," I remarked.

We walked into the post office, about half the size of the cafe. The fellow behind the desk looked at our postcards addressed to Texas.

"Don't send many things out to Texas."
"Well, I guess most Texans stop in Colorado."

STUDY QUESTIONS

1. What does the police car with dummies indicate about the spirit of the place the author is writing about? Why did the author single out this peculiarity of the town of Centennial to recount?

2. Does the woman at the Chuck Wagon Cafe play a similar role to the one that Wana plays in earlier narrative chapters? What do you make of her life? Is she provincial? When the author asks her if she misses going to a movie or a fancy restaurant, she says: "I think about it, but I don't miss it. Never have lived in a city to miss it." Is she living in the stage of naive prejudice? Do you pity her? Admire her? What does she represent for the author?

FOR FURTHER READING

Luchetti, Cathy. *Women of the West*. In collaboration with Carol Olwell. New York: Norton, 2001.

"The Sweet Science." Photo by author, 2007.

Twelve

THE SWEET SCIENCE
AND
THE COMPETITIVE SPIRIT

> As I shared his bounty I thought of all his contemporary lawn-tennis players, laid away with their thromboses, and the golfers hoisted out of sand pits after suffering coronary occlusions. If they had turned in time to a more wholesome sport, I reflected, they might still be hanging on as board chairmen and senior editors instead of having their names on memorial pews. I asked Mr. Ray how many fights he had had and he said, "A hundert forty. The last one was with gloves. I thought the game was getting soft, so I retired."
>
> When I was last in Hanover, New Hampshire, faculty members were dropping on the tennis courts so fast that people making up a doubles party always brought along a spare assistant professor.
>
> A. J. Liebling
> *The Sweet Science*

> In life, as well as in play, we must pursue our goals as if what we did really mattered, knowing full well that we are also precisely that person who can take a standpoint from which such seriousness can be undermined.
>
> Randolph M. Feezell
> "Play and the Absurd"

It never fails. Whenever I find myself at a gathering of people who detest football, basketball, and even baseball (George Will, where are you when we need you?), watch only Masterpiece Theater on television or refuse to own one at all, and fancy themselves the very images of gentility and culture, I always say something about how much I love a good heavyweight boxing match.

I even wrote an op-ed piece a number of years ago on the moral superiority of boxing over tennis. Whatever happens outside of the boxing ring—and I'd be the first to admit that the sleazy wheeling and dealing and the multi-million-dollar hype surrounding every major fight would be enough reason to ban boxing without even considering the violence—when you step in the ring, the only thing that will do you any good is good boxing. Verbal and psychological shenanigans enter the ring, to be sure; but there is, to say the least, a means of recourse. "Protect yourself at all times" means that if you start whining to the referee, you're liable to get your jaw broken in the process. When you give a guy your best shot and he takes it, or even if you knock him out cold, you've got to respect him for standing up to you. And if the guy knocks you out cold, well, he was better on that day, or maybe on all days—and any man who doesn't respect someone who is better at something, well, he's liable to get knocked out again.

There's no net between the fighters, and no racket and ball between the blows they throw at each other. There's something clean and heroic about that, something clear-cut and uplifting, even if frightening and brutal. It brings us down into and through the violence that is in us all and back up into a kind of civility that comes from a hard-won mutual respect and from a look into the jaws of mortality, not from all sorts of barriers and mock politeness and bowing to the Queen in the royal box.

It's true, the medical evidence is mounting that boxing is indeed brutally dangerous, even though, statistically speaking, the chances of serious injury are greater in buggy racing. And it's certainly too corrupt. And perhaps the corruption and the danger can't be eliminated, although Olympic-style boxing does a pretty good job with both. Perhaps I'm overstating the case to make a point, and, in all honesty, the injuries and deaths do give me pause. But the catechismal condemnation of the violent sports that I've had occasion to hear at many an intellectual social gathering is indeed, in far too many cases, nothing more than a knee-jerk litany, and another sure-fire sign of pseudo-intellectualism—that is, a sure sign of the absence of thinking, of signifying social membership and pooh-poohing those who fall outside of that society. This prejudice is certainly not universal among cosmopolitan intellectuals, but in certain circles it is mandatory to condemn the violent sports, even sports in general, and indeed the whole idea of competition.

The rejection of competition comes in part from the warmed-over Marxism lurking in the minds of many cosmopolitan intellectuals. Competition, as the heart and soul of capitalism, must be rejected in all its manifestations. And of course much of our sports culture does embrace a view of competition that is ruthlessly Hobbesian—the gridiron is a battlefield, winning is everything, and opponents are enemies to be annihilated. And the proponents of the winning-is-everything attitude do believe that life is competition, but competition understood as war: on the playing field, in a capitalist economy, in love, and in war, to the victor goes the spoils. The widespread admiration for Callicles and Thrasymachus on the playing fields certainly contributes to the idea that competition is inherently dehumanizing. On this view, competition is inherently bad, and all forms of play in which there are winners and losers are unethical, psychologically destructive, educationally ineffective. That leaves two choices: either a wholesale rejection of sports or, a prevalent ingenuity in youth athletics, a call for noncompetitive sports. Sports are acceptable only if they are organized, coached, and taught in such a way that winning—and therefore talent and ability—doesn't matter at all. On this view, "having fun" is the only thing that matters. Give everyone a trophy at the end of the tournament. Give all team members equal playing time regardless of ability. And so on. Not far beneath the surface of this attitude toward sports is a Rousseauian view of human nature, that we are by nature wonderful loving, communal beings, and that we need to remake society to be in touch with that communal nature. The current political twist on this Romantic view of humans is that it is not the state as such that has corrupted us, but Western individualism and capitalism, which make a virtue of selfishness and the competitive drive to win.

The sad thing is that those who embrace and those who condemn the Hobbesian view of competition are both missing the point of competition. There's a middle ground between the winning-is-everything view and the fun-is-everything view—at its best competition pushes the competitors to levels of excellence they could not achieve individually. Competition properly understood is, as Drew Hyland puts it, a "mutual striving for excellence."

In the *Republic* Socrates suggests that gymnastic untempered by music produces savageness and hardness and a lack of self-control, but that music without gymnastic produces softness and tameness and a lack of courage. For the modern cosmopolitan intellectual the latter is by far the greater danger, but let's return for a moment to Homer's Phaeacians. They represent high culture cut off from unruly nature, but they also represent a culture which emphasizes *musikē* over *gumnastikē*, or, rather, a culture in which *gumnastikē* has been transformed into *musikē*—or, even better, one in which *musikē* and *gumnastikē* both function as highly civilized forms of pleasurable play.

Indeed, the Phaeacians are certainly not without *gumnastikē* in the ordinary sense of the word—in fact, civilized athletic games of all sorts are an integral part of their life of high culture. And yet they have less taste for the games that relate to war and strife:

> We are not blameless in boxing or in wrestling,
> But we do run nimbly in races and are best in ships.
> Feasting is dear to us always, the lyre, and dances,
> Changes of clothes and hot baths, and the bed.

Odysseus reminds the Phaeacians of the relation of athletic play to the dead-serious matters of violence, of war, of death. At first he refuses to participate in the games, pleading great sorrow and homesickness. When Euryalos accuses Odysseus of being a merchant sailor, "an overseer of cargoes," and not an athlete at all, he is thinking of athletics as a sign of a culture of pure leisure. The Phaeacians are sailors too, but their ships glide effortlessly over the water, without rowing, without cargo, without martial intent—the forerunners, I suppose, of yacht clubs and social-set marinas. Angered, Odysseus picks up a weight, larger than the ones that the others had thrown, and hurls it far beyond the longest throw of the Phaeacians. He refuses to fight the son of his host, but of the others he says—and he is no doubt looking at Euryalos when he says this—"I should like to know them and try them out face to face." I don't think he had Olympic-style boxing—or Phaeacian—in mind. He goes on to explain that, even though

Philoctetes once surpassed him with the bow, now he is the best of all living mortals. He explains by saying that he would be the first to hit his man among the enemy, reminding his hosts that archery bears a relation to warfare, to killing a man rather than hitting a bull's-eye. Alcinoos, the Phaeacian king, wisely suggests that someone go find Demodocos and his lyre for a bit of song and dance.

Are the Phaeacians, who've expunged the violence from sport, truly a superior culture? Contrast the games that take place in the *Iliad* to honor the death of Patroclos—and, in anticipation, the fated death of Achilles. The competition reaches such a furious level that a boxer is knocked silly, Achilles must step forward to stop Odysseus and Ajax from wrestling a third fall so that they won't injure each other, and the Achaians put a halt to the close combat with bronze spears for fear that Ajax will be killed. For the Achaians athletic contests were sacred games that bore a direct relation to death, not just pleasurable pastimes but moving reminders of human excellence and of human finitude, of human victory and human defeat, of courage and cowardice. As Randy always reminds me, sports can build character, but more often than not they reveal it. For the Greeks sports revealed something about human character, but also about the relation of the human and the divine. In sports the Achaians found not just pleasure, but truth.

In fact, it is a great moment in the *Odyssey* when Demodocos unknowingly sings of the Achaians' great deeds at Troy, and, to the surprise of Alcinoos, brings tears to Odysseus instead of pleasure. For the Phaeacians, neither sport nor song bore a relation to truth, at least until Odysseus ventured upon their shores. When Odysseus finally tells his own story of suffering and wandering, they are spellbound. Poetry, too, brings the pathos of truth, not just pleasure—and in some cases deeply tragic, downright painful truths. As Homer has it, both *gumnastikē* and *musikē* are much more than educational tools for building good character.

The Phaeacians have escaped the toils of the seasons like farmers escaping the toils of the farm for the bright city lights, the violence of the Cyclopes like intellectuals fleeing from inner-city public schools. They pride themselves on their cultural superiority to merchants and to warriors, to those who toil and to those who wage war. Odysseus has something of the Cyclops in him, for he certainly responds to Euryalos' witty taunt with the threat of bodily injury (at least as I read his remark); and recall that Odysseus has also encountered one of the Cyclopes, who ate several of his men. Odysseus escaped under the belly of a ram, calling himself "no one," but not before he had put out the Cyclops' single eye with a smoldering wooden spike. Were the Cyclopes the first rednecks? Was Odysseus? The Phaeacians, I contend, were the first pseudo-intellectuals, the first cosmopolitan intellectuals, the first metrosexuals—except that they chose to completely separate themselves from the masses of bread-eating men, much as the Phaeacians of our day have made of the very concept of worldliness the means for a ruthlessly closed, ruthlessly inbred society, reflected in the best schools, right neighborhoods, and even in their acceptable regions of the country.

The Phaeacians refined art, sport, and life into experiences of abstracted aesthetic pleasure—what Gadamer calls "aesthetic differentiation." They abstracted not beauty, but the aesthetic experience, from truth. The songs which produce pathos in Odysseus are but a pleasurable repast for the fateless Phaeacians. The very same athletic games which mark the death of Patroclos, which mark the religious festivals of the Greeks with the pathos of human excellence in the face of human finitude and mortality, are marks of cultural superiority and the means of the most sophisticated, but ultimately meaningless, pleasure for the Phaeacians.

Bill Bradley, a Rhodes scholar who returned from England to play a remarkable career of NBA basketball before he went on to become a senator, explained why he played the game. He said that he didn't play for the fame or the money, but for those moments of truth when everything comes together. It is easier to see in the ritualistic religious connections of the Greek athletic games that something important is going on, that some truth might arise from the playing of the games. It is easier to see the connection of seemingly frivolous play to the seriousness of life and death in boxing, in Odysseus' description of archery. But even in the seemingly frivolous play of basketball, something important happens. In the very separateness of sport from life, paradoxically, we do not escape life, but see it in an uncommon way, in a way that is not ordinarily available to us in the busy-ness of living it day-to-day.

That's why, to answer the old saw, it's not whether you win or lose that matters, or even how you play the game—but how the game is played. Something happens in the game that is more significant than merely winning or losing. The competitors who play to win do indeed make the game possible, but through their efforts they become participants in something greater than the sum of their individual efforts. They give to the game, and to each other, their efforts to win, but they take from it—or they can if they play technically and morally well—more than winning. Ultimately, sport is a ritual that affirms the play of life—a playing and playing out that includes excellence and failure, comedy and tragedy, luck and fate, and death. The seriousness of the Greek games was more readily apparent, but I would suggest that even the modern games without the overt religious and cultural connections reflect, in the serious playfulness with which they must be played, back upon life—not as an escape from it, but as a mirror of its essence as dead-serious play.

In fact, a number of thinkers have suggested that understanding play will help us understand the truthfulness of art as well. Gadamer says that art is the "transformation of play into structure." The play of the athletic games is unpredictable, unique each time; the play of drama may vary with different interpretations in each performance, but the same play is nonetheless repeated—the play is given a structure which is repeatable. In a painting the play of shape and light and color is transformed into a structure that is permanent. In art play becomes a work, an *ergon*. I'm tossing around a lot of philosophical baggage here, but I would suggest that the play of sport and the play that becomes a work of art are more in touch with the essence of life than either the work ethic which sees life as work in the sense of mere toil (*ponos*) or the pseudo-intellectual aesthetic which sees the play of art and sport as a means of abstracted pleasure, free of toil, death, and truth. Life, if I may heap bald assertion upon philosophical baggage, ought to be lived as a dead-serious, playful game—not a game that some people win and others lose, but as a game in which there is truth, in which something is recognized, even if that something is not altogether pleasurable. We see the comedy and tragedy of life, in the play of sport and in the play of art, when we experience the way things are. There is a good deal of the way things are to be gleaned from a Sophoclean play, from a painting by Van Gogh, from a Hollywood movie about a forsaken sheriff, from a Greek athlete giving his all in a sacred festival, from a perfectly executed pick-and-roll, from a stiff left jab, even from those moments when two tennis players lose themselves in the greater reality of the contest which their competitive spirits make possible. We live a life worth living, we live nobly, when we live in the face of the way things are, not as Camus's rebel in defiant revolt against the absurdity of it all, but as Sophocles' Oedipus seeing the truth in the very moment of putting out his own eyes, as Odysseus choosing his mortal fate over Circe's eternal bliss and the Phaeacians' life of leisure, as Achilles and Socrates doing what they must, with "good hope toward death," knowing full well they must die for it—perhaps, when all is said and done, by embracing, if not the absurdity of Camus's indifferent universe, then the meaningful irony of being human. We live life nobly when we play it out in the face of its impenetrable mystery like the pure shooter in a pick-up basketball game who releases the eighteen-foot jump shot, the pure scrapper who fights through a pick, the forty-year-old point guard who dishes off to the wing on a fast break as if his life depended on it.

Should we, like the Achaians, stop the boxing and the close combat of football before the sacred ritual of play is desanctified by senseless death or injury? Perhaps. But let us think about them first, and, even if we ban them, let's remember that the meaning that came out of them was more than the titillation of horror-movie blood and guts; and let's not assume, as a matter of class identification, that the more gentrified athletic pursuits or the oxymoronic noncompetitive ones are in all respects superior. The answer of course is not simply to embrace the more violent sports—let's keep in mind that even violent sports can elicit some pretty unreflective snobbery. The enthusiasts of the truly violent sport of bullfighting, for example, insist it's not a sport at all, but art. How many of them, I wonder, have any idea what art is, or even sport? The question of the morality of violence aside, if we fail to recognize in our games, athletic or artistic, the deeper sense of who we are—or who we all are, in our individuality and in our communal relations; if we see in ourselves only the fabricated sign of a civilized superiority that bears no relation to the tragic and comic play of individual and common humanity, we aren't thinking.

I keep taking a slightly political turn here, losing track, as it were, of Gadamer's "ontological" interpretation of play, which has greatly influenced all of these reflections. In more mundane terms, I always find the experience of getting in there and sweating and struggling, of triumphing over some and being dominated by others, and of sharing the getting in there and sweating with both, a profoundly democratic experience. When all of the participants get in there and sweat on equal terms, some are always better and some always worse, but there is a kind of equality in the very participation, in sharing equally in the event of the game, in doing your part, in accepting your abilities and your limits. It is a democracy of equal participation, equal shared respect for the getting in there and giving it your all—and it is a democracy in which unequal excellence not only is tolerated, but required.

Having identified myself as a peculiar sort of liberal (that is not entirely to be distinguished from a peculiar sort of conservative) for a good many years now, I've found myself constantly complaining about the great number of brie-eaters with whom I share the label. I'm not sure if this principle applies to conservative intellectuals, but I've always maintained that one of the features that separates a good number of the crusty, broader-minded liberals from the knee-jerk variety is a certain sense of comically tragic human reality, derived from living a life of the jock manqué. I think of two Southern boys who cut their political and literary teeth in Texas. Read Willie Morris's overly nostalgic, but genuinely felt autobiographical sports stories in *Always Stand in Against the Curve*. Even his book on Marcus Dupree is a journey back into his own sports-filled childhood. It's his love of a good story and his love of a good ball game that keep him from falling prey to the liberal's ever-present temptation to drift off into hopeless, even vindictive, idealisms. Read Larry King's essay about his high school football coach in West Texas, and you'll know why there's something of that rip-roaring, go-for-broke West Texas football spirit in his best writing. Of course, I identify with the Southern species more strongly, but take the old head-banger of a liberal from New York, Norman Mailer, who once referred to himself as a "left conservative." He would have given his left testicle to be a great boxer. Hemingway's love of boxing and the bullfight was perhaps excessive, as was his battle with the darker side of life's play. But there's something there, too, for as one critic said, Hemingway's writings about "our nada who art in heaven" were not an affirmation of nihilism but a powerful portrayal of the battle with it. He lost the battle in the end, but he played out a life of great pathos and insight in the process.

My wife reminds me that all of this sweaty-jock worship does little for most women, and, for that matter, for a goodly number of crusty, phronetic, tragedy-conscious male intellectuals. Some women get into getting in there and sweating with the best of them, but many don't; many men don't, and I surely don't want to condemn anyone, male or female, on the basis of a sweat test. Many folks get that sense of participation in struggling humanity, in the breadth of life's comedy and tragedy, through a good crusty lower or middle-class upbringing, from raising unruly kids or coming to terms with parents, from war, from a life working with their hands in dirt or wood, from do-or-die giving it their all in the inner-city public schools. Get it where he or she will, the 21st-century intellectual is usually in dire need of some hearty, if not violent, *gumnastikē*. And one thing is certain: intellectuals, conservative or liberal, who think about life have to see that calling famous tennis players by their first names doesn't necessarily make them superior to the fellow who sits in the first row of Madison Square Garden and yells out to his favorite boxer, "Kill the bum!"

༺༻

STUDY QUESTIONS

1. The author refers to an article he wrote about the moral superiority of boxing over tennis. Although this claim seems to be somewhat tongue-in-cheek, what arguments does he give? What do you think and how would you argue for your position?

2. Do you view competition as positive or negative? If someone says about another person that he or she is "competitive," do you take that to be a positive or negative comment? Hobbes thought that humans are inherently selfish and that their natural state is competitive, what he called the war of all against all. Rousseau thought that one of the fundamental human emotions is empathy, that we are fundamentally social. Are humans by nature competitive, selfish, individualistic, altruistic, compassionate, social? Is there a basic human nature?

3. The author explains some of the antagonism of intellectuals toward competition as "the warmed-over Marxism lurking in the minds of many cosmopolitan intellectuals." What is Marx's criticism of capitalism? Is it a criticism of the competitive nature of capitalist culture? Is the competition that classical capitalist economic theory embraces similar to, parallel to, the competition in sports? Is the competitive spirit in sports a result of the competitive nature of our capitalist economy? What is the author's position?

4. The author quotes Drew Hyland's remark that athletic competition, properly understood, is a "mutual striving for excellence." It's easy to see athletic competition as a striving for excellence—the athletes are trying to be as good as they can be at the sport. But what about this striving is "mutual"? In your athletic experiences, when have you performed at your highest level, when you've had a weak opponent or a strong one? Is the traditional sportsmanship value of respect for opponents outdated?

5. Ordinarily, we think of sports as enjoyable diversions from work. Baseball is the "national pastime." But the author talks about art and sport as forms of play that are truthful: "We see the comedy and tragedy of life, in the play of

sport and in the play of art, when we experience the way things are." Does it make sense to say that we learn something about ourselves through the play of sport? Does it make sense to see sport and art as closely related in this regard?

6. The author says that life should be lived as "dead-serious play." Is that an oxymoron? Much of American culture treats life primarily as a matter of work: the work ethic, doing God's work, the American Dream of working hard to get ahead. From that perspective someone who "plays at life," someone who thinks that life is "nothing but a game," comes off as childish, cynical, irresponsible. Does the author manage to stake out a middle ground between those two views of life?

FOR FURTHER READING

Bradley, Bill. *Life on the Run*. New York: Vintage, 1995.

Clifford, Craig and Randolph M. Feezell. *Coaching for Character: Reclaiming the Principles of Sportsmanship*. Champaign, Ill.: Human Kinetics, 1997.

Feezell, Randolph M. *Sport, Play, and Ethical Reflection*. Champaign: University of Illinois Press, 2006.

Hyland, Drew A. *Philosophy of Sport*. New York: Paragon House, 1990.

Liebling, A. J. *The Sweet Science*. New York: Viking, 1982 [1956].

    Liebling's tribute to boxing.

Trout, Medicine Bow National Forest, Wyoming. Photo by author, 2003.

Thirteen

THE HALFE-ARS'D ANGLER

Rainbow

I caught my first fish
and watched it fish-wriggle and flip-flop on the grass,
like the cook was already flipping it on the griddle pan,
glinting sun silver, butter gold.
We weren't prepared, neither one of us,
he'd left the buckets and ropes back at the house.
Do you want to let it go, he asked.
But it was getting dark, so I said no.
And when his mom cooked it up in golden corn meal,
the kitchen's fluorescent rods beamed down
and licked the dining room with silver light.
Dinner was great that night.

Mallory Young
August 1981
Annapolis

I was almost embarrassed by my Zebco spinning reel. Some fellow in Centennial had talked me into this plastic bubble and a few flies. The bubble would float the end of the line and give enough weight for casting to simulate fishing with a fly rod. It was an awkward, conspicuously awkward rigamarole that I wouldn't have been caught dead with on the Brazos River. Of course, I didn't give a damn what I was caught with on the Brazos, or the Palo Pinto, or on Squaw Creek—I managed to find times and places there so that I didn't have to worry about anyone else.

When the afternoon shower eased up, I got on my duck-hunting waders and thrashed about with my Zebco and my vulgar looking bubble. As I worked my way up the Little Laramie River—hardly a creek by East Texas or Louisiana standards—I discovered that it branched off and rejoined itself endlessly, with great convolution and thus, on my part, great confusion. I was never quite sure whether I was still on Wana's place, and I wasn't entirely sure whether Wyoming ranchers felt the same way West Texans do about trespassers. The river ran through the broad valley that sloped up into the mountains, and on each side of it and in the countless islands formed by its forks and re-unions a thicket of trees and shrubs thrived on the moisture. Looking down from the highway, I had seen a thin line of dark green; standing in the river bed, I saw thicket. I felt the same disorientation I'd felt in East Texas forests. I knew I was within a hundred yards of the cabin, but occasionally I'd find myself in quickness of pulse and breath, transported back to the piney-woods campground east of Houston. I'd lost my way there at the age of ten or so, wandered senselessly, in a near panic, for an hour or two until I'd found a paved road. I guessed directions and started off down the road. Luckily, I guessed right and I ended up back in the campground. Of course, I've also been known to make a U-turn into a filling station in order to get the gas tank on the right side, and then pull out going the direction I ended up facing. On many a two-lane in Texas, or anywhere else, how can you tell the difference? Roads, after all, do run both ways.

I reached a fork in the river, casting without hope along the way. My dad's friend Shoestring Martin, an old hand at fishing the Louisiana bayous and swamps, says you have to have your bait in the water to catch a fish. Outdoor Man says you have to believe you're going to catch a fish or you won't. I was more concerned that I wasn't living up to some aristocratic fisherman's ideal of primitive purity. Hell, I'd never even held a fly rod. I was more concerned that some effete Wyoming fly fisherman, or some fly-fishing aficionado from Cornell, would see me with my Zebco; or that Outdoor Man or some other blue-collar Texan or some skillet-fishing Cajun would be transported to Wyoming and see me with this damn plastic bubble.

I looked up one branch of the river and saw two fully decked-out fly fishermen up to their waists in the deep pool of the next bend. One, the older one, was explaining to the other how to negotiate the overhanging limbs, in order to lay the fly delicately in the shaded pool beneath them. I didn't know anything about trout, but I'd sure as hell expect a bass to hang out there—as Outdoor Man always puts it, if I were a fish, I'd be hanging out there. The other one, the younger, flicked the long line three-quarter armed, his head cocked half-sideways almost as if he were looking down the rod as he brought it around—the fly popped into a limb and hung up, no more than four inches above the water. "Darn," he said.

"Damn," I thought. I turned into the other fork, although it looked less promising. But, with my rig, and my lack of faith in it, I could have been casting on the bank. I lumbered through shallow rapids, then deeper rapids, remembering stories of duck hunters drowning in irrigation canals when their chest waders filled up with water. I reached another fork, a three-way. I had no idea which way to go, or even where I would end up if I went back to the last fork. I had been wandering around for over an hour, taking river forks less traveled by maybe half a dozen times by now. Where on earth was I? I looked back down the river, and I saw water and overhanging thicket. I heard a tireless rumble and roar of water over gravel and rock and sand. I was standing in the middle of a river in Wyoming, lost as a Baptist at a Catholic bingo, holding a slim black pole with a plastic bubble and tiny artificial insect dangling into the water. I was gasping for air, partly in exhaustion from the hike and partly in that age-old childhood near panic. I had no idea how to get back to the cabin.

I looked down to remind myself that I always think best in a near panic. I saw an instantaneous streamlined streak of color, a goddamn huge trout swimming, no, streaking, against the current as if there wasn't one. Damn, I thought. I looked up again, saw the same water and thicket, then turned to look again at the treble fork in the rippling waters. Out above the trailing off of one of the forks, nestled in the open cut that the water made in the horizon, stood those unmistakable peaks of the Snowy Range. I knew then exactly where I was, not more than fifty yards from the cabin. I knew then that the land sloped up to the ranch house off that direction. I stepped up onto the steep bank and headed off like a compass to the cabin. Lewis and Clark could navigate in rivers; I couldn't.

When I crossed the final leg of the river behind our cabin, I saw Mallory coming up the road with a middle-aged man wearing hip boots, a khaki-colored fishing vest, a bag slung over his shoulder with a long strap. As he approached I noticed that he was carrying a light graphite rod with a spinning reel—true, an open spinning reel of considerably higher status than my Zebco 20/20, but no fly rod.

Mallory introduced her prize catch. "I told him you needed a few pointers."

"I need more than a few."

I explained, as if I needed to, that I didn't know trout fishing from throwing horseshoes.

"I've never done any fly fishing," I went on. "The fellow in town said to try this contraption. I can see you don't believe in that technique."

"I've been coming up here from Denver for fourteen years, and you can take it from me, all you need is the rod and reel you've got there and a few of these." From his vest pocket he pulled out a couple of small spinner baits—a sixteenth-ounce rooster tail with a brass-colored blade and a black and yellow tail, a Mepps spinner with a couple of brass balls and a red plastic sleeve above the tiny treble hook, and a number-two Martin spinner with a yellow and red bead. "Here, take these."

"Thanks. Thanks a lot."

"You can get more in town. You'll need them. I lose two or three on every outing."

"And these work as well as flies?"

"Better for here. I fly-fished for years here, and I finally just gave up. The river is so narrow and with the trees and bushes overhanging, you just can't get the fly into the shadows underneath the tree limbs. If you want to spend your time figuring out how to cast in impossible circumstances, and retrieving your flies from trees, that's fine. But I like to catch fish."

"I'll be damned."

He motioned for me to follow him. He walked out on the sandy point below our cabin. "Let me give you a couple of other pointers. As you work your way up the stream, make five casts from each position, starting downstream then working your way upstream. You see there where the rapids make a V with the backwater?"

"Yes."

"That's always a good place. Now, if you catch one, there's probably another one, but usually you'll have to come back later to catch him. They spook pretty easily."

"I really appreciate it."

"Good luck," he said as he finished reeling in the last demonstration cast. He stepped up out of the stream and headed up the road without another word.

"Goddamn. Where did you find him? That's two years of experience crammed into a five-minute lesson."

I had about a half hour left before dark. I cut off the plastic bubble chandelier, tied on the rooster tail, and headed up the river. The sun was already dropping behind the trees, and the river turned to a cool shadowy tint. At the first bend I cast up into the rapids and worked the spinner just beneath the surface at about a forty-five-degree angle. The next cast dipped into the edge of the backwater that my accidental guide had described. I lifted and reeled slowly. A tiny streak hit the spinner. I was too stunned to hook him well. He was gone as quickly as he appeared. That got my heart beating a few beats faster. I cast farther back into the backwater pool. Another lightening strike. I jerked back violently, the fish came out of the water, and the hook pulled loose. These aren't five-pound hybrids, I coached myself. They don't have a mouth like a bass.

I worked up the stream as the evening chill settled down on the water. I had four or five strikes, small ones, but unmistakable. I got one about halfway in before he got off, but I couldn't quite get the feel. First too light, then too hard. I knew everyone was waiting to eat. It would have been nice to bring back half a dozen respectable brook trout, but there was always the left-over chili from last night.

As I got back to the cabin I saw my mentor coming out of the thicket just downstream. He saw me and walked over.

"This is what you're looking for," he said, pulling a fourteen-inch brown trout out of his bag. He pointed to the markings. "The browns have dark spots on a light background, and the brookies are just the opposite."

"I had a few strikes with the spinners you gave me, but I couldn't get them in."

"Gotta have the right touch. They're tricky."

The next morning I hit the river at sunrise. I had on layers upon layers of T-shirts and sweaters, but my fingers were so cold I could hardly feel the rod in my hands. As the sun climbed above the trees, the warmth brought up a mist on the water. The myriad species of insects fly fishermen try to imitate danced on the water. I walked and cast, walked and cast. I peeled off the sweater and tied it around my neck. Every time I cast into the V between the rapids and a backwater, I'd find myself breathing rapidly in anticipation. I was beginning to believe.

Behind a beaver dam I hooked a small one and gently brought him in. I stood waist-deep in the swift current, the waders bubbling out in the water. I reached down gingerly and removed the tiny brook trout from the hook. He was only about six inches long, so I turned him gently back into the water. I cast under the limbs at the outside of the bend. Another strike, but I lost him. I walked on around the bend and snagged another small one in the middle of the rapids. Still too small for my taste—I turned him back, too.

About ten o'clock I headed back to the cabin. I could have stayed all day, but we had a hike in the mountains planned.

In the evening I decided to give it one more try, just before dinner. "Get the fire going—I'm going after dinner," I announced confidently. And, sure enough, I ran into my mentor again.

"Caught a few small ones this morning. Where'd you find that fourteen-incher you had yesterday?"

"Work those spinners slow."

"How do you do that in the those shallow rapids without getting hung up on the rocks?"

"All right, all right. Go up this way. The big ones are in the deeper pools."

Of course, I should have known that, but I had images of standing in the very thick of the rapids and hooking a record-breaking monster that would leap above the tumbling white water, hang photogenically in the air, fight like an old pro, then finally wear down enough for me to get him in.

I crossed the rickety bridge behind the big barn and headed off in the direction he'd pointed. I didn't like the looks of the first bend—too much moss to work the lure. I cut across the pasture to the next leg of the river. The water was slower, darker, deeper. I crawled over a fallen tree, half-rotted, and perched on a fairly tall bank. The water backed up against a huge beaver dam. Across the way I could see a fallen tree trunk running from the high bank into the deep pool. It cast an inviting shadow just beneath it. My first cast was short. I reeled in quickly. The second gently nicked the bottom of the tree trunk and settled smack in the center of the shadows. Before I could get my rod tip up, a heavy thud radiated up the line. I knew I finally had a keeper. I worked him across the deep pool behind the dam, giving when he made his determined runs, reeling when he paused. I got to my knees when I got him to the bank, stretched down to the water's edge to pull him out. He was a bit over a foot, a ruddy streaked brook—no monster, but respectable for a brook trout in that river.

It was fast approaching nightfall as I unhooked him. One fish wouldn't make much of a supper for four adults, one food-inhaling seventeen-year-old, and a hungry seven-year-old. I thought momentarily about throwing him back, recalling the public television special on fly fishing I'd recently seen on which the announcer, playing to the Masterpiece Theater crowd, suggested that all fly fishermen turn their fish back. They fish, he said, for the sport of it.

There's no way in hell I'm turning this goddamned fish back, I muttered to myself, as I turned and stomped off down the bank with the meager results from two days of hard fishing. I knew I was getting the hang of it, and that I would catch my fair share in the few days remaining, but this one was the one I'd been looking for.

STUDY QUESTIONS

1. This chapter begins with an epigraph from the author's wife, a poem about her catching her first fish and eating it; and it ends with the author finally catching a fish and declaring that he's not going to turn it back. How does this recurring theme of catching and killing fish connect to the larger philosophical discussion of cosmopolitan versus rooted intellectuals? To the discussion of the relation of culture and nature in chapter 12?

2. Are there fishing prejudices? The author is embarrassed by his Zebco spinning reel and the plastic bubble that enables him to cast weightless artificial flies with spinning gear. The fly fishermen would laugh at his cheap spinning reel, and his blue-collar fishing friends in Texas would laugh at the plastic bubble. Are there local fishing customs that deserve respect? How is the fisherman from Colorado who gives the author advice a symbol of a kind of "phronetic" approach to fishing this particular stream?

3. What is the significance of the author's story about losing his bearing while fishing—and of how that reminded him of getting lost in the woods as a child? The peaks of the Snowy Range return once again in this story when the author finds his bearing as result of looking up and seeing them in the distance. What do they represent in this context?

FOR FURTHER READING

Gordon, Caroline. *Aleck Maury, Sportsman.* Carbondale: Southern Illinois University Press, 1980 [1934].

A novel based on the life of Gordon's father as hunter and fisherman.

Hemingway, Ernest. "Big Two-Hearted River: Part I" and "Big Two-Hearted River: Part II." In *The Short Stories of Ernest Hemingway.* New York: Scribner's, 1938.

Ostensibly a story about a fishing trip, but, beneath the surface, a haunting reflection on the human condition. One of Hemingway's finest works of fiction.

On the "Chiantigiana" between Siena and Florence, Italy. Photo by author, 2005.

Vineyard on Mosel River in Germany. Photo by author, 1978.

Prosciutto di cinghiale (cured wild boar), Tuscan bread salad, and Brunello di Montalcino, Montalcino, Italy. Photo by author, 2005.

Grilled rack of pork, Stephenville, Texas. Photo by author, 2006.

Fourteen

BLOOD SPORTS AND HAUTE CUISINE

> Killing cleanly and in a way which gives you aesthetic pleasure and pride has always been one of the greatest enjoyments of a part of the human race. Because the other part, which does not enjoy killing, has always been more articulate and has furnished most of the good writers we have had a very few statements of the true enjoyment of killing.
>
> Ernest Hemingway
> *Death in the Afternoon*

> Eschew soft crabs in tony seafood restaurants which, invoking haute cuisine, insult the soft crab with "a light blanket of béarnaise," or "an exotic sauce of sherry and toasted almonds." Please.
>
> A beaten biscuit can't be made in a food processor, and a soft crab can't be fully appreciated without as strict adherence to rite and custom as the modern world will allow. It is the very essence of a Maryland summer.
>
> Cecelia P. Clark
> "Soft Crab Factor"

To be sure, many culture-vulturing pseudo-intellectuals look down on all hunting and fishing, on anyone who kills "poor defenseless animals," as the phrase usually runs. In certain circles, though, a certain kind of fishing is not only allowed but becomes itself another means of pseudo-intellectual snobbery. If my high-energy physics professor was a fisherman, he was surely a catch-and-release fly fisherman. Had Randy and Barbara admitted to him that they had been fishing for lake trout with worms, he would certainly have dismissed them as "bait fishermen," just as the narrator's brother in *A River Runs Through It* condemns the narrator's brother-in-law for bringing along a coffee can full of worms on a fishing trip to the Big Blackfoot.

Most of my fishing in Texas has tended to be of the blue-collar variety—fill your skillet and your freezer. I bear with the early spring "water hauls" because I know that sooner or later we'll catch the sandies or the crappie on their feeding-frenzy spawning runs and fill the boat with fish. I love riding around Palo Pinto Lake watching for the white splash, the slapping sound, of the sandies schooling on the surface; seeing a school come up right on top of us, surrounding the boat by the hundreds, one of them hitting a lure hanging from an extra rod off the front of the boat . . . honest; finding a school of hybrids on Lake Proctor and hauling in four- and five-pounders on every pass until three of us have caught enough fish to feed half of Stephenville for the next year, back before the five-fish limit, that is. I even love the feel of never finding a damn fish, of just flat giving up, of setting the rods down, leaning back with a beer and watching in total defeat and humiliation as the sun sets with a Sartrean indifference, but spectacularly, in the western sky.

But, to be honest, I did eventually get hooked on fly fishing myself. I'm too much of a sucker for athletic challenge, for physical finesse, for gear and equipment and how-to books, and books that talk about sport in order to think about life. So many writers I admire are adamant fly fishermen, and downright uppity about it. John Graves's story about pulling a fly fisherman out of a swollen Brazos River is filled with erudite disquisitions on the etiquette of fly fishing; of course, his subject is not fishing, but mortality and the delicate ways we respect each other's coming to terms with it. I told him I'd fished for trout in Wyoming with a Zebco spinning reel, and he responded: "You'll really have to try fly fishing. It adds to it." He loaned me a copy of Caroline Gordon's *Aleck Maury: Sportsman* with the recommendation that it is the only thing worthwhile to come out of the whole Southern Agrarian movement. "It doesn't go anywhere, but I love how it doesn't go anywhere." Aleck Maury, modeled on Gordon's father, lived an entire life for fly fishing.

Hemingway's "Big Two-Hearted River" just wouldn't work if Nick had been fishing with a blue-collar rig he'd bought at K-Mart; of course, he uses live grasshoppers as bait, not handcrafted dry flies. The artistry of fly fishing somehow lends a deeper gloom to the burned-out forest and that final swamp stretch of the river that Nick is afraid to enter. Ralph Ellison says that he learned to fish and hunt by reading Hemingway, and even survived a few stretches of the starving artist's existence on the game.

In *Open Season* William Humphrey included a series of stories about fly fishing in Europe that rivals Twain's innocents abroad. Of course, they're stories about humans, not fish. "The Spawning Run," for example, ostensibly about salmon fishing in England, carries a tongue-in-cheek symbolism to the pinnacle of human comedy, as it parallels the mating habits of the fish with those of the fishermen's wives who are left alone at the inn while their husbands are off fishing. A good Texas boy from way back, he half apologizes for devoting much of the book to "aristocratic fishing," and I admit that I liked the half-fantastical tales of hunting with his father during his boyhood in East Texas best of all, but the fishing tales are finely hewn and that Twainian squint on the world would never have worked without a meticulous knowledge of the blue-blooded art of fly fishing.

Norman Maclean's *A River Runs Through It* begins with this fly-fishing invocation:

> In our family, there was no clear line between religion and fly fishing. We lived at the junction of great trout rivers in western Montana, and our father was a Presbyterian minister and a fly fisherman who tied his own flies and taught others. He told us about Christ's disciples being fishermen, and we were left to assume, as my brother and I did, that all first-class fishermen

on the Sea of Galilee were fly fishermen and that John, the favorite, was a dry-fly fisherman.

Certainly, there's a kind of self-effacing snobbery in this passage, but it's awfully appealing, especially when it leads into a story of haunting vision—a vision in which fly fishing is the thread that ties together brothers and father and, in a final epiphanic moment, brothers and fathers and nature's mysterious murmurings.

In the end, you have to concede that fly fishing is not a matter of snobbery for Norman Maclean; it is, like religion at its best, a way of understanding who we are. If you're really serious about fly fishing, as opposed to being serious about trying to impress people by telling them you're a fly fisherman, it's hard to be snobbish about something so humbling, so revealing of our finitude:

> Well, until man is redeemed he will always take a fly rod too far back, just as natural man always overswings with an ax or golf club and loses all his power somewhere in the air; only with a rod it's worse, because the fly often comes so far back it gets caught behind in a bush or rock.

Maclean continues:

> My father was very sure about certain matters pertaining to the universe. To him, all good things—trout as well as eternal salvation—come by grace and grace comes from art and art does not come easy.

Fly fishing was for the Maclean family about truth and beauty and goodness, and about human frailty and tragedy, and, the comments about the bait-fishing brother-in-law notwithstanding, the Macleans didn't do it in order to seem or to feel superior to anyone.

By contrast, though, the following statement in the credits to Robert Redford's movie version of *A River Runs Through It* is an appalling bit of holier-than-thou pseudo-intellectual prejudice:

> No fish were killed or injured during the making of *A River Runs Through It*. The producers would like to point out that, although the Macleans kept their catch as was common earlier in this century, enlightened fishermen today endorse a "catch and release" policy to assure that this priceless resource swims free to fight another day.

And according to *The Internet Movie Database*:

> Trout used in the movie were pond-raised in Montana and were kept in a specially aerated and cooled tank truck until their big moment in front of the cameras. No hooks were used, and no blood was drawn. A line was tied

to each fish's lower jaw under the careful observance of the Montana Humane Society.

Let's be more precise. The Macleans didn't just keep their catch; they killed and ate them. "Catch and release" may now be a necessity because of the hoards of Orvis-clad fishermen assaulting the rivers that Norman Maclean grew up on, not to mention the pollution. But to suggest that this practice is somehow more enlightened and morally superior to what the Macleans did is really more about flashing your union card in front of the people who judge movies than it is about caring for the well-being of fish. Assuming for the purposes of argument that we should be worried about the emotional trauma of fish, which is a stretch to say the least, then wouldn't jerking a fish around with a string tied to its lower jaw in order to make it look like Brad Pitt knows how to fly fish be less humane than catching a fish, killing it quickly, and eating it? And the standard catch-and-release practice, which involves using a barbless single hook that can easily be removed from the fish with minimal damage—why is catching a fish and jerking it around on the end of line for the mere sport of it morally superior? If you eat fish, why wouldn't it be an honorable thing to catch your own—to kill your own, that is—and eat them?

The first time I asked Outdoor Man where he and Ron had caught the sixty sand bass that Ron had been bragging to me about, he said, "In the water." After I had dropped countless not-too-subtle hints, he finally took me up to Tin Top on the Brazos in early spring. We put in five or six miles upstream from Lake Granbury and headed upstream about a half-hour's boat ride until the water was too shallow to go any further.

When I explained that I had never fished for sand bass before, he looked in my tackle box and pointed to a small chartreuse tail. "Put that on a sixteenth-ounce jig head, an eighth if it's windy."

"How do you fish it?"

"In the water."

"Thanks."

I watched him studiously and imitated his every move and manner. Soon he'd caught half a dozen and I'd caught none.

"Let it sink to the bottom, then work it back."

"Won't I get hung up?"

"Yeah."

I cast up against the bank and watched until the line went slack. I lifted the rod slightly, then reeled a few turns. I let the line sink once again. When I pulled up I felt a slight tug, almost as if I had hung up on some moss. I jerked back, half expecting to feel the dead weight of the proverbial hunk of weeds. The line took off sideways, the pole bent, and my fingers felt the determined vibrations of a fish.

"There's old sandy," Outdoor Man said approvingly.

I hauled him in and made another cast. I felt the lead jig head settle on the bottom again. I lifted and came up against a whale of a resistance.

"Oh, yeah, I forgot to tell you. There are some pretty bad rocks right here." He jerked back and the telltale sideways movement of his line suggested that I hadn't learned the whole routine.

"How can I let it sink to the bottom if the bottom's full of rocks?"

"Well, that's a problem. You gotta be careful."

It took a dozen trips to get half of Outdoor Man's secrets out of him. Even with years of practice now, I rarely give him a run for his money; but rest assured, when I do, there's no greater pleasure on earth than discovering that a certain color or a certain lure is the only one that will work and that Outdoor Man doesn't have any of those. Ten-cent plastic tails suddenly cost two dollars.

To this day I still marvel that he can find a ledge or a drop-off in the middle of a five-hundred-acre lake of absolutely indistinguishable water, tell one grassy bend in a river from another. I can do it, but I have to do it consciously, methodically, triangulated from the radio tower and the marina, or remembering the exact configuration of trees on the river bank, or the color of the clay bank, or the smooth rock just beneath the surface; he does it intuitively. I figure out where I am; he knows where he is.

My childhood memories of fishing are strictly blue-collar. My dad always lacked the patience for fishing, but he'd occasionally arrange a fishing trip back to Louisiana. His older brother Perkins took us cat-fishing with his three sons on a deep irrigation canal next to a pumping station. The fins of the huge channel cat scared me to death. For several of his teenage years my dad was raised by his older brother, and although my dad was known to indulge rather regularly in less-than-genteel-language, he wouldn't have even thought of cursing in front of his brother. A deacon in the Baptist church, Uncle Perkins was straight as an arrow and as strict as a sergeant with his sons. While we were fishing one of them uttered the word "damn," barely above a whisper, standing a good fifty yards away from Uncle Perkins. He rushed over and pounced with the wrath of the Old Testamental God. It scared the hell out of me.

Once Uncle Bud, my great uncle by marriage, took my dad and me out to the Atchafalaya Basin, hired us the best guide around, and sent us off through the murky endless waters, a thick jungle of cypress and cattails that covers several thousand acres of south Louisiana. How the guide knew one cut from another, one clump of lazy cypresses from another, I had no clue. We didn't fill the boat, but we caught a good icebox full of sac-à-lait. It didn't occur to me until years later that the name meant "sack of milk." The first time I saw the Texas name "crappie" in print, I didn't realize it was the same fish, let alone how to pronounce it. Many of the creatures I'd learned to name as a kid had different names in Texas, but I'd grown up with Louisiana parents.

Duck hunting, not fishing, was my father's passion, and for that reason my most vivid outdoor childhood memories involve greenheads and teal and pintails. Even before I was old enough to hunt, I was waking up to the smell of pin feathers singeing over a gas burner, my head resting on a pillow stuffed with down feathers from my father's ducks. I carried an empty .410 for a year to learn to carry it safely, that is, without ever pointing it at a human being I didn't intent to shoot whether it was loaded or not. When I was old enough to start hunting, my father's explanations of the mathematics and physics of leading a bird on the wing never turned me into the natural that he was, but I was good enough not to embarrass myself or him. I would practice the soft chuckling sound of the mallard feeding call for hours on the old Faulk's duck call my dad handed down to me, even though I knew he would never let me call as long as he was in the blind to call for us. In the eighth grade, I broke my leg playing sandlot football, and, even though I couldn't hunt, I went with my dad on a hunting trip to Louisiana. We stayed on a houseboat anchored in the middle of the Louisiana coastal marsh, and I managed to get the plaster cast on my broken leg so wet that the doctor decided to take it off two weeks early rather than redo it. I remember how the Cajuns my dad hunted with called spoonbills "smilin' mallards." They were considered poor eating, so if you killed one, presumably by accident, you had to whittle the bill down to normal size, wrap it with a five-dollar bill, then donate it to the camp.

In the years of intensified cosmopolitanism, I gave up hunting, thinking—or emoting—it was not fitting for a life of the mind. I came back to it, though, as I gradually groped my way back to a life lived with both feet on the ground. Living in Annapolis, I'd head home Christmases for duck season. It took several years and thousands of spent shells to get it all back. On the first duck hunt after a lay-off of ten or so years, I ran my brother-in-law a close race for emptying your gun the most times to no avail. We both shot over two boxes of shells to kill maybe four or five ducks each. My dad suggested that we'd probably killed those with the ejected hulls that had filled the sky.

In certain circles hunting is a touchy subject. You know, the fellow is limply lifting the artistically sculpted, diminutive silver knife to place a dab of goose liver pâté, extracted from Alsatian geese whose feet have been nailed to a board, upon a morsel of bread delicately torn from an exquisitely slender French baguette which has been baked in authentic wood-burning brick ovens in an authentically upwardly-mobile strip shopping center in, well, Fort Worth or Austin or Houston.

I say something about goose season opening next week and he, mouth agape and silver knife clinking against china plate, queries in unmistakably accusatory tones: "You mean you actually shoot those poor birds with a gun?"

"Well, I shoot at them."

In the presence of a featherless biped of the Masterpiece Theater-watching variety such as this, I usually revert to the Cajun Theory of Expressive Hunting. This theory, I explain, requires that you hunt with a three-shot gun. A double-barrel simply won't do. The first shot, I say with flawlessly straight face, is to kill; the second is to maim; and the third is to communicate a socially ungraceful remark having something to do with the reproductive act as the bird is flying rapidly and well beyond range into the receding horizon. The reason for requiring the plugging of five-shot pumps and automatics, I continue, is not to protect the bird populations, but to prevent an escalation of hunting vulgarity beyond the bounds of all, even hunters', civility.

Vegetarians are at least consistent, and some of the arguments for vegetarianism I can take seriously. The folks who inhale pounds upon pounds of plastic-wrapped grocery-store meat and then rail against the moral depravity of hunting I cannot. In order for meat eaters to have meat to eat, animals must die, and, to put the point directly, someone must kill them. Farm folks and small-town folks grow up with slaughtering and butchering. But city folks who eat meat would do well, would do morally well, to go out every now and then to kill some of the meat they are eating, to face squarely the deaths that our meat eating requires. Ancient rituals of various kinds—from the sacrificing of blood or organs to Olympian deities to the Hebrew codes that prohibit boiling the calf in its mother's milk—acknowledge this cycle, this necessity. Modern rituals of various kinds, from plastic wrap to catch-and-release fishing, cover it up.

From the animal's point of view, isn't it more honorable to live in the wild and die in the hunt than it is to be force-fed and mechanistically terminated in the slaughterhouse? Human civilization being what it is—and I certainly don't mean to say we should all don loin cloths again—domesticating animals for food purposes is a part of life we can't do without; but the overly sanitized, technologized version is a far cry from our grandparents wringing the backyard chicken's neck. It makes us forget a part of ourselves. Hunting and fishing magazines that refer to the killing of game as "harvesting," I might add, are making their contribution to the plastic-wrap view of the world. To my mind, it is spiritually healthier to eat something you have killed with your own hands. It has something to do with near-primitive ritualistic meanings, with murmurings of our earlier selves, I know, but I sense these murmurings with dead certainty at times.

To be sure, there are hunters who aren't in touch with these reasons, who blaze away in drunken splendor, who wound, maim, and mutilate without concern, who leave dead game to rot in the field. There are hunters who become obsessed with the sheer sport of shooting, and I would be the first to argue that taking the life of a bird for the mere sport of skillful shooting is immoral. If you're just interested in winged marksmanship, shoot trap or skeet and leave the live ones alone. The purpose of good shooting in hunting is always tied in some degree to sheer shooting prowess, but it also has something to do with killing cleanly the food you will eat, and the hunter who does not feel a twinge of guilt as the occasionally unavoidable wounded prey flutters or hobbles away doesn't understand what hunting is about. Indeed, hunting for big-game trophies transforms the "grain-giving earth" into the adventurer's playground—another sort of high culture profoundly out of touch with nature's deeper meanings.

Hunting done well, done, if you will, meditatively, can keep a person in touch with natural cycles and rhythms in a way that modern life doesn't often allow. Hunting of the serious variety requires a kind of reverent attunement to the prey, a kind of union between hunter and prey that primitive folks knew something about. In order to kill, to kill cleanly, you watch, you listen, you intuit—wind, sun, clouds, the lay of the land, the color of grass and trees, the telling flash of light upon the wristwatch you forgot to take off, the feel of the bird's wing as it turns into the northwest wind. You learn. You begin to know that the teal will make another pass before they set their wings for their landing; that the single mallard drake will circle half-a-dozen times before he floats in; that the dove on the horizon will curve your direction, follow the tree line, come in from the left; that when you stand to shoot, the dove will veer this way and not that. You see yourself in the yellow-brown maize stalks, blending in as if you are a part of the field, see yourself as the dove sees you. You see the curve of the hill, the reflection of light on the tank, as the dove sees it from fifty yards above you. You see in a way that you don't if you are just watching. Even if it is but a convenient fiction, you see as the hunter who must attune himself to the prey, who must see in order to eat. For a moment, you are ordered within the natural world—its births, its flashing beauty, its brutal deaths, its cycling timeless ways—and not an existential abomination against it.

John Graves's thoughtful ambivalence perhaps expresses the greater truth:

Saint Henry David Thoreau, incisive moral anthropomorphist that he was, implied that blood sports were for juveniles, not men, and was conceivably right. Prince Ernest Hemingway implies the opposite. . . . One's nature, if he owns more than a single mood, implies both views at one time or another and sometimes in cramping conjunction.

Hunting and fishing done well represent two kinds of rootedness: they brings us face to face with a more general connection to the earth, to nature's cycles, to mortality; but they also grow out of a specific locale, the flora and fauna and terrain of a particular place, and they also tend to involve family traditions, something passed down from one generation to the next. I grew up hunting ducks because I was born in and my father had grown up in south Louisiana, and because ducks, at least back then, were plentiful in the rice country south and southwest of Houston. For the last twenty or so years of my father's life, one of the things we did together every winter was go duck hunting. I can't think of my relationship to him without thinking about duck hunting. Typically the people I run into who despise hunting and guns of all shapes and sizes have never had that experience. Sometimes they have, and sometimes they arrive at anti-hunting and anti-gun conclusions through a consideration of the evidence and the issues involved; but too often the stance is arrived at without the slightest experience or understanding because it is obligatory for those who wish admittance to the community of intellectuals.

One of my colleagues, who hails from the Great Northeast, was appalled at the fact that her children's elementary school was auctioning off a deer rifle to raise money. "What is that going to teach these kids?" she demanded to know. I said it would teach them that a good deer rifle is a good thing to have, and that a lot of people in these parts want one, or a second or third or fourth one, bad enough to buy raffle tickets. "I know," she said condescendingly. In order to get a high school diploma, I continued, all children should have to learn how to safely and accurately use firearms, and that they should have to live off of food they killed themselves for a six-month period. End of that conversation.

And then, ou-là-là, there's the question of cuisine, or, as we say in Texas, grub. Haute cuisine has always been one of the weapons of regional, class, and pseudo-intellectual bigotry. In certain circles pointing out that someone eats fried food calls up images of barefoot illiteracy and burning crosses. The prejudice is directed especially at Southern regionalism, but it is often a prejudice against regionalism of any kind, at least American regionalism of any kind, and it is based on the equation of culture and some vague notion of worldliness.

A couple of years after the high-energy physics professor proclaimed to us in the Medicine Bow Mountains that there was no good food in the West, I had a similar experience with a new colleague. Being congenitally hospitable Southwesterners, my wife and I invited a new colleague to dinner to welcome her to the community. Originally from New York City, she showed all of the signs of having already condemned our regional university and our small-town community without giving them a chance. We were determined to show her just how cultured we were. I spent the entire afternoon preparing a gourmet meal, gourmet in the classically French sense of the word. That evening she sat on our patio eating it quite gleefully as she badmouthed the town, our students, and the state. Near the end of the meal, after polishing off several courses of my food, she proclaimed, and I quote, "You know, there's just no good food in Texas." I started to ask her if she had ever met a high-energy physics professor from Cornell, but I didn't. Like him, her intention was not to condemn us. She was not condemning my food, for that matter. She was uttering a cosmopolitan prejudice so bold in its sweeping generality that you'd think she'd recognize that one good counterexample, like the meal she had just eaten, would reveal its absurdity. The truth is, like the physics professor, she expected us to nod in knowing agreement. After all, we were all professors. I did not nod in agreement, and suffice it to say she was never invited back to our home. And I now know to respond to this kind of condemnation by saying to the intruder: that makes you either really stupid for accepting the job here or an incredible loser because you couldn't get a job somewhere you approve of.

Robert MacNeil underwent a re-education in the English language; I had to undergo a re-education in food. It's more complicated these days, but for my generation establishing your intellectual and cultural superiority meant, in the arena of food, learning about and devoting yourself to European foods and wines, especially French food and wine. What I was taught right along with Plato's dialogues in college and graduate school was that I would become "worldly" by embracing classic European cuisine. As a good graduate student obedient to the call of cosmopolitanism, I became fascinated with French and German wine, ironically largely through the influence of a Yale PhD originally from Oklahoma, and I studied Hugh Johnson's *World Atlas of Wine* right alongside Plato's *Gor-*

gias and Heidegger's *Sein und Zeit*. I began to learn to cook about the same time, and between watching Julia Child on TV and sifting through countless cookbooks and watching and stealing from the accomplished Francophile cooks that clustered around my university environment, I managed to get along pretty well.

Then, ostensibly to learn German well enough to read Heidegger in German, I went to Europe for the summer, mainly to Germany but also to a bit of France and Switzerland. What did I discover? French and German food, even at the highest levels, comes out of earthy, localized regions, out of country and peasant traditions. Paris is their New York, and in Europe folk traditions get lost in lofty cuisines, but, still, French food comes from French people. People in different regions eat their own regional foods, which reflect the soil and the climate and the habits. People in different regions drink primarily the wines or beer made in their particular region. Ernst Wolfgang Orth, a philosophy professor we stayed with in Trier, made the rounds each year to all of the vineyards on the hills above the town—most of the wine in his well-stocked cellar came from the hillsides you could see from his house. A philosophy professor, world traveler, comfortable in German, French, and English, and pretty handy with classical Greek and Latin to boot—was he provincial?

Just think about wine, if you will. More than any other drinkable substance it reflects its region, its province. The worldly Hugh Johnson sums it up this way:

> The relation between maps and wine is a very intimate one. Wine is, after all, the unique agricultural product whose price depends entirely on where it comes from. The better the wine, the more exactly it locates its origin—down, eventually, to one diminutive field in a simple village lying under what Stendhal described as 'an ugly dried-up little hill': named Romanée-Conti.

When I read in Hugh Johnson that the wines of the northern Rhône reflect the crumbling granite cliffs, the wines of the southern Rhône the broad, sun-baked terraces, I swear, I could taste them. Compare what happens to Merlot in Saint-Émilion and neighboring Pomerol, or even in the sandier western part of Pomerol as opposed to the eastern part bordering Saint-Émilion. Look at the Mosel Rieslings as opposed to the Rheingau. The Rieslings from the Saar tributary to the Mosel have a flintier, green-apple sharpness than the middle-Mosel wines from less than a dozen miles away. During my summer of culinary *Bildung*, on a hill overlooking Bernkastel and, across the river, the sister town of Kues in which Nicholas of Cusa lived, I took a few steps and walked from Bernkasteler Graben into Bernkasteler Doktor. I stood among the vines that produce the grapes of Bernkasteler Doktor and watched a man drive a tractor along a winding road at the bottom edge of the vineyard. Wine growers, I remarked to myself, are farmers.

When I returned to Europe a few years ago for the first time since graduate school, I had a similar experience in Italy. Staying with our friend Chiara in a little village on the Adriatic coast at the northern edge of Marche, most of the food we ate came from the sea a stone's throw away or from the nearby countryside. Maria, who had worked for the family for thirty years, contributed fresh lettuce and arugula from her garden. All of the food was cooked with olive oil from the trees on the family land just outside of town. The homemade wine we drank every day was made by a neighbor from local grapes. In the local market, even most of the commercial wines were from the immediate region. When we asked about the Brunellos from Tuscany, one of the "great" wines of Italy, some of the people we talked to knew about them. But they talked of them as if they were from a foreign country, even though Montalcino, the home of Brunello, was only a few hours to the southwest.

And when we made our mandatory tour through southern Tuscany, we found, once again, that the local custom was to drink the wine from the immediate locale. Montalcino and Montepulciano are maybe twenty miles apart, but when you're sitting in a restaurant in Montalcino you'll be drinking Brunello di Montalcino or Rosso di Montalcino with your *chingiale*, and when you're sitting in a cafe in Montepulciano for a late afternoon snack, you'll be sipping Vino Nobile di Montepulciano with your caprese. Certainly those wines are similar, and they are both similar to Chianti Classico just to the north of there. Brunello is 100 percent Sangiovese, and Sangiovese is the dominant grape of Vino Nobile and Chianti. But the differences are distinctive. The hint of cedar in many of the Brunellos tells you exactly where you are—or, like Proust's *madeleine*, it will transport you to the place it's from and the time you were there if you're drinking it back home in Texas.

I still drink some French and German wine, and to this day they still vividly recall that summer I spent in Europe nearly thirty years ago, even the particular *Weinstuben* and restaurants I drank them in. And nowadays I drink a lot of Italian and California wine. I still talk about which wines are the very finest in the world, and I occasionally run up my credit card debt to experience them. But, in a certain way, I've lost faith in the very idea of a "finest in the world" in abstraction from the occasion and the location of the drinking of it. And I remind myself of what my "re-education" in food and wine taught me, that if a knowledge of and taste for things French makes me worldly, it does so, not because France or French food or wine is worldly, but because I have broadened my experience to another province—and, for that matter, to a province that values the same kind of attachment to place I was supposedly trying to overcome. The French, dear intellectual, are about as provincial as a people can be, in the good sense of being rooted and in the bad sense of being chauvinistic about it. Which I suppose is why I tend to prefer things Italian these days, but the point is the same: how does it follow from my admiration of their rooted provincialism that I should reject my own rootedness and my own province?

That's why I occasionally drink Texas wine, even though Texas does not yet produce wines that are among "the finest in the world," and maybe never will. And, in addition to learning and loving countless European recipes, I've mastered family recipes out of Louisiana and Missouri for duck gumbo and chicken 'n dumplin's, and I've personalized and fancified regional Texas recipes for barbecued brisket and wine-simmered doves and tear-starting chili. True, I don't eat a lot of traditional Texas fried food, because it doesn't do good things to my intestines, or, I hear, to my blood vessels, but every now and then I do stop in at Jake and Dorothy's for a big, greasy chicken-fried steak covered an inch deep in cream gravy you could stand a fork up in.

And sometimes I ponder this dilemma, too: I once thought the culture climb was one-way, but after a bit of globe-hopping among the provincial folks of Europe it occurred to me that a Frenchman who wants to become worldly can't accomplish anything by eating brie, quiche, and baguettes or drinking a 1982 Cheval Blanc. It was obvious that a Frenchman who wanted to become worldly and cultured would have to reverse the process by coming to Texas to eat chicken-fried steak and chili. Hell, for a Frenchman, I reckoned, chili was *haute culture*. After what the French have done for us, we owe it to them to keep up the traditions of local Texas cuisine.

One perfectly understandable response to food snobbery is to reject haute cuisine altogether—and to assert that not only is the list of ingredients on the side of a cereal box of equal literary value to Shakespeare at his best, but that a Big Mac is the equivalent of a Chateaubriand with a sauce béarnaise, and a diet Coke the equal of a Chateau Margaux. Or, a more intellectually respectable alternative, to eat only the hoi polloi food of the local province—in my case, barbecue, Tex-Mex, chicken-fried steak, and the like. But, I can't help it, I love to cook; I love good food and wine far too much to give into that form of throwing the baby out with the bathwater.

Recent American popular culture, perhaps no surprise, has shown considerably more wisdom on this subject than intellectual culture. It's a sad state of affairs, but I prefer the attitude of some of the TV chefs to the attitude of some of my fellow intellectuals. The best of the TV chefs, especially the current generation, have done wonders for exposing the food snobbery prejudice for what it is—and for overcoming it. They overcome it not by rejecting the very idea of haute cuisine but by basing it on the genuine love and knowledge of good food rather than the calculative desire to display visible signs of cultural superiority. This may well be a characteristic of many of the great chefs we don't see on the Food Channel, but we get to see it in full force with some of the TV chefs.

Not coincidentally, in my own experience the worse food snobs generally aren't good cooks at all. The pretenders to high culture who are so quick to condemn someone else's low class grub are the kinds of cooks—if they cook at all—who slavishly follow a recipe, who decide what recipe to cook before they know what ingredients are available and then complain to high heaven because the local supermarket didn't have some exotic ingredient that a good cook would quickly figure out a substitute for, who cook to impress rather than impress because they love to cook.

What we find out from some of these "classically" trained TV chefs is that the genuine, as opposed to the strategic, love of good food cuts right through all of the regional and cultural barriers that our prejudices have erected. If you can cook good food, the Anthony Bourdains and Emeril Lagasses and Sara Moultons and Bobby Flays and Tyler Florences aren't going to have a problem with where you're from or what kind of accent you have. These classically trained New York chefs cut through the usual regional and ethnic barriers and prejudices because their acceptance of differences is based on a genuine appreciation of something excellent and beautiful and rooted in place and history.

So, yes, Emeril, who started his career in a Portuguese bakery in Fall River, Massachusetts, earned a doctorate at Johnson and Wales, and polished his skills in Paris and Lyons, really appreciates the complexities and intensities and the cultural resonances of down-home Cajun food raised to the level of haute cuisine. And when he does a show on "comfort food" and cooks classic pork fat-laden Southern dishes, again raised to a higher level but still in touch with the roots and origins (no, I'm not going to say when he "kicks it up a notch"), his ecstatic enthusiasm for the food is real. And, here's the point: if he's doing the show down South and his guests savor their elongated vowels as much as their pork fat, Emeril takes that in right along with the food. If the food is good, he wants to know how you made it, not why you say "y'all" and "I'm fixin' to" while you're cooking it.

When Bobby Flay, who grew up in Manhattan and studied at the French Culinary Institute, waxes poetic about Southwestern cuisine as a distinctly American culinary style, about the intensity and complexity of the seasoning and the ingredients, it's the food equivalent of Gershwin embracing the blues as indigenous American music worthy of its place alongside the indigenous European classics.

And, even though, generally speaking, Tony Bourdain is not all that focused on American regional cuisine, there's one classic episode of *A Cook's Tour* that brings home the point I'm trying to make. Bourdain heads down to Louisiana because he wants to eat alligator. He asks around and finds out about this Cajun who lives out in the swamps and hunts alligators. I'm doing this from memory so lets call him Boudreaux. Boudreaux tells Bourdain that if they're going to eat alligator they've first got to kill one, so off they go in Boudreaux's flat-bottom boat to kill a baby alligator. The babies are more tender, he explains. Bourdain turns to the camera as they're motoring through the swamps and says, "Animals *were* harmed in the filming of this show." They get back to Boudreaux's place, and Boudreaux proceeds to butcher, marinate, and cook the alligator. At some point, a grease fire engulfs the stove, and Boudreaux puts it out with a huge fire extinguisher. Bourdain leans in close to the camera and says, grinning ear to ear, "This is my kind of people!" OK, he was having fun, maybe poking fun, but on some fundamental level he meant it. Good chefs embrace the full range of the food process, from slaughter to presentation, and people who hunt alligators in order to eat them *are* their kind of people. It was Bourdain, after all, who penned the following passage in *Kitchen Confidential*:

> Vegetarians, and their Hezbollah-like splinter faction, the vegans, are a persistent irritant to any chef worth a damn. To me, life without veal stock, pork

fat, sausage, organ meat, demi-glace or even stinky cheese is a life not worth living. Vegetarians are the enemy of everything good and decent in the human spirit, an affront to all I stand for, the pure enjoyment of food.

Food breaks down the regional barriers and prejudices, but, by the same token, the TV chefs I'm discussing teach us, over and over, that great food comes from particular places and localized traditions. Great chefs learn to elevate traditional food, but they embrace the power of place and region. And in embracing the power of place and region in great food, they display the kind of respect for other cultures that is based on getting involved in them rather than just proclaiming them all of meaningless equality.

Bourdain's globe-trotting search for the most exotic foods in the most distant foreign lands illustrates this principle as well. Although *A Cook's Tour* is certainly an exercise in a certain kind of xenophilia, Bourdain goes in search of good food, not high status, and he embraces the relation of food and place, whether foreign or domestic. And as his mugging-for-the-camera grimaces often reveal, he doesn't like food just because it's foreign. Of course, for the purposes of overcoming the food snobbery that I'm talking about, Bourdain's shows in America, like the episode I just described, are more to the point. And tracking down rich regional American food is central to shows like Bobby Flay's *Food Nation, Emeril Live*, and Tyler Florence's *My Country, My Kitchen* and his episodes of *All American Food Festivals*.

What impresses me about the TV chefs I'm talking about is that they teach us that a genuine love of good food, as opposed to food snobbery, means that it's OK for Americans to embrace American traditions and customs, to appreciate the relation of food and place in our own regional cultures, to realize that being human means, at least in part, being provincial.

Of course, to a great extent American cuisine in general has gone this direction, not just TV chefs. There has been an explosion of elevated regional and ethnic cuisines in the United States over the part few decades, some of it bordering at times on the silliness of all mass fads and trends. But the phenomenon I'm talking about has to do with the genuine love of good food leading to the genuine respect for American regional and ethnic traditions, based on the same principles of good cooking that led to the elevation of provincial French and Italian dishes to the status of haute cuisine.

When my wife visited her French cousin in Lyons a few decades ago, he bragged about the different regional foods in France. Provincial, for him, is good. But he remarked that America doesn't have regional foods like Europe does—all steak and potatoes, presumably. During the era of my childhood I suppose we deserved that stereotype. But even back then Emeril was growing up on the coast of New England eating Portuguese seafood dishes adapted to the availability of ingredients and other American influences; I was growing up eating my mother's wild duck gumbo, which she learned growing up in South Louisiana; and Southern Americans, black and white, were eating fried chicken with cream gravy, boiled collard greens, fried okra, and grits.

I might be pushing this a bit far, but I think these TV chefs offer us a model for how to approach the issue of "multiculturalism." There are two ways to go wrong on this issue, and I think they avoid both of these extremes.

On the one hand, we often underestimate the differences of our regional and ethnic cultures (and, by the way, I say "regional" and "ethnic" as if I'm talking about two different things, but, as food will teach you quickly, they're inextricably intertwined). On this view, we're all one big happy family, and we just need to hold hands and love each other. One version of this attitude as it manifests itself in the food world is "fusion" food, which I distinguish from the natural cross-fertilization that happens in all locales, especially in American locales that are infused with the experience of immigrants from all over the world.

On the other hand, we sometimes overemphasize the differences, to such an extreme that it seems pointless to try to understand or appreciate each other. In *The End of Education* Neil Postman calls this version of multiculture the "god of tribalism"; the term "balkanization" has perhaps been overused, but it does reflect the direction this view leads us in. Ultimately, if we're that different, then it ends up being all about power.

But contrast to these unreflective polar extremes Anthony Bourdain getting excited about eating Cajun alligator, Tyler Florence talking to black Southerners about how to cook greens, Bobby Flay soaking up everything he can learn about the blending of Hispanic and Anglo cultures in the American Southwest—that's a model for multiculture that accepts and relishes the differences but touches the kind of humanity that dissolves the prejudices that our differences naturally give rise to.

Bread and wine partaking marks my memory of family, friends, communities, places. True, high cuisine is one of the universal languages of the cosmopolitan intellectual, and I speak it. But I love food and wine because it means more than social or intellectual status; every partaking is a symbolic act of communion, or re-union, with a silent earth. In addition to hunting and fishing, I fight squash bugs, spring floods, and summer droughts to remind myself that tomatoes grow in dirt, not supermarket vegetable bins. But partaking of earthly sustenance symbolizes, realizes, fosters, another kind of communion. The dinner or supper table is the central place the family comes together. Or at least it used to be.

I associate food with rituals of family identity. My wife's grandmother, from a Hassidic Polish family, brought over the ritual of boiled potatoes early in the Passover ceremony, from the days when the service lasted long enough to starve the most faithful. But the faithful were sensible too. For the friends we now share seder with each year, "Lea's potatoes" are the high point of the evening, and Lea is present at our table because of this ritual even for people who never knew her. In my family, Christmas dinner was always chicken 'n dumplin's, served Cajun-style over rice, made by my grandmother in the old Lafayette house where my mother grew up and she and my father met when he boarded there after coming back from World War II. Even when my grandmother moved from her house into an apartment and started spending Christmases at my parents' in Texas, she still made the chicken 'n dumplin's. When my mother announced one year that she would cook a turkey for Christmas instead of having my grandmother make the traditional family meal, I, a supremely rational student of the principles of logical argumentation, threw a John McEnroe tantrum and insisted that we had to have chicken 'n dumplin's because we always have chicken 'n dumplin's. How much more logical could I be? Now I make them each year at my mother's house, even though I never know if I've kneaded the dough long enough or if I've rolled it out as thin as my grandmother once did.

As we enter adulthood, we reject the handed-down ceremonies of our elders and ancestors, certain that we can make our own decisions, think all things out on our own, act rationally and autonomously. That is a necessary process; but eventually we come back to the traditions, looking for those lost irrational parts of ourselves. We turn our reasoning independence back upon the traditions—thinking them through, we make them our own. We might still reject some of them, or change them, but we come to see ourselves in terms of them. We come to terms with them.

Why is repetition and ritual so important? It has to do with identity, I think. Family traditions, and even the larger traditions such as our religious ones, define us, give us a sense of being this and not that, give us a sense of belonging. To a large extent, the identity of a person, the character of a person, is a matter of habit and ritual. I talk a certain way, I walk a certain way, I go home for chicken 'n dumplin's for Christmas out of sheer habit; but how I walk, talk, and eat on Christmas makes me, not entirely but in a great part of me, the person that I am. Rituals and ceremonies locate us in a larger context, too. Making the traditions our own, we accept ourselves as participants in a larger process, standing between past and future generations.

This is as true of the accidental traditions and ceremonies as it is of the ones with reasons and deeper meanings behind them. Even accidental traditions often hold more meaning than they first seem to. Chicken 'n dumplin's at Christmas seems a mere accident of family history, but it is a silent thread for me leading back from my grandmother in Louisiana to her mother, a McCoy, who came from Kansas, and probably back to some Scotch-Irish cookery that I would never have dreamed of as a boy growing up in the fifties in Houston, Texas.

Holiday meals keep me in touch with family traditions. But Thanksgiving dinners and Christmas dinners have to do with the broader sweep of things as well, of cultural and religious ceremonies that mean on many levels at once, that point to historical events, to religious beliefs, and to natural cycles. As the days shrink down to the winter solstice and grey-brown dominates the land, Christians bring evergreens into their homes. Jews light candles, commemorating a historical event, but also continuing an ancient ceremony by which the light of the shortened day is extended into the long nights, or perhaps as a way of welcoming in the lengthening daylight soon to come.

I suppose one might argue that pointing out the pagan roots of our various religious ceremonies undermines the purity of religious belief. I like to think instead that the common threads of harvest thanksgiving, of life and light in the dark of winter, of death and rebirth, unite us all in our humanity and in our common ability to see spiritual significance in the rhythms of natural cycles. We humans live, as humans, not among mere Newtonian stuff, but among meanings. One meaning is the calculability of things which we find in our science and our technology; but there are others, less manageable, elusive, sometimes dangerous, but important. There is a meaning in things that I see as I pull the dead tomato plants from my garden, as I rake leaves from the back porch, as I watch the winter sky sunless and iron grey—it is a meaning that is in me as well, and I see myself in these things. Each of us deals with these meanings in his or her own way—with pagan rituals of reverence, with religious conviction, or with dauntless nihilism—but we share in them nonetheless.

I also associate friendships with rituals of food and drink. When I think of good friends, I automatically think of good meals or good drinking we've shared.

Thanksgiving with Angelo's family in Rhode Island. Every Italian dish you've ever imagined all sitting before us. Ten kids and four or five odds and ends from the neighborhood, a few extra relatives—everyone screaming at the top of their lungs. "Where are youse from?" his mother asked.

Brewster and Carol over for barbecued ribs in Buffalo for the 4th of July. All of us thinking we were above such unsophisticated rituals, deciding at the last minute to do it anyway, and ending up having a hell of a time drinking up Brewster's prized bottles of smoky Saint Joseph because it went so well with barbecue.

That first night in Trier, a week after Professor Orth's father had died. His wife and kids were still with the rest of his family. He picked us up at the train station and took us to a small restaurant on the square. The Fachwerk buildings overhung the tiny streets; the vine-clad hills gently ringed the horizon. I remember almost thirty years later the veal and wild mushrooms I ate as if they were on my tongue this very minute. Orth's colleague, the geology professor Herr Negendank, having all of us over for dinner and keeping us there arguing about politics and positivism and philosophy and science until five in the morning by taking us through a bottle of every wine he had in his cellar, from *Kabinett* to *Spätlese* to *Auslese*.

Sitting in Jim and Cel's backyard in Galesville, Maryland, eating steamed crabs. After dinner we walked down to the docks. We stood on a century of shucked oyster shells, and Jim pointed out to his young son an American bittern hiding, frozen still, in the marsh grass. In his *Daughter of the South County* Jim had written of these very marshes, of herons and mallards and gulls, of cattails and shoal creeks; in *Chesapeake Country Life*, a magazine all four of us were helping write into bankruptcy, Cel had written about the role of regional food in the fiction of Maryland's Eastern Shore. On another occasion, Jim's chilied pork that he'd learned to make during his younger years in New Mexico and El Paso. And one year an Easter meal of Chihuahuan green-olive soup; stacked West-

Texas enchiladas; chicken mole; Tex-Mex frijoles, thrice refried; homemade flour tortillas; and sopaipillas with honey.

When we visited Stephenville a couple of summers before we moved here, one of the professors we met responded to my admission that I'd like to move back to Texas and start hunting again by dragging us and a bunch of colleagues over to cook up his last batch of quail from the previous season. The swamp cooler struggled against the furnace heat of the hot kitchen and the August night, and the Texas twangs floated across the table and into my oldest memories. Since moving here, we've counted the years with Mike's dove pie, venison chili, and smoked wild turkey, but that first spur-of-the-moment meal—fried quail, mashed potatoes, well-peppered cream gravy, and big hunks of cornbread to sop it up— I can still remember after living here for nearly a quarter of a century.

Years ago, on a trip through South Louisiana orchestrated by my father and his childhood friends, Bayou Broussard served a mountain of boiled crawfish, potatoes, and corn on the cob on a table covered with brown paper. He sat next to Mallory and, with the expertise of long experience, peeled enough tails for both of them to eat a filling meal, leaving me, with the ineptitude of minimal experience, to fend for myself. Every year here in Texas, when our friends Linda and Tim throw a big crawfish and shrimp boil, in honor of Linda's Louisiana background and Tim's love of all things Gulf Coastal, I think of Bayou and the childhood haunts of my parents.

Some of our local food lore is of the comic failure variety. Don Zelman, indefatigable backyard grillmeister, once invited fifteen or twenty guests for a meal, including some local dignitaries he was trying to impress. He had eaten a beef tenderloin at our house that I had grilled to perfection in the heat of the summer on a large charcoal fire in about thirty minutes. For reasons that still escape me and him, he tried to grill a huge standing rib roast on a fire of maybe a dozen briquettes in the middle of the winter. The air temperature was around freezing. Don took the meat out to cook it. After about an hour, with no sign of Don, the dignitaries were starting to take off their ties and chow down on the chips and dip. Finally, Don came back into the house and asked me to help. "I don't think it's going to get done," he said. I asked for a meat thermometer, which he produced. We walked out into the backyard with the meat thermometer showing the room temperature of the house, around seventy degrees. I plunged the thermometer into the center of the large roast sitting on the grate above the diminutive fire, and the needle shot down to forty-five degrees. I suggested that we cut the roast into ribeye steaks and cook them under the broiler inside. We ate about ten o'clock. This story is repeated now every time Don invites people over for grilled meat.

When we visited Mark and Lisa after they moved from Stephenville to Annapolis, Mark served fried okra, which I had scrupulously avoided for years thanks to my culinary erudition. I was reminded that I had not eradicated all of my own cosmopolitan prejudices. Good okra cooked well is damn good, so why had I quit eating it? Now I grow it every year and cook it in a variety of dishes all summer. It is, after all, one of the few vegetables that will grow right through the deadly heat of a Texas summer. And when my xenophilial friends turn their noses up at it, I point out that it's originally an "indigenous" African food, which causes in them a severe case of culinary dissonance.

I've already mentioned the local origins of the food and wine we had with our friend Chiara in central Italy a few years ago. Nowhere I've ever been is a meal so central to the relations of family and friends as it is in Italy. Meals with Chiara's family were communal events. Early in the morning, Maria would let herself in to clean the house and start preparations for the noon meal, mixing the pasta dough and sometimes starting a stove-top pork roast with fresh rosemary or a big pot of braised squid and green peas. It was our good fortune that César, an old family friend, was also visiting. Originally from Mexico City, he has worked as a professional chef all over Europe. Around noon each day César would roll out the dough that Maria had mixed and kneaded, then cut and cook the *tagliatelle*; for a second course he would pan-fry veal cutlets or put the finishing touches on whatever dish Maria had left simmering on the stove top. Chiara, her sister Pia, and her brother-in-law Gianfranco would come home from work; Pia and Gianfranco's children, Laura and Francesco, would come home from school; and we would all gather at the big table with César and Signora Russo to eat the multi-course meal and drink the local wine out of simple glass tumblers.

One day César had to leave unexpectedly and left several pounds of beautiful shrimp that he had planned to cook that evening. I volunteered to make a pot of shrimp gumbo, an ambassadorial gesture of culinary exchange and, I hoped, a way of expressing my gratitude that would make more sense than my stumbling attempts at Italian. Making the chicken stock was pretty straight forward, and I made the roux with the local olive oil and flour. Finding the right Cajun spices posed a challenge, though. Luckily, Chiara remembered that César had stowed away some Mexican spices. I found some comino, but no cayenne or Tabasco. I substituted lots of black pepper and some crushed hot red peppers. A pot of rice and we were set to go. It was such a hit that Pia, Chiara's sister, wanted the recipe. Since Pia didn't speak English, I spent the next morning with an Italian-English dictionary writing out the recipe in Italian as best I could. God only knows what I really wrote down or how it came out if she's ever made it from that recipe.

When Chiara and her fiancée, Davide, took us to Venice for three days, needless to say the postcard beauty and historical resonances of the town were imprinted in our memories forever. But most vivid in my associations with our friendship are several of the meals, not so much because of the food itself but because a meal in Italy with friends is like an act of communion. In the Jewish ghetto of Venice, the oldest Jewish ghetto in Europe, we sat under a huge umbrella alongside a small canal and ate Kosher food. Davide, who grew up in Trieste just to the northeast of Venice, relayed for us the history of the Venetian Jews, and my wife talked of her mother and grandmother escaping from the Nazis to South America and then to America. The last night in Venice, out of sheer exhaustion, we decided not to venture back into the main part of the city, but to find a place to eat near our out-of-the-way hotel. Around ten o'clock, in a neighborhood street without a tourist to be seen other than ourselves, we stumbled upon a local restaurant that looked good, Osteria al Garanghèlo. Tables and chairs were literally set up in the street. Davide ordered a round of "spritz," a local aperitif, and then engaged the waiter in a fairly lengthy conversation in Italian. I understood enough to know he was asking for the freshest local food and ordering a local wine. By the time we made it leisurely through *l'antipasto*, *il primo*, and *il secondo*, the waiters had already moved all of the other tables and chairs inside getting ready to close up, but they seemed to enjoy our enjoyment of the food and our interest in the local fare and showed no signs of rushing us off. Our waiter brought us complimentary glasses of *Verduzzo* as the time approached midnight. My wife and I didn't know the names of half the food we had eaten and we were thousands of miles from familiar turf, but sitting with our friends in the slowly cooling and musky Venetian night air we felt at home.

I could go on, but it's making me hungry and making me miss too many friends in faraway places. It's also making me see some common threads that tie together this culinary reflection. I see how much food and wine played a part in my search for worldliness, how the search for distant cuisines united me with fellow intellectuals. But I also see how many of the meals that mark off important friendships and important experiences at home and abroad were made up of food and drink not just from the earth, but from particular traditions rooted in particular patches of earth. What appealed to me, even as I thought I was merely becoming worldly, was the identification of my worldwide friends with their own local, family, ethnic traditions—their being at home in their homes, and with their traditions. With most of these friends, I've shared meals from all sorts of foreign places, not just from our respective homelands, but of course, even then we were broadening our horizons through the sampling of different provincial ties with the earth's bounty, not by eating "worldly" food.

The intellectual's culinary landscape has of course changed since my coming of age, and it has become as xenophilial as the rest of that landscape. A couple of years ago a new colleague complained about the absence of Ethiopian restaurants in this rural north-central Texas town of 15,000 people. I tried to explain that there are no Ethiopian restaurants here because there are no Ethiopians here, and that there probably weren't Texas barbecue places in Ethiopia. But, by God, the big city she had once lived in had Ethiopian restaurants so why didn't we? French food is no longer foreign enough, and of course French food is European, and everything European is Eurocentric and imperialist and suspect. I imagine that the indigenous culture of Ethiopia is just as Ethiopia-centered and Africa-centered as any European culture is Europe-centered, which is of course what makes them interesting. And if we had an Ethiopian restaurant here, à la Anthony Bourdain, I would try it. And I find it interesting that the American landscape is dotted with Thai, Korean, and Vietnamese restaurants, not just Chinese. My point is not to reject good food from foreign lands, but to reject food snobbery—and to reclaim the right to have my own roots.

The particular prejudices of intellectual food snobbery have changed since my culinary re-education, but the point is the same: overcoming the limitations of one's native province is a necessary part of the educational process, and to that end travel and foreign food and such are all essential experiences; but worldliness that obliterates the native province is sheer foppery. That's why I opt for "provincial" French cooking over Parisian pomp, Italian over French in general, and regional American over the latest foreign exotica—that's why I opt for high cuisine that reflects a province and dismiss the nouvelle and fusion cuisines that don't, just as I prefer Faulkner to Henry James and Mark Twain to the purist strains of New England transcendentalism. You might think of it as my way of reviving and expanding the old Paleface-Redskin debate in American letters to food, language, and life. It's become something of a prejudice in me, I know, but there's good reason in it, too.

There's something important about food, though, that has nothing to do with high cuisine, even of the rooted regional kind. What makes a place feel like home to some people and like Mars to others has a great deal to do with local accents and local grub, with habits and everyday ways. It's not just my grandmother's holiday chicken 'n dumplin's, but plain old everyday food too.

In a way, our move back to Texas said it all. On the three-day trip from Maryland, we decided to avoid all chain restaurants and eat only in the greasiest of greasy spoons in the smallest of small towns.

On the first day, we pulled into a small motel diner on the outskirts of Nitro, West Virginia.

"I'll just have a cheeseburger and some fries. And some coffee."

There wasn't another soul in the place. The neon sign flashed across the wall above the grill as the waitress flipped the hamburger patty.

"Here you go, honey."

I looked down at the plate and saw a piece of meat, a piece of cheese, a bun, and some French fries.

"Could I get some lettuce and tomatoes with this?"

"You gotta speak up, honey. You can have it any way you like, you know, just like Burger King. Just speak up."

The next day in Danville, Kentucky, we drove up to a combination gun store and greasy spoon cafe. Stuffed deer heads lined the wall and old men in hunting caps lined the lunch counter. What with all the Kentuckians who had come to Texas, I figured my hamburger would surely come with lettuce and tomato, so I ordered, simply, a cheeseburger again. I ended up getting a more irritated version of the same speech about asking for it the way you want it.

The next day in Carlisle, Arkansas, I ordered a barbecue sandwich to go, but it was that chopped-up gooey pork slop that Arkansans call barbecue, worse than a hamburger without lettuce and tomato. I threw it out the window after two bites. That evening we zipped by the "Welcome to Texas" sign, grumpy as hell, without remark. After dark we pulled into a cafe with a wall-to-wall concrete floor and walls of genuine pseudo-wood paneling, wishing we could have found a Howard Johnson's.

"A cheeseburger, and, damn it, I want lettuce and tomato on it."

"Honey, it *comes* with everything on it," the waitress drawled in astonishment.

❧☙

STUDY QUESTIONS

1. The chapter opens with the author's explanation for how he eventually got hooked on fly fishing, largely because so many of the writers he admires are fly fishermen and write about fly fishing. How does the author distinguish between fly fishing snobbery and the love of fly fishing that these authors embrace? What is it about fly fishing that appeals to the literary mind? Have you ever been persuaded to change your mind about something, to take up a new activity, as a result of reading literature?

2. The author says that it's hard to be snobbish about fly fishing because it reveals our finitude, and he quotes several passages from Norman Maclean's *A River Runs Through It* in support of that claim. How does fly fishing reveal our finitude? Is it a good thing to experience our finitude?

3. The author says that fly fishing "is, like religion at its best, a way of understanding who we are." Based on this comment, how do you think the author would distinguish between religion at its best and religion at less than its best? The focus of religion would seem to be knowledge of, faith in, and worship of God, rather than self-knowledge—and, in many religions, the goal for the believer is salvation rather than self-knowledge. In what way could religion help us understand who we are?

4. The author contrasts Norman Maclean's attitude toward fishing to the one expressed at the end of Robert Redford's movie version of *A River Runs Through It* which claims that today "enlightened fishermen" practice catch and release. What is the author's argument for seeing Redford's comment as an example of pseudo-intellectual prejudice? Is he being fair to Redford? Are current catch-and-release fishermen more "enlightened" than the Macleans were? What is the author's complaint against catch-and-release fishing?

5. How does the author defend hunting? When he remarks that in contrast to meat eaters who condemn hunting, vegetarians are at least consistent, what does he mean? Why, in spite of crediting vegetarians with consistency, does the author reject vegetarianism? Why does he align himself with the passage he quotes from Anthony Bourdain's *Kitchen Confidential* proclaiming vegetarians

"the enemy of everything good and decent in the human spirit." What arguments could be given for vegetarianism? What arguments could be given against it?

6. The author identifies hunting well with hunting "meditatively." What would that mean? Would it mean the same thing as hunting "phronetically"? What are the different possible approaches to hunting? Does its make sense to talk about living life meditatively?

7. Much of this chapter has to do with the relation of humans to nature. One aspect of 20th-century existentialist thought is based on the idea that nature is indifferent to human purposes. Coupled with a rejection of traditional religious ideas of life's meaning deriving from God, this view led Camus to view human life as fundamentally absurd. The author says of a hunter focusing on the prey: "For a moment, you are ordered within the natural world—its births, its flashing beauty, its brutal deaths, its cycling timeless ways—and not an existential abomination against it." He later remarks: "We humans live, as humans, not among mere Newtonian stuff, but among meanings." How do you see the relation of humans and nature? Is there an unbridgeable chasm as a result of our need for meaning and purpose and nature's indifference to our purposes? Is there meaning in nature? Is there meaning without God? Are meanings fictions or constructs created by humans? Are humans natural? Are they animals? Is a relation to nature important for humans? Can experiences like the ones the author describes in this chapter connect us to nature?

8. The author claims that going to Europe got him to see the "contradiction" in his quest to become worldly by embracing European foods which are themselves rooted in particular locales. Is there a contradiction? Obviously, cuisines can be exported, but in what sense are they connected to particular places? What is the author's point is stating that wine growers are farmers? What does it mean to become "worldly"? Can a human life be full, good, and virtuous if it is not worldly?

9. How does the author explain his "re-education" about food as analogous to Robert MacNeil's re-education about the English language that he describes in chapter 4? Why does the "phronetic" understanding of food not result in a wholesale return to the author's native food and a rejection of all foreign food? How does he reconcile his love of foreign cuisines and his attachment to his native culture?

10. The author talks about eating food as a kind of "communion," both with the earth and with friends and family. What is the significance of this religious term in this context? The author also embraces the importance of family and friendship rituals and traditions. The Enlightenment championed reason over the authority of tradition. From the Enlightenment perspective, traditions and rituals are irrational, perhaps even anti-rational. What is the author's defense of tradi-

tions? Does he endorse an uncritical acceptance of traditions? Is the bifurcation of reason and tradition legitimate? Hans-Georg Gadamer says in *Truth and Method* that reason is always historically situated and that tradition is the result of many acts of reason, acts of conscious preservation—that there is no reason without tradition and no tradition without reason. Does living the examined life that Socrates called for require the rejection of ritual and tradition? Did Socrates refrain from all traditional rituals?

FOR FURTHER READING

Bourdain, Anthony. *Kitchen Confidential: Adventures in the Culinary Underbelly*. New York: Harper Perennial, 2001.

Gierach, John. *Sex, Death, and Fly-Fishing*. New York: Simon and Schuster, 1990.

Hemingway, Ernest. *Green Hills of Africa*. New York: Vintage, 2004 [1935].

> Hemingway's exploration of big game hunting in Africa.

———. *Death in the Afternoon*. New York: Scribner, 1996 [1932].

> Hemingway's tribute to bullfighting.

Humphrey, William. *Open Season: Sporting Adventures*. New York: Delacorte Press/Seymour Lawrence, 1986.

Mailer, Norman. *The Fight*. New York: Penguin, 2000.

> Mailer's account of the 1975 championship fight in Zaire between Muhammad Ali and George Foreman.

McClane, A. J. *A Taste of the Wild: A Compendium of Modern American Game Cookery*. New York: Dutton, 1991.

> A beautifully written cookbook, with a sense of history and a deep appreciation for nature. The kind of cookbook you sit down and read.

Fifteen

BREAD AND WINE

> Bread is a fruit of Earth, yet touched by the blessing of sunlight,
> From the thundering god issues the gladness of wine.
> Therefore in tasting them we think of the Heavenly who once were
> Here and shall come again, come when their advent is due;
> Therefore also the poets in serious hymns to the wine-god,
> Never idly devised, sound that most ancient one's praise.
>
> Friedrich Hölderlin
"Bread and Wine"

I've only got one, and he isn't all that big." I pulled the trout out of my bag. As I cleaned him, Evan watched half-fascinated and half-repulsed, his face screwed up into a look that only a seven-year-old can muster.

"We've still got some of the chili left over. A little chili, a little trout, a couple of sliced cucumbers from the Feezell garden, and a lot of beer."

It didn't take long to get the fire going. The chili gurgled in the big pot. The trout crackled in the iron skillet, the Little Laramie River hummed like a Buddhist chant, dusk crept in among the trees. I had visions of half-a-dozen brook trout in the skillet, one for each of us. Perhaps tomorrow.

We gathered around the big timber table in front of our cabin, counting adults and baby and everyone in between, seven all told. Mallory dished out the chili while I contemplated strategies for cutting up one small trout into six pieces. It wouldn't work, I concluded.

"Here. Let's just pass the skillet around. Everybody take a bite."

Barbara flaked off a piece with her fork. The meat was pink. She murmured a sign of approval and passed the skillet on to Randy.

"Good. Real good. Here, Travis."

"I'm glad we weren't depending on fish for the whole meal," Travis said as he took his bite. "Here, Ev."

Evan shook his head. "I don't want any." He squirmed in his chair.

"Evan, it's fish," Barbara said. "You like fish."

Randy, the philosopher, appealed to the categorical imperative of hunting and fishing. "Evan, if you're going to go fishing, you have to eat what you catch."

"I don't want any."

"Evan, you wimp," Travis interjected.

Mom took charge. "All right, all right. Give it to Mallory."

Mallory took the skillet, extracted a carefully sculpted bite, placed it just so on her plate, looked approvingly at the arrangement of cucumber slices and chili and the one small piece of trout, and finally ate the fish with an air of great deliberateness.

"Come on, come on." I took the skillet and flaked off the last piece. "Sure, Evan?" Evan groaned. I ate the fish without ceremony, but with considerable pleasure. "Not bad at all."

After we'd gobbled up the chili and sloshed down enough beer to soothe our singed palates, we opened a German *Auslese* and settled into various postures of slouching comfort. Barbara fed the baby while we sipped and talked. Randy and I talked wine, or, rather, we talked about wines we had drunk together in Buffalo. I retold the story about standing in the middle of Bernkasteler Doktor and looking out across the river at the hacienda of Nicolaus Cusanus. Travis was talking to Mallory about foreign languages, about majoring in English or languages or even Classics.

I sat in wonderment as Travis discussed the possibilities of graduate school, his interest in journalism and writing, his honors English class in high school. I remembered going off to the University of Texas as a math major in the liberal arts honors program—what else could someone with a high score on the math section of the SAT and a notebook full of juvenile poetry do in college? I abandoned math after one semester, fled pre-law when I read Plato's *Gorgias* during my third semester, and ended up a PhD in philosophy writing half-literary, half-philosophical essays in an age which detests the word "essay." Travis was an eighteen-year-old with a mind full of questions, but he seemed to have a better idea of what he was up to than I had.

"How did your Frank O'Connor paper turn out, Travis?" I quizzed him.

"OK, I guess."

"You never sent me a copy like you promised."

"Well . . . actually, I've got it here. Dad made me bring it—"

"Come on, Trav—" Randy defended himself.

"I brought some of my sports columns too."

"What did you think of the stories?"

"I thought the ones about kids relating to their parents were great."

"It's funny, you know, he had such an insight into children and parents, but he was pretty much of a jerk to his own kids. Myles has never recovered from it. Of course, just being the son of a great writer would mess you up some even if he wasn't a jerk. You'll have to meet Myles someday. He can tell some great stories about his old man."

"I'd like to."

Night had fallen imperceptibly. We piled more wood on the fire. We drank the cool sweet wine as the night chill crept in.

"Now might be a good time to give Travis his graduation present, don't you think?" I asked Mallory.

"Sure."

I went into the cabin, pulled on a jacket, and picked up the two books we'd transported from Texas to Wyoming for the occasion.

"Since you're going to be a literature major, I figured a couple of good books might be a good send-off for college."

Travis looked slightly embarrassed. He flipped open the first one and read the inscription.

"Oh, yeah. Dad has this one."

"John Graves lives right down the road from us, in Glen Rose. That's his first book. It's about a canoe trip down the Brazos River. The best book to ever come out of Texas. I'm not talkin' horse opera either. It's a work of art, first-rate."

"Thanks."

"And that's the second-best book to come out of Texas—"

He grinned as he looked at the cover of the other book.

"Your dad has that one too, but I figured you deserved your own copy. You don't have to read it, but I thought you ought to have one. It does have some pretty good stories about Myles and his dad, though—a few about your dad. You can quote it for your next paper on Frank O'Connor. Besides, you can show off at college and tell everybody you know the guy who wrote it."

"Thanks, really, thanks," Travis said politely. He flipped through the pages in the soft light of the fire.

He's growing up fast, I thought.

STUDY QUESTIONS

1. This chapter begins with an epigraph from Friedrich Hölderlin's poem "Bread and Wine," which talks of poets singing "hymns to the wine-god." Would you characterize the narrative chapters of this book as a kind of hymn? Why or why not?

2. This chapter picks up the thread of the author's fishing experiences in Wyoming from chapters 7 and 13. Finally, he and his friends eat the one fish his several days of fishing have produced. How does this chapter, along with chapters 7 and 13, provide a narrative representation of the discussion in chapter 14? How does the comic nature of two families sharing the one small trout the author has managed to catch complement or conflict with the seriousness of the argument in chapter 14?

3. In talking about Travis, the author reflects on the choices he had made at Travis's age and about the choices Travis is about to make. What is the significance of focusing on Travis near the end of the book?

FOR FURTHER READING

Capon, Robert Farrar. *Food for Thought: Resurrecting the Art of Eating.* New York: Harcourt, Brace, Jovanovich, 1978.

Sixteen

IDOLS OF THE ACADEMIC THEATER

> Lastly, there are Idols which have immigrated into men's minds from the various dogmas of philosophies, and also from wrong laws of demonstration. These I call Idols of the Theater, because in my judgment all the received systems are but so many stage plays, representing worlds of their own creation after an unreal and scenic fashion.
>
> Francis Bacon
> *Novum Organum*

> One is desperate to see people of independent mind willing to enter the academic world. On the other hand, it is simply the case they will be entering hostile and discriminatory territory.
>
> Alan Kors, quoted by David Brooks in
> "Lonely Campus Voices"

Many cosmopolitan intellectuals are not professors, but there is nowhere on earth with a higher concentration of cosmopolitan intellectuals—pseudo-intellectuals, that is—than among the professors. And a high concentration of cosmopolitan intellectuals who thrive on membership in this prestigious club means that universities have become—or perhaps always have been—centers of what Stephen Balch calls academic orthodoxy. Balch explains this phenomenon in terms of the majoritarian system of governance in university departments. That majorities of any kind will favor their own and naturally strengthen themselves when they have the authority to do so is certainly a plausible explanation. Cosmopolitans, then, would naturally hire and promote cosmopolitans, admit cosmopolitan graduate students, and permit cosmopolitan perspectives on dissertations. A number of critics of the current academic orthodoxy have also pointed out that when people only associate with others who agree with them and share their values then all of them tend to become more extreme. I would add that they also tend to become more certain of their monopoly on the truth, which is what led John Stuart Mill to speak of the tyranny of the majority and to claim that all suppression of dissent amounts to an assumption of infallibility.

On the other hand, if this majoritarian power structure was populated by professors who believed in intellectual pluralism, wouldn't they strengthen the value of pluralism? I'm not sure exactly what causes what, which is the chicken and which is the egg, but what is strengthening itself among too many of the professoriate is unreflective group affiliation and what is lacking is a phronetic wisdom, a Socratic spirit to call into question the power of prevailing opinion to stifle thought and discussion. I've already remarked that if Socrates were to come back to life, intellectuals would certainly condemn him again—professors, I'm afraid, would lead the charge. Those who profess and possess wisdom, and sell it for a fee—even if that wisdom consists of the higher truth that all wisdom is nothing but a construct of those in power—never take well to someone who has the arrogance to think for him- or herself and the humility to believe that the highest level a human can rise to is the love of wisdom, rather than the pretense of its possession.

My reflections on this topic have largely derived from my own personal experiences coming up in and trying to survive in the intellectual world. For that reason, I have focused on the prejudices that have been leveled at me and prejudices I was expected to adopt, which, as I've remarked, are still pretty much with us even though the landscape has changed considerably since I first knocked on the door to the intellectual life. But I'm also concerned about the prejudices that my students who choose the academic life will have to adopt in order to gain admission—and about the new ways in which cosmopolitan intellectualism manifests itself today.

It strikes me that the idols of the academic world are even more extreme now than they were when I was coming up, that the orthodoxy is more virulently imposed and more widely accepted, that the conviction of infallibility among the orthodox is stronger, and that the prejudices one must accept are more stridently political.

As I've recounted, I had to reject my Texas and Louisiana roots and embrace the Great Northeast, French wine, and classical European music. My students who aspire to be professors will likely not only have to reject their localized roots in north-central Texas, but also to condemn everything American, nay, everything European; and they will have to mimic a xenophilial obsession with "post-colonial" literature, indigenous cultures fighting against the corrosion of American globalism and capitalism, Ethiopian food, and a sloganistic concept of diversity; and, if they are in the humanities, they will have to kowtow to the postmodernist dogma that all reality is a construct in language that furthers the interest of those in power. And, although political liberalism was mandatory for my generation of professors, the overtly political character of the prevailing concepts of today is unmistakable: post-colonial literature, male hegemony, Eurocentrism, to name a few.

Joseph Conrad's *Heart of Darkness* was for my generation a book about the existential darkness that resides in the human heart, most centrally illustrated by Kurtz, a European; now, proclaims Chinua Achebe, Conrad is a "bloody racist." Achebe has argued for that position—unconvincingly, I think—but this way of reading literature of the colonial period has become inscribed into the academic literary culture as something beyond argument. If you have any doubts about the politicization of the humanities, open a program for a meeting of the Modern Language Association and count how many presentations deal with race, class, or gender.

My evidence here is largely based on personal experience, what the social scientists dismissively like to call anecdotal evidence, but a number of recent studies focusing on political party affiliation, voting patterns, and the like have shown just how lopsided the academic world is along political lines. The dominant academic orthodoxy is much broader and deeper than party affiliation and voting patterns show, but it is unabashedly political.

To a great extent I embrace the new interest in literature from India and Africa and other former European colonies, and it's arguable that the various forms of "globalization" obligate us to learn about parts of the world that most of my generation never paid any attention to. And, to a great extent, some of these changes in the literary canon were originally the result of thoughtful reexamination, to be sure. I approve of the tradition of self-criticism that makes it possible for us to call into question our sacred texts, to reinterpret them in light of new situations, to argue for the inclusion of works that were previously excluded on illegitimate grounds. But I'm not going to condemn Stephenville, Texas, because it doesn't have an Ethiopian restaurant, and I'm not going to quit teaching Hemingway's "Hills Like White Elephants" to my honors seminar, in which women typically outnumber men about three to one, because Hemingway has been pronounced a bloody sexist by the current literary establishment. When one of my colleagues gave a presentation on a movie short based on "Hills Like White Elephants" at a conference a few years ago, a graduate student came up to her afterwards and proclaimed that she wouldn't have come to the session if she had known that it was about a Hemingway story.

What really matters is whether we're thinking about these issues or just learning to mimic the authority figures in the community we're trying to gain admission to. What really matters is when those who profess to be guided by an abiding suspicion of all prejudice and bigotry make snap judgments based on group affiliation, stereotypes, and ideological orthodoxy. Isn't it possible that the new canon and newly canonized ways of reinterpreting traditional literature could become so enshrined that the spirit of self-criticism could be extinguished? Isn't it possible that the same charge that was leveled against the traditional canon, that it expressed the power structures rather than literary merit, could be leveled at the contemporary orthodoxies? Or do we want to go to the postmodernist extreme and embrace the idea that it's all about power, that there is no such thing as literary or philosophical merit, or, for that matter, justice or injustice? That is a common refrain in the halls of the academy, but it is morally bankrupt.

Academic orthodoxy results in a kind of informal ideological litmus test. How many times have I read or heard stories of or, I'm sorry to say, witnessed firsthand the wholesale rejection by members of my profession of someone for being conservative? Or religious? How many times each day does a professor somewhere in the United States of Academia say that only a stupid person could be religious or Republican? That there are more liberals in academia because liberals are smarter?

I've dwelled on the prejudices launched against me, but, as I've explained, in many areas I have certainly possessed and continue to possess the proper papers. At least in my younger days, I could condescendingly make fun of religious fundamentalists, conservatives, and the like with the best of the cognoscenti. I marched against the war in Vietnam, and, since childhood, I've only gone into a church for funerals and weddings of people I respect, or as a tourist traveling in Europe. But what would it be like for an academic aspirant who, like me, hails from Texas, speaks with a Texas accent, likes country music, hunts and fishes and shoots military weapons for fun—and, on top of that, worships in a Baptist church, voted for George W. Bush, and supported the invasion of Iraq?

Even if some hotshot social scientist were to show that on average atheists were smarter than religious people and less prone to violence, wouldn't the automatic dismissal of someone for being religious or conservative still be just one more form of bigotry, not unlike rejecting a black or Hispanic American for an academic position because studies have shown that on average they score lower on standardized tests and have lower graduation rates? Was Thomas Aquinas stupid? Immanuel Kant? Dante? John Milton? Bach? And are we of the liberal creed that dead certain that a religious perspective or a politically conservative perspective does not need to be heard? I may not agree with a fair amount of what George Will says, but do I want to say that he's stupid? Or if I admit that he's a pretty bright guy with a good education, am I certain that he's always wrong and that I'm always right?

The great irony of ironies is that one of the chief tenets of the current academic climate is a commitment to diversity, and yet, as my experience and a growing number of more scientific approaches have shown, the spirit of intellectual diversity—what we used to called intellectual pluralism—is in grave danger. And the quickest way to academic hemlock these days would be to call into question this notion of diversity. If diversity of perspective has educational value, which is one of the central arguments in favor of ethnic diversity in higher education, then why is it that so many professors claim that the political orientation of faculty members doesn't matter since, as scholars, they don't let their politics enter the classroom or their research? It's arguable that to assume different skin pigment necessarily adds up to a different perspective is racist, but it does make sense to say that a reasonable diversity of cultural backgrounds and perspectives among students and faculty contributes to a rich educational environment. So wouldn't that also be true of backgrounds and perspectives in the areas of politics, religion, and the like?

What's wrong with academic orthodoxies of whatever kind? Mill is instructive here. The greatest threat to free speech in a democratic society, a majoritarian society, he says, is prevailing opinion. So when all of the faculty members of such and such department are sitting around the coffee room day after day, and they all agree on virtually everything they talk about—at least everything that matters to them—they will naturally come to be more and more certain that they couldn't be wrong, and they'll come to be ever more extreme in their pronouncements and condescensions. Shouldn't the first premise of all human inquiry be that humans, especially like-thinking groups of them, are fallible? And even if the beliefs of the coffee-room professors are true and morally superior to those of the Red State rubes they teach or the president of the country they despise, even a true belief—and this is Mill's greatest insight—will turn into a "dead dogma" or "mere superstition" if it is not challenged by a dissenting opinion well argued. If they all agree, there will be no need for coming up with reasons for their beliefs. There will be no reason to think.

It's doubtful that even the most conscientious professors can keep their politics or views on religion out of the classroom when their subject treats of those topics—as is the case in many courses in political science, sociology, philosophy, literature, and history. But, aside from that issue, the level of intellectual and scholarly discussion suffers when the dissenting opinions are few or nonexistent. All of us should be Socratic enough in spirit to interrogate ourselves, to play devil's advocate, to fabricate the dissenting opinion and argue for it well when there isn't one, as Mill recommends; but human nature, even among professors, tends toward the security of sophistry rather than the fearlessness of Socrates. That's why Mill advocates an encounter with opposing arguments that are put forward by someone who truly believes them. Diversity is valuable in an intellectual context not so that we can all hold hands and sing "Cumbayah" but in order to create the kind of contentiousness that demands investigation, thought, and argumentation.

In the end, education is the crux of my topic, for cosmopolitan intellectualism is the product of education. Cosmopolitan intellectuals want to reproduce their cosmopolitanism in their children and, if they are teachers, in their students. It is, in a well-meaning way, the solemn duty of teachers to rip the rug of homegrown prejudices out from under their backwater students and, in my day, give them French food, the Queen's English, Henry James's literature, and the cul-chuh of Manhattan—and nowadays to give them a xenophilia that rejects not only the hometown roots but their civilization. The professors, even if they truly reach only a small percentage of their students, reproduce their prejudices in hundreds, who go on to be professors, community leaders, editors, writers, and consumers of mass quantities of *injera*.

For Americans raised on Burger King and *I Love Lucy* or, nowadays, Quiznos subs and video games, it is the professor who wakes them from their localized childhood sleep, the professor who prods them from the naive to the cosmopolitan stage. There's no more exciting time in the lives of intellectuals. In the face of inescapable *aporia*, up against the limits of their world view, they hunger for learning, for a broader view, for knowledge in place of opinion. Discovering a world out there, a geographical one and a spiritual one, spurs them in that great burst of uninhibited intellectual enthusiasm. From the later years of jaded cynicism or even of self-assured achievement, we look back upon those days with great nostalgia.

It is indeed the professor's responsibility, in fact the responsibility of all intellectuals, to inspire, prod, even trick the next generation into the cosmopolitan stage. But a little learning can well be a dangerous thing. It is also the professor's responsibility at the very least to lay the foundation for a move to the third stage of the intellectual's life. The move from that youthful thirst for finality, for the absolute, to the acceptance of *phronēsis* as a fundamental intellectual principle requires a good deal of the wisdom of age, of that learning by suffering that Aeschylus so encapsulated in his famous dictum. But there are hints that can be dropped.

In more concrete, more emotional terms, the hindrance to the student's move to the phronetic stage is often a matter of the cosmopolitan professors' rejection of the importance of the students' local origins and attachments. In a fine essay in *The Chronicle of Higher Education*, "The Rootless Professors," Eric Zencey diagnosed the problem with great wisdom:

> There is a difference, then, between the perspectives we share as a "cosmopolitan" class and the perspectives of the majority of the students who attend colleges and universities in their home states. That difference is worth looking at and worth talking about for the effects it has on education and, through education, on the outlook and characteristics of what is supposed to be the best-informed and most educated portion of the American public. I suggest that as cosmopolitans we may be systematically blind to some of the crucial elements of an integrated life—the life that is one of the primary goals of a liberal-arts education—and to the values of the connectedness to place.
>
> The primary value in connectedness to place is, of course, a sense of belonging, of being located in space and time. We may say that there is educational value in being uprooted, in being asked to entertain new ideas of self and self-in-relation-to-world, but I wonder sometimes if this truth isn't covered by a patina of rationalization.

Just as Robert MacNeil's confessions on the Queen's English bespeak a move to a phronetic understanding of language, Zencey's indictment of the rootless professors bespeaks a great insight into the cosmopolitan concept of education. And it is the cosmopolitan concept of education which produces cosmopolitan intellectuals in the first place. Good teachers may be born, but cosmopolitan intellectuals are made. The university is the very heart, if not the black hole, of my subject.

Zencey recounts a story of an acquaintance who got his degrees in his native state, taught a few years as a temporary lecturer at a university in that state, and then was told by the chairman of his department that he was "too much of a native" to ever become a permanent faculty member. I have read this same story and heard it from friends at other universities countless times, and I've even seen it happen with my own eyes a few too many times.

Just after arriving at the regional state university where I've taught for nearly twenty-five years now, eager to be back among my natives, I witnessed a similar development. To be sure, the cosmopolitan tribe had not taken over, but the fact that it had made inroads even in a rural university in God-forsaken Texas was a wake-up call for me. In reviewing candidates for a position, two of my colleagues systematically ruled out any candidates who were from or had degrees, not just from this state, but from this part of the country—because we were too "inbred" already. The argument that ensued was enlightening. I confessed at the outset a gut desire, that might count as prejudicial at least in its intensity, for more natives—preferably natives who had studied abroad as I had. I pointed out, first of all, that in the subject we were hiring this person to teach, including courses on the Texas variety of that subject required by the state legislature, we currently had no one from Texas or from a Texas university, and, secondly, that almost all of our students come from Texas, most of them from one part of Texas. One of my colleagues backed off to an admission that he too, a non-native, was probably prejudiced in his direction. We met in the middle with the agreement that if native roots wouldn't count in favor, at least they shouldn't count against—and even agreed that our students need exposure to foreign folks with foreign points of view *and* to natives who know the feel of the weather and which end of a cow gets up first, all the while displaying a living of the life of the mind.

The other colleague never saw the issue. He remained, even after reading Zencey's fine essay, adamantly convinced that his was the position of unadulterated reason. The purpose of a liberal education is broadening the mind, overcoming prejudice—and since prejudice is the product of the local culture—ergo, hire non-natives. Quod erat demonstrandum. There's certainly some truth in that position, but there's also some bigotry in it.

Is liberal education merely a matter of exposing students to teachers who share none of their values or perspective? If so, why just hire out-of-state professors? Why not hire all foreigners? (Nota bene: I mean that last comment to be sarcastic, but it occurs to me that, given the rampant xenophilia among the professors, that the answer in some quarters to that question will be a resounding "yes.") How is it then that the very model of liberal education, Socrates, engaged only his fellow citizens and the traveling sophists who happened into his hometown? Knowing the prevailing opinions of his homeland all too well, he saw his gadfly role as a sacred calling in service to his city. Exposing students willy-nilly to "otherness" is not a liberal education. What's more, it seems that the urgency of hiring non-natives always seems greater in rural universities in places like Texas. After all, the values of these students are just wrong-headed and need to be changed. Rural Texans seem to need an exposure to "otherness" much more than, say, silver-spoon students at the Cornells and MITs and Harvards. Do the faculty at U. Mass.–Amherst insist on hiring conservative, gun-totin' rural Texans so that their students will be broadened by an exposure to "otherness"? I doubt it.

Nearly a quarter century later, I find that even a few of the natives here have bought into the inbreeding phobia. One member of a search committee grew up two hours away and earned all of his degrees at the university in his hometown, but he insisted that anyone with a background or degree from this state would have to be remarkably better than all of the other candidates to even get an interview. When I asked about one candidate who had grown up in the area, but done his PhD a thousand miles away and had taught for twenty years three states away, he dismissed him by saying that he just wanted to come back to his old stomping grounds. Why would that be a bad thing? I guess the institution needed just enough inbreeding for this member of the search committee to keep his job, but no more.

One more recent example: when the historians at my university brought in an outside evaluator to conduct a "program review," he proclaimed that too many of our historians had their doctorates from "a Texas university," including in a couple of cases PhDs from the same school, and that "such a concentration risks the development of an in-grown intellectual culture, with insufficient input from sources outside the state." For the next vacancy to be filled, he recommended that we "conduct a national search with a premium placed on hiring candidates with PhDs from universities outside the state of Texas."

That sounds oh-so-reasonable to academic ears, but not because it is the result of careful consideration. It sounds reasonable because it conforms to prevailing academic opinion. First of all, it assumes that all universities in Texas turn out graduates with similar views, which is as unsupported by evidence and as bigoted as assuming that all blacks think alike. Would a graduate of the University of Texas doctoral program in history who had grown up in China have the same perspective as someone who grew up in Denton and got his undergraduate and graduate degrees from the University of North Texas? And, for that matter, as heretical as this may sound, it occurs to me that two graduates from the same school, especially if the department is large and diverse, might be as far apart in their perspectives and approaches to the subject as they could possibly be. If I were trying to hire an analytic philosopher to complement my areas in continental and ancient philosophy, it would be nonsensical to exclude someone with a degree from my graduate institution, which, at least in my day, was a pluralistic battleground of different approaches to philosophy. Someone who concentrated in analytic philosophy would be as different from me as, well, Quine from Heidegger. And, since we're trying to think about these issues rather than worship the idols of our tribe, would someone from the same program I graduated from twenty-six years ago share the same perspective? Most of the professors I studied with are either retired or dead. Maybe they were successful in shaping the future of the department in their images before they left; maybe they weren't.

But the underlying prejudice in all of these assaults on "inbreeding" is the rejection of local roots, especially if they're Texan or Southern or Midwestern or Western, and the call for monolithic cosmopolitanism. The irony is that all of the talk of going outside the state or region to combat inbreeding means not that the goal is genuine intellectual diversity, but precisely the opposite. Surely people with different backgrounds will bring that background to bear in their thinking and perspective, but, with rare exceptions, what the detractors of inbreeding really want are more professors like themselves, rootless cosmopolitans who will agree with them on all of the things they care about, most importantly that rejecting redneck rootedness is of the very essence of the intellectual life.

Zencey, no idealist, accepts that professors in this day and age are going to be uprooted folks, at least in the literal sense that they are going to end up teaching wherever they can get a job and it's usually not going to be anywhere near their hometown. He argues that the rootless professors ought to respect the connectedness of students to their place, even as they seek to broaden them. Professors ought to include "local" content in courses, ought to teach students to think about their origins, come to terms with them, instead of willy-nilly rejecting them. Many cosmopolitan professors radiate a kind of resentment for their displacement, that they got stuck in the boonies instead of New York or some other City of the World—and even, I suspect, in strange perverse ways, deeper down in their all-too-human psyches, that they themselves have been ripped from hometown and family with nary a chance of return. That resentment often comes through in the classroom as a kind of profound disrespect for the students.

Zencey concludes:

> What is needed is a class of cosmopolitan educators who cultivate a sense of place and exemplify in their teaching and in their lives a successful resolution of the tension between the local and the universal, the particular and the abstract. To do less is a disservice to our students.

"In their lives"—that is the problem. Zencey rightly complains that most uprooted professors know nothing of the natural environment of the universities in which they teach. Most, he accurately reports, could not even describe the watershed in which they live. One solution for overcoming the alienation of uprootedness, then, is for rootless professors to truly put down roots in their new place—place in the fullest, earthy sense of the word. Learn the customs, the land, the people. Accept, among other things, that the fate of an academic life has decreed that your children's hometown is the town you teach in, not the university. How often do cosmopolitan professors say, instead, how much it horrifies them that their children will be Texans or Mississippians or Arkansans—of, if they're immigrants, that their children will be Americans? Accept that you must integrate your citizenship in the community of intellects with the plain reality that you are an immigrant in a local community. Even if you teach at a university like Cornell, which draws from all over the country, what are you teaching your students by the example of your own life when you say that you are *from* Cornell, and not Ithaca—and wouldn't even think of mentioning the town you grew up in? Just what you want to teach them, I know, but you are doing them a disservice.

This dual citizenship is no easy matter, for cosmopolitan intellectuals will never overcome their disdain for the new local culture, their resentment, unless they first come to terms with their original local culture. No student with the sense God gave a mule will fall for the teacher who learns the ropes of the new hometown, dances the local dances, but doesn't remember where he or she is from—originally, in the sense of having origins, a mother, a father, a childhood. That's another kind of dual citizenship, which I guess gives us triadic citizenship—the city of the intellect, the new hometown, and the original hometown. Hate it if you will, never go back to visit, mourn your connection to it—but understand it you must if you will understand who you are. An integrated human being is one who integrates origins with aspirations. It has become a commonplace catechism for cosmopolitan professors from humble unintellectual locales to say, "I knew from an early age that I wasn't really from . . ." Clever, but wrong. Whatever piece of ground you landed on when you came out of the womb, that's your native soil; and wherever you grew up will always be the place you grew up.

The intellectual's aspirations are Olympian, but the intellectual's origins are, for want of a better metaphor, as Ithacan as those of Odysseus, even if we opt for Tennyson's Odysseus over Homer's. Milan Kundera reminds us in *Ignorance* that "Odysseus, the greatest adventurer of all time, is also the greatest nostalgic." He is "nostalgic" because he longs for his homecoming, his *nostos*.

There is another option, though. My wife and I never could feel at home in Annapolis, Maryland, partly because the sleepy Southern hometown that my best friends there had grown up in had long since been converted to a condo bedroom community, a snobbish historic district run by carpetbaggers both Northern and Southern, and an aquatic parking lot for party yachts. Partly because my wife taught at the U. S. Naval Academy, a fine academic institution populated by Yale PhDs and students with SAT scores on a par with the Ivy League, but a national institution that required a very abstract sense of national purpose and prevented any sense of local belonging. It's a noble job, and somebody's got to do it, but I think we left the job in competent hands, albeit in a few cases stylishly cosmopolitan hands. But mainly we didn't feel at home in Annapolis because it wasn't home. Our home and our families were a full three-day drive away, so we chose—to the astonishment of many of my wife's colleagues and many of our academic friends—to go back home, or at least close to home.

We now teach at a regional state university, and many of the kids we teach come out of small-town high schools far less sophisticated than my big-city high school in Houston. But the Texas identity is so pervasive that even three hundred miles from where I grew up the students, some of them at least, very much remind me of myself at their age. Had I gone a slightly different route, I might have ended up at a Cornell somewhere. But I didn't, and I don't regret that I now teach Plato to students whose accents make me feel at home, in a town that reminds me now of the sleepy small-Texas-town feel that my rural neighborhood outside of Houston had in the 1950s and 1960s when I was growing up. There are some students here as smart as students at Cornell, and they see through Euthyphro and Meno and Anytus and Meletus with a freshness of philosophic spirit that many scholars can't muster. Many are not, but so be it—like students anywhere the students here suffer under the agony of *aporia*, some for the better, some for naught. Some suspect me of bookishness and are convinced I'm a Yankee, but, if they listen to me, they find out I'm something else as well. And when some of our budding intellectuals hear me talk about hunting and guns, they suspect me of being an Ag professor who's wandered into the wrong building; but that suspicion disappears as soon as I hand out the syllabus. Indeed, I may never belong here the way my students belong. Sometimes that's alienating, but mostly it's not. And in a certain way I do belong. And in a certain way I feel closer to many of my students than I do to many of the professors in my profession.

Of course, my solution to the need for rootedness—actually returning to my roots—is not the only one. And there is a certain value to our Ivy League centers of uprooted, no-holds-barred, neurotic intellectualism—for some folks that's the true road they must travel. And for those who are on it, sometimes there's no getting off. I know there are thousands of stories of high-energy physicists from Arkansas and Jewish refugees from Europe and high-tone Texans and such who live happily ever after at the Cornells of the world. But you've heard those stories plenty of times before; you recite them to yourself on your starry, starry nights. I'm trying to inscribe into the book of the intellectual a few other possibilities that will suggest, if not the total falsehood then at least the narrow-mindedness of certain intellectual assumptions. I hope I've made it clear that my argument is not that rooted intellectualism requires my particular roots and proclivities, although I hope I've also made it clear that many of those roots and proclivities are the most conspicuously under attack. You can certainly be phronetic about the importance of roots without sharing the specifics of my experience—being from Texas, going back to your childhood haunts, killing some of your own meat; likewise, you might very well share my particular experiences and proclivities and still be a cosmopolitan intellectual, as I myself have been at various times and in varying degrees. There are no check lists that will guarantee anything in this arena.

One more story, if I may. My wife's graduate school friend Karen went back to graduate school somewhat late. Having grown up around Albany and having spent all of her adult life in a small town in the hills south of Buffalo, her daughters finishing up high school and her own life twisting and turning in the winds off of Lake Erie, she chose the State University of New York at Buffalo—which, as it turned out, was at that time a haven of post-structuralist, deconstructionist Francophilial pseudo-philosophical literary criticism. (By the absolute yardstick of hotshot literary programs, that means it was topnotch, first-rate, upper-echelon, or whatever you wish to call it.)

After considerable personal sacrifice and travail, she finished up her course work and a theoretical dissertation in literature. She met a man from Chicago who was teaching English at Fredonia State University right down the road from her hometown, and she started teaching there part-time. Lo and behold, Dartmouth, no slouch of a school on the old cosmopolitan intellectual yardstick, offered her a job. She said she couldn't take it unless she could work out her personal life. Dartmouth said *take a year to think about it*—the job would still be open. She thought about her friends and relations, intellectual and otherwise; about the hills of humble Upstate New York and nearly forty years of her life invested in them and they in her; about the young men and women coming out of those hills with the same window on the world that she had grown up with. She turned Dartmouth down, no doubt with some trepidation, but with well-considered resoluteness as well. She struggled through a few years of part-time drudgery at Fredonia—and, yes, it could have ended with her slaving her life away for $1,500 a course—but as soon as a few personal and political realignments took place, she was granted a full-time job and tenure in one fell swoop. And, as fate and resolute choice would have it, she married the man from Chicago, and she spent her entire career teaching at this unprestigious "regional" university—that is, teaching students who were nurtured by the same soil and local customs that had nurtured her. Now retired, should she think back on her lifetime as a failure? A number of years ago she remarked to me that however highly she may think of Dartmouth, she has never regretted not going there.

I think she made the right choice, and my point is simply this: the knee-jerk intellectual would think she was crazy, or, at least, that necessity dealt her a terrible blow. As a professor you look at that great intellectual ranking of universities in the cosmopolitan sky and you sacrifice family, friends, roots, heterosexuality, or whatever it takes to climb to the highest rung you can.

Socrates claimed that he had received from the oracle at Delphi a sacred charge—to awaken his fellow Athenians from the sleep of false wisdom, to live out his love of wisdom in his native land, to devote himself so thoroughly to his homeland that he would choose death, at the very hands of his fellow citizens, over exile. He struggled with native and visiting intellectual tyrants, rhetoricians, soothsayers, and other sophists for the souls of the young Athenians. Some of these young men were as brilliant as students at a Yale or Cornell; some were not. Some of the antagonists with whom he fought for those souls were brilliant sophists, some were cheap tricksters, and some were just not too smart. His classroom was the *agora*, and the people in whom his gadfly sting elicited the experience of *aporia* were not unlike the students and faculty members at a rough-at-the-edges state university. Socrates could conceive of no other life.

The choice to stay back home with your own kind, or to go back home to teach the kids who come out of the same upbringing and circumstances that you came out of, appears to the cosmopolitan intellectual as a sure sign of mental weakness. I offer a plea that the resentful displaced professors, the ones seeing their friends off on a journey of homecoming or the ones in a position to hire the homecoming native, respect the choice as an honorable one—even if indeed the opposite choice may in many cases be honorable too. The native son or daughter who wants to give himself or herself to the mother- and fatherland, just as Socrates gave himself to his, should receive from fellow intellectuals not derisive condescension or patronizing sympathy, but a phronetic, reflective respect. Intellectuals who give themselves in Socratic fashion will likely elicit some of the same contempt from their homelanders that Socrates received from his—it's no easy life—but the calling is a noble one.

No, the Socratic intellectual should never rest unreflectively with the inherited views of the province. But I want to call at least a few intellectuals back home in the most localized and literal sense, and I wonder, too, if that calling might not be true to the spirit of American democracy that the mythical framers unleashed upon the world—and, simultaneously, to that democratizing spirit of the Socratic imperative that the unexamined life is not worth living *for a human being*, not just for the brightest or the economically luckiest. Certainly individuals differ tremendously in natural ability for Socratic reflection, for thinking things through on their own; but that doesn't mean that learning and thinking are not of value to the health of the soul and the political health of the country, any more than differences in athletic ability mean that *gumnastikē* is of no value to the health of the body and soul. Yes, what happens at the best of the best universities has an enormous effect on the life of the nation; but a lot of life goes on out here in the great expanses of bad food, and occasionally we think on our own, not even giving a damn what someone at a Yale or a Harvard or a Cornell thinks all good intellectuals should think. To the extent that the elite universities take on the role of national gadfly, as opposed to the role of self-serving factories of pseudo-intellectual prejudice and group-think orthodoxy, we ought to give a damn; to the extent that they don't, we shouldn't. One prejudice that the great minds at the great universities ought to repeatedly shoot down is the belief that nothing which happens in the rest of the universities matters.

It's about time we balance the wanderlusting, escape-your-childhood intellectual model with a Socratic gadfly who unmercifully devotes himself to the hearts and souls of his homeland. The comparable homeland for Karen was not the nation, but the western end of Upstate New York. In my book, now literally as well as figuratively, she is an intellectual hero, harkening back to that first, and I hope perennial, hero of Western intellect. Canonizing heroes is an act of prejudice, but I think we can think our prejudices through, even rework them a bit, and, if you will, choose our heroes to a certain degree. Having thought, I choose to admire a new one and reaffirm an old one.

༄༅

STUDY QUESTIONS

1. The author says: "Good teachers may be born, but cosmopolitan intellectuals are made. The university is the very heart, if not the black hole, of my subject." How does this claim follow from the discussion of the three stages of the intellectual life in chapter 2? In what sense are cosmopolitan intellectuals made?

2. In *Regents of the University of California v. Bakke*, a 1978 U.S. Supreme Court case, the Medical School of the University of California at Davis cited the

educational value of diversity as a defense for a special admissions program that gave preference to candidates from ethnic minority groups. Is there an educational value to a diverse student body for a medical school? For an undergraduate university? Is there educational value to a diverse faculty? If so, what kind of diversity?

3. The author claims that there is a growing uniformity of perspective among professors, that is, that they share the prejudices of the cosmopolitan intellectual world view. Assuming for the purposes of argument that this is the case, is that a problem? What is the author's reason for objecting to this uniformity? Do you agree? What would the effects of this uniformity be on the professors themselves? On the students they teach?

4. Do the political or religious views of professors matter? Should professors bring their political or religious views into the classroom? Should they conceal them? Is it possible for professors to keep their political or religious or philosophical perspectives out of the classroom in subjects like literature, political science, history, and philosophy? One view is that professors are scholars who relay objectively to their students the scholarship and scientific evidence. On that view, the personal beliefs of the professors should not and need not come into play. At the opposite extreme is the view that professors should be activists, should try to make the world a better place. Where does the author stand on this issue? Is there a middle ground?

5. The author says that his "evidence here is largely based on personal experience, what the social scientists dismissively like to called anecdotal evidence." What experience does the author have with respect to the academic world he is discussing in this chapter? The term "anecdotal evidence" is typically used to imply a logical fallacy, generalizing on the basis of an inadequate sample. Is it illegitimate to draw conclusions from personal experience? Is the author generalizing on the basis of personal experience? Or is he reflecting on his personal experience? Or illustrating his general point with examples from his own experience? In one sense, this entire book is a "personal" essay, and yet it purports to address a broad cultural phenomenon. What is the relation of the personal and the philosophical?

6. As evidence of the prejudice among professors against rootedness, the author recounts several personal experiences with university search committees that refused to consider candidates from the region or in some cases from universities in the region. The dominant view, according to the author, is that hiring natives produces inbreeding, and students, especially at regional universities, need to be exposed to non-natives. The author clearly rejects the idea that natives should be excluded. What should the criteria be for hiring professors? Should the criteria be the same for all universities, from Ivy League schools to regional state universities at which most of the students are from that region of the state? What

does it mean to hire the best available candidate? Is it legitimate to quantify the criteria for hiring and promoting professors: an Ivy League PhD gets more points than a regional state university; articles in blind refereed academic journals get more points than articles in newspapers; and so forth? Is it legitimate to consider whether a potential faculty member will be able to relate to the students of a particular university?

7. The author approvingly quotes Eric Zencey's call for "a class of cosmopolitan educators who cultivate a sense of place and exemplify in their teaching and in their lives a successful resolution of the tension between the local and the universal, the particular and the abstract. To do less is a disservice to our students." Should professors introduce "local" content into their classes or focus their efforts on exposing students to other cultures and perspectives? Or should they, as Zencey claims, exemplify a resolution of the tension between the local and universal? How does Zencey's claim echo the discussion in chapter 8 of reaching the universal by way of the particular?

8. This chapter ends with the author's story of a friend from graduate school who turned down a job at Dartmouth to stay at a regional state university in the area where she had grown up. Not unlike the judgment that universities make about hiring professors, professors sometimes have a choice about which university to teach at. In the abstract the best teaching jobs and the best students would seem to be at the "best" universities, but the author's friend based her judgment on any number of intangible aspects of her own life. How does a wise person, a person of *phronēsis*, make difficult decisions about which course in life to follow? How does a wise person weigh the competing values of professional ambition, the opinions of colleagues and friends, regional and family attachments, a sense of belonging?

9. At the end of this chapter the author says that we can "choose our heroes to a certain degree." Do humans need heroes? Is there a danger to having heroes? Shouldn't a rational human being make each decision based on the particulars of the situation rather than trying to emulate a hero? If heroes are necessary, what are they necessary for? How do they function? Is it possible to choose our heroes or is that something that our gut does for us?

FOR FURTHER READING

Balch, Stephen H. "The Antidote to Academic Orthodoxy." *The Chronicle of Higher Education*, April 23, 2004.

Bloom, Allan. *The Closing of the American Mind: How Higher Education Has Failed Democracy and Impoverished the Souls of Today's Students*. New York: Simon & Schuster, 1987.

Klein, Jacob. "The Idea of Liberal Education" and "On Liberal Education." In *Lectures and Essays*. Edited by Robert B. Williamson and Elliott Zuckerman. Annapolis: St. John's College Press, 1985.

Mill, John Stuart. Chapter 2, "On the Liberty of Thought and Discussion." *On Liberty*. Indianapolis: Hacket, 1978.

>Perhaps the greatest defense of free expression ever penned.

Solomon, Robert C., and Jon Solomon. *Up the University: Re-Creating Higher Education in America*. New York: Addison-Wesley, 1993.

>A rare fountain of reasonableness on the purpose and state of American higher education.

Steele, Shelby. *White Guilt: How Blacks and Whites Together Destroyed the Promise of the Civil Rights Era*. New York: Harper Perennial, 2007.

Zencey, Eric. "The Rootless Professors." *The Chronicle of Higher Education*, June12, 1985. Reprinted in *Virgin Forest: Meditations on History, Ecology, and Culture* (Athens: University of Georgia Press, 1998).

Seventeen

WESTWARD I GO FREE

The truck was packed, except for the two fishing rods that were propped against the side of the cabin. We gave the cabin a quick sweeping, moved the two wooden chairs that stood by last night's campfire coals back inside. Early-morning dew dampened our shoes, and a sharp chill turned our breath to misty vapors. We surveyed the setting, the small clearing in front of the cabin where we had gathered each evening for over a week, the sandy gravel point just below the trees where Evan had caught his first fish and Mallory had read *A River Runs Through It*, the tip-tops of the mountains just visible above the trees, the "path" leading off behind the cabin, the tunnel of a dirt road leading out of the river thicket up to Wana's house.

"Head 'em up, move 'em out," I concluded our reverie. I put the rods in the back of the truck. We climbed in, and started up the hill. We drove past the Feezells' empty cabin—they had left for home a few days earlier—and on up to the ranch house to settle with Wana.

"I won't charge for the fishing. A couple of the fellows who come here every year said it wasn't very good. In fact, it sounds like you did as well as anyone. You must have done some fishing before."

"Yes, ma'am. Not for trout though. That fellow from Denver gave me a few pointers."

I wrote out a check for the cabin, and thanked her for the hospitality.

"I'm glad you didn't find the cabin too rough. Some people get here and they're real disappointed. Now, make sure you stop by the campus on your way out."

"Yes, ma'am. We plan to."

We said our goodbyes and drove on up the hill. At the highest point, just as the road turns back around toward the highway, we stopped and took a last look over our shoulders. Wana was still standing on her front porch. Her son was down in the pasture below us loading his pickup with firewood from a huge pile of scrap lumber and old fence posts. Helen was back with Menelaus in Sparta, no worse for wear. Odysseus was back in Ithaca, wondering about winnowing fans but content for now. We were going back home, purged of all desire ever to set foot in a Wal-Mart again—revitalized, inspired. And up there, somewhere up in the Snowy Mountain Range, the gods were holding peaceful council, all of their perennial feuds and jealousies for the moment simmered down to a glorious reflection of early-born, rosy-fingered dawn upon the broad heavens and the grain-giving earth.

A week or so after we returned from Wyoming, Randy and Barbara called with some news about Travis's college plans. As a high school senior torn between talents in baseball and schoolwork, he had struggled to decide between a first-rate academic institution and a roundabout baseball career. Not quite good enough in America's game at the end of high school to make a topflight division-one baseball college, say, an Oklahoma University where his father had played or a University of Texas, he had foregone Ivy League academics for a nationally scouted baseball training camp of a junior college in Florida. After a year, he'd either make it into the baseball big time at a school with good academic credentials or just transfer to a good school, baseball aside.

As luck had it, the coach at the junior college up and quit while we were all hiking about Wyoming, the baseball program collapsed, and, a week before the beginning of the fall semester, Travis was back at square one. Randy and Barbara shuddered at the financial prospects of Travis turning his thoughts back to a Yale or Harvard. Deep down they were loyal to that crusty cross-section of life that a big state university provides, especially one in Oklahoma or Texas, or even Nebraska. But they also felt the pressure of the intellectual prejudice that says you send your children to the best school money can buy, come hell or bankruptcy, no matter that that school might do little to teach them to think, and much to indoctrinate them in the vain superiorities of intellectual prejudice.

"I think I'll go to the University of Wyoming," Travis announced out of the blue.

STUDY QUESTIONS

1. What is the effect of the author's use of Greek gods and Homeric language in this final chapter—and in the book as a whole? What is the relationship of contemporary American culture to ancient Greek culture? Is it a relationship of familiar to foreign, analogous to the relationship, say, of contemporary American culture and contemporary Chinese culture?

2. The author says he's returning home "revitalized, inspired." What has he gotten out of his experiences? Is he referring to the fact that he got the idea for this book out of his experience in Wyoming—or is he referring to something else?

3. What is the significance of ending the book with a narrative chapter in which Travis decides to go to college at the University of Wyoming? Will he face the same prejudices at the University of Wyoming that the author describes in chapter 16? Based on the information you have, did Travis make a good decision? What do you expect him to end up like?

FOR FURTHER READING

Stegner, Wallace. *Wolf Willow: A History, a Story, and a Memory of the Last Plains Frontier*. New York: Penguin, 2000 [1966].

Highway 130, Centennial, Wyoming. Photo by author, 2003.

BIBLIOGRAPHY

To the extent that I have used "sources" for this book, I try to document them here, at least those that have played a direct and explicit role in the writing of this book—especially those works I've quoted from or discussed in some depth. I should explain, however, that I make no attempt to cite all of the works that have influenced the writing of this book, or for that matter every work I mention or allude to, especially in the case of long-established and readily available classics. I do make a special effort to diligently include works that are in some way more idiosyncratic, less familiar, and harder to track down.

Finally, in the interest of promoting the reading of these works, rather than the scholarly scrutiny of their publication data—and, for that matter, in the interest of providing a partial map of my peculiar intellectual acreage—I cite the editions I have used, which are in some cases the definitive scholarly edition and in other cases not. In cases of historical significance, I include the original date of publication in brackets.

❧☙

Abbey, Edward. "Down the River with Henry Thoreau." *Down the River*. New York: Dutton, 1982.
Achebe, Chinua. "An Image of Africa: Racism in Conrad's *Heart of Darkness*." In *Heart of Darkness: An Authoritative Text, Background and Sources, Criticism*. Edited by Robert Kimbrough. London: Norton, 1988.
Adams, Robert M. "The Bard of Wichita Falls" (review of Larry McMurtry's *Texasville*, *Lonesome Dove*, and a paperback reissue of *The Last Picture Show*). *The New York Review of Books*, August 13, 1987.
Aristotle. *Nicomachean Ethics*. Translated by Martin Ostwald. Upper Saddle River, N.J.: Prentice Hall, 1999 [1962].
Artusia, Pellegrino. *Science in the Kitchen and the Art of Eating Well*. Translated by Murtha Baca. Toronto: University of Toronto Press, 2003 [1891]. Originally published as *La Scienza in Cucina e l'Arte di Mangiar Bene: Manuale Practico per le Famiglie* (Firenze: Giunti, 2003 [1891]).
Bacon, Francis. *Francis Bacon: A Selection of His Works*. Edited by Sidney Warhaft. New York: Odyssey Press, 1965.
Balch, Stephen H. "The Antidote to Academic Orthodoxy." *The Chronicle of Higher Education*, April 23, 2004.
Berry, Wendell. *Recollected Essays 1965–1980*. San Francisco: North Point Press, 1981.
———. *Standing by Words: Essays by Wendell Berry*. San Francisco: North Point Press, 1983.

Bloom, Allan. *The Closing of the American Mind: How Higher Education Has Failed Democracy and Impoverished the Souls of Today's Students.* New York: Simon and Schuster, 1987.
Bourdain, Anthony. *Kitchen Confidential: Adventures in the Culinary Underbelly.* New York: Harper Perennial, 2001.
Bradley, Bill. *Life on the Run.* New York: Vintage, 1995.
Brooks, David. "Lonely Campus Voices." *The New York Times,* September 27, 2003.
Brooks, Cleanth. *The Language of the American South.* Athens: The University of Georgia Press, 1985.
Capon, Robert Farrar. *Food for Thought: Resurrecting the Art of Eating.* New York: Hartcourt, Brace, Jovanovich, 1978.
―――. *The Supper of the Lamb: A Culinary Reflection.* New York: Doubleday, 1969.
Casals, Pablo. *Joys and Sorrows: His Own Story as Told to Albert E. Kahn.* New York: Simon and Schuster, 1970.
Clark, Cecelia P. "The Soft Crab Factor." *New Bay Times* 4, no. 35 (August–September 1996).
―――. "Togus Leaf and Green Grape Catsup: Food in the Fiction of the Eastern Shore." *Chesapeake Country Life,* June 1983.
Clark, J. Wesley. *Daughter of the South County.* Annapolis: Free State Press, 1979.
Clifford, Craig. *In the Deep Heart's Core: Reflections on Life, Letters, and Texas.* College Station: Texas A&M University Press, 1985.
―――. *The Tenure of Phil Wisdom: Dialogues.* Lanham, Md.: University Press of America, 1995.
Clifford, Craig, and Randolph M. Feezell. *Coaching for Character: Reclaiming the Principles of Sportsmanship.* Champaign, Ill.: Human Kinetics, 1997.
Clifford, Craig, and William T. Pilkington, eds. *Range Wars: Heated Debates, Sober Reflections, and Other Assessments of Texas Writing.* Dallas: Southern Methodist University Press, 1989.
Conrad, Joseph. *Heart of Darkness: An Authoritative Text, Background and Sources, Criticism.* Edited by Robert Kimbrough. London: Norton, 1988.
Dahlberg, Edward. *The Sorrows of Priapus.* New York: Harcourt, Brace, Jovanovich, 1972.
Dante Alighieri. *The Divine Comedy.* Translated by Allen Mandelbaum. New York: Knopf (Everyman's Library), 1995.
DeVoto, Bernard. *Mark Twain's America.* Westport, Conn.: Greenwood Press, 1978 [1932].
Didion, Joan. *Slouching Towards Bethlehem.* New York: Simon and Schuster, 1979.
Dillard, Annie. *Pilgrim at Tinker Creek.* New York: Harper's Magazine Press, 1974.
Duncan, David James. *The River Why.* New York: Bantam, 1984.
Dylan, Bob. *Lyrics: 1962–2001.* New York: Simon and Schuster, 2004.
Ehrlich, Gretel. *The Solace of Open Spaces.* New York: Penguin, 1986 [1985].
Ellison, Ralph. *Going to the Territory.* New York: Random House, 1986.
―――. *Shadow and Act.* New York: Random House, 1964.
English, Sara Jane. *Wines of Texas: A Guide and a History.* Austin: Eakin Press, 1986.
Epstein, Joseph. *The Middle of My Tether: Familiar Essays.* New York: Norton, 1983.
―――. *Once More Around the Block: Familiar Essays.* New York: Norton, 1987.

———. *Plausible Prejudices: Essays on American Writing*. New York: Norton, 1985.
Faulkner, William. *Absalom, Absalom!* New York: Random House, 2002 [1936].
———. *The Sound and the Fury*. New York: Everyman's Library, 1992 [1929].
Feezell, Randolph M. "Play and the Absurd." *Philosophy Today* 28 (Winter 1984): 319–29.
———. "Play, Freedom, and Sport." *Philosophy Today* 25 (Summer 1981): 166–75.
———. *Sport, Play, and Ethical Reflection*. Urbana: University of Illinois Press, 2006.
———. "Sportsmanship." *Journal of the Philosophy of Sport* 13 (1986): 1–13.
Gadamer, Hans-Georg. *Heidegger's Ways*. Translated by John W. Stanley. Albany: State University of New York Press, 1994.
———. "Interview: Historicism and Romanticism," *Hans-Georg Gadamer on Education, Poetry, and History: Applied Hermeneutics*. Edited by Dieter Misgeld and Graeme Nicholson. Translated by Lawrence Schmidt and Monica Reuss. Albany: State University of New York Press, 1992.
———. *Truth and Method*. Translated by Joel Weinsheimer and Donald G. Marshall. New York: Continuum, 1989. (*Wahrheit und Methode: Grundzüge einer philosophischen Hermeneutik*. Tübingen: J. C. B. Mohr [Paul Siebeck], 1960.)
———. "Die Unfähigkeit zum Gespräch." In *Variationen*, Vol. 4 of *Kleine Schriften*. Tübingen: J. C. B. Mohr (Paul Siebeck), 1977.
Gierach, John. *Sex, Death, and Fly-Fishing*. New York: Simon and Schuster, 1990.
Goethe, Johann Wolfgang von. *The Autobiography of Johann Wolfgang von Goethe* (translation of *Aus meinem Leben: Dichtung und Wahrheit*). Translated by John Oxenford. Chicago: University of Chicago Press, 1974.
Gordon, Caroline. *Aleck Maury, Sportsman*. Carbondale: Southern Illinois University Press, 1980 [1934].
Graves, John. "Going Under." *Texas Monthly*, March 1981.
———. *Goodbye to a River*. New York: Knopf, 1979 [1960].
———. *Hard Scrabble: Observations on a Patch of Land*. New York: Knopf, 1980 [1974].
Griswold, Charles L., ed. *Platonic Writings, Platonic Readings*. New York: Routledge, 1988.
Hazan, Marcella. *Essentials of Classic Italian Cooking*. New York: Knopf, 1992.
Hazlitt, William. *Selected Writings*. Edited by Jon Cook. New York: Oxford Univesity Press, USA, 1999.
Heaney, Seamus. *Poems 1965–1975*. New York: Farrar, Straus and Giroux, 1980.
———. *Preoccupations: Selected Prose, 1968–1978*. New York: Farrar, Straus and Giroux, 1980.
———. *Station Island*. New York: Farrar, Straus and Giroux, 1985.
Heidegger, Martin. *Basic Writings*. Edited by David Farrell Krell. New York: HarperCollins, 1993.
———. *Being and Time*. Translated by John Macquarrie and Edward Robinson. New York: Harper and Row, 1962. Originally published as *Sein und Zeit* (Tübingen: Max Niemeyer, 1927).
———. *Discourse on Thinking*. Translated by John M. Anderson and E. Hans Freund. New York: Harper, 1969. Originally published as *Gelassenheit* (Pfullingen: Günther Neske, 1959).

———. *The End of Philosophy*. Translated by Joan Stambaugh. New York: Harper and Row, 1973.
———. *Erläuterungen zu Hölderlins Dichtung*. 4th ed. Frankfurt: Vittorio Klostermann, 1971.
———. *Existence and Being*. Translated by Douglas Scott. Chicago: Henry Regnery, 1970 [1949].
———. "Gespräch mit Martin Heidegger" [interview with Martin Heidegger]. *Der Spiegel*, May 31, 1976.
———. *Hebel: Der Hausfreund*. Pfullingen: Günter Neske, 1957.
———. *Holzwege*. 5th ed. Frankfurt: Vittorio Klostermann, 1972 [1950]. Epigraph translated by David Farrell Krell in the introduction to *Basic Writings* and "Der Ursprung des Kunstwerkes" translated by Albert Hofstadter as "The Origin of the Work of Art" in *Poetry, Language, Thought* (also appears in abridged form in *Basic Writings*).
———. *Nietzsche*. Vol. 2. Pfullingen: Günter Neske, 1961.
———. *Poetry, Language, Thought*. Translated by Albert Hofstadter. New York: Harper and Row, 1971.
———. *Vorträge und Aufsätze*. 3 vols. 3rd ed. Pfullingen: Günter Neske, 1967 [1954].
———. *What is Philosophy?* Translated by William Kluback and Jean T. Wilde. New Haven: College and University Press, 1956. Originally published as *Was is das—die Philosophie?* (Pfullingen: Günther Neske, 1956).
Hemingway, Ernest. *Death in the Afternoon*. New York: Scribner's, 1996 [1932].
———. *Green Hills of Africa*. New York: Vintage 2004 [1935].
———. *A Moveable Feast: Sketches of the Author's Life in Paris in the Twenties*. New York: Scribner's, 1964.
———. *The Short Stories of Ernest Hemingway*. New York: Scribner's, 1938.
Hobbes, Thomas. *Leviathan*. Edited by Edwin Curley. Indianapolis: Hackett, 1994.
Hölderlin, Friedrich. *Poems and Fragments*. Bilingual edition. Translated by Michael Hamburger. Ann Arbor: University of Michigan Press, 1968.
Holmes, Oliver Wendell. *The Autocrat of the Breakfas-Table*. Teddington, Middlesex: Echo Library, 2006 [1858].
Homer. *The Iliad of Homer*. Translated by Richard Lattimore. New York: University of Chicago Press, 1951.
———. *The Odyssey: A New Verse Translation*. Translated by Albert Cook. New York: Norton, 1967.
———. *The Odyssey of Homer*. Edited by W. B. Stanford. London: Macmillan, 1974.
Humphrey, William. *Home from the Hill*. New York: Knopf, 1977.
———. *Open Season: Sporting Adventures*. New York: Delacorte Press/Seymour Lawrence, 1986.
———. *The Ordways*. New York: Knopf, 1965.
Hyland, Drew A. "Competition and Friendship," *Journal of the Philosophy of Sport* 5 (1978): 27–38.
———. *Philosophy of Sport*. New York: Paragon House, 1990.
Jackson, Girard. *Theresa Bernstein*. Stamford, Conn.: Smith-Girard Gallery, 1985.
Johnson, Gerald W. *South-Watching: Selected Essays by Gerald W. Johnson*. Edited by Fred Hobson. Chapel Hill: University of North Carolina Press, 1983.

Johnson, Hugh, and Jancis Robinson. *The World Atlas of Wine*. London: Mitchell Beazley, 2001 [1971].
Kant, Immanuel. *Critique of Judgment*. Translated by J. H. Bernard. New York: Hafner, 1951.
Ketchum, Jonathan. "The Silence of Socrates." Private monograph. Oakstone Farm, 1977.
———. *The Structure of the Plato Dialogue*. Draft of PhD diss., photocopy. Oakstone Farm, 1975.
———. *The Structure of the Plato Dialogue*. PhD diss., State University of New York at Buffalo, 1981.
———. "What is Philosophy, and What Is It For? Oakstone Farm, Twenty Years." Private Monograph. Oakstone Farm, 1979.
King, Larry. "A Coach for All Seasons." In *Warning: Writer at Work—The Best Collectibles of Larry L. King*. Fort Worth: Texas Christian University Press, 1985.
———. *None But a Blockhead: On Being a Writer*. New York: Viking, 1986.
———. *Of Outlaws, Con Men, Whores, Politicians, and Other Artists*. New York: Viking, 1980.
———. *The Old Man and Lesser Mortals*. New York: Viking, 1974.
Klein, Daniel B., and Charlotta Stern. "Political Diversity in Six Disciplines." *Academic Questions* 18, no. 1 (March 2004): 40–52.
Klein, Daniel B., and Andrew Western. "Voter Registration of Berkeley and Stanford Faculty." *Academic Questions* 18, no. 1 (March 2004): 53–65.
Klein, Jacob. *Lectures and Essays*. Edited by Robert B. Williamson and Elliott Zuckerman. Annapolis: St. John's College Press, 1985.
———. "On Liberal Education." Lecture given at St. Mary's College, California, March 25, 1965. Photocopy, St. John's College Bookstore, Annapolis, Md.
Knox, Bernard. *The Oldest Dead White European Males: And Other Reflections on the Classics*. New York: Norton, 1993.
Kumin, Maxine. *In Deep: Country Essays*. New York: Viking, 1987.
Kundera, Milan. *Ignorance*. Translated by Linda Asher. New York: HarperCollins, 2002.
Liebling, A. J. *Between Meals: An Appetite for Paris*. San Francisco: North Point Press, 1986.
———. *The Sweet Science*. New York: Viking, 1982 [1956].
Lopate, Phillip. "The Essay Lives—in Disguise." *The New York Times Book Review*, November 18, 1984.
Luchetti, Cathy. *Women of the West*. In collaboration with Carol Olwell. New York: Norton, 2001.
Maclean, Norman. *A River Runs Through It, and Other Stories*. Chicago: The University of Chicago Press, 1976.
MacNeil, Robert. "It's Not I but Me, and I Say: Leave American English Alone." *The New York Times Book Review*, September 14, 1986.
Mailer, Norman. *The Fight*. New York: Penguin, 2000.
Martin, George. *Verdi: His Music, Life and Times*. New York: Dodd, Mead, and Company, 1963.
McClane, A. J. *A Taste of the Wild: A Compendium of Modern American Game Cookery*. New York: Dutton, 1991.

McCrum, Robert, Robert MacNeil, and William Cran. *The Story of English*. New York: Penguin, 1986.
McMurtry, Larry. "Ever a Bridegroom: Reflections on the Failure of Texas Literature." *Texas Observer*, October 23, 1981. Reprinted in *Range Wars: Heated Debates, Sober Reflections, and Other Assessments of Texas Writing* (Dallas: Southern Methodist University Press, 1989).
———. *Horseman, Pass By*. New York: Penguin, 1979 [1961].
———. *In a Narrow Grave: Essays on Texas*. Austin: Encino Press, 1968.
———. *The Last Picture Show*. New York: Penguin, 1987 [1966].
———. *Lonesome Dove*. New York: Simon and Schuster, 1985.
———. *Texasville*. New York: Simon and Schuster, 1987.
Melville, Herman. *Moby-Dick or, The Whale*. New York: Penguin Classics, 2002.
Mencken, H. L. *The American Language*. New York: Knopf, 1977 [1919].
———. "The Sahara of the Bozart." In *Prejudices, Second Series*. New York, 1920.
Mill, John Stuart. *On Liberty*. Indianapolis: Hackett, 1978.
Montaigne. *Montaigne's Essays and Selected Writings: A Bilingual Edition*. Translated by Donald M. Frame. New York: St. Martin's Press, 1963.
Morris, Willie. *Always Stand in Against the Curve*. Oxford, Miss.: Yoknapatawpha Press, 1983.
———. *The Courting of Marcus Dupree*. Garden City, N.Y.: Doubleday, 1983.
———. *North Toward Home*. Boston: Houghton Mifflin, 1967.
———. *Terrains of the Heart and Other Essays on Home*. Oxford, Miss.: Yoknapatawpha Press, 1981.
Nieli, Russell K. "Enhancing Intellectual Diversity on Campus—The James Madison Program at Princeton." *Academic Questions* 18, no. 2 (March 2005): 20–48.
Nussbaum, Martha C. *Love's Knowledge: Essays on Philosophy and Literature*. New York, Oxford: Oxford University Press, 1990.
Oates, Joyce Carol. *On Boxing*. Garden City, N.Y.: Dolphin/Doubleday, 1987.
O'Connor, Flannery. *Mystery and Manners: Occasional Prose*. Edited by Sally and Robert Fitzgerald. New York: Farrar, Straus and Giroux, 1984 [1969].
O'Connor, Frank. *Collected Stories*. New York: Knopf, 1981.
Pilkington, William T. "Contemporary Texas Writers and the Concept of Regionalism." *The Texas Humanist*, April 1980.
———. *Western Movies*. Edited by William T. Pilkington and Don Graham. Albuquerque: University of New Mexico Press, 1979.
Plato. *Euthyphro, Apology, Crito*. Translated by F. J. Church (revised by Robert D. Cumming). Indianapolis: The Library of Liberal Arts, Bobbs-Merrill, 1956 [1948].
———. *Five Dialogues: Euthyphro, Apology, Crito, Meno, Phaedo*. Translated by G. M. A. Grube. Indianapolis: Hackett, 1981.
———. *Gorgias*. Translated by Terence Irwin. Oxford: Clarenden, 1979.
———. *Gorgias*. Translated by W. C. Helmbold. Indianapolis: The Library of Liberal Arts, Bobbs-Merrill, 1952.
———. *Meno*. Translated by Benjamin Jowett. Indianapolis: The Library of Liberal Arts, Bobbs-Merrill, 1949.

———. *Plato*. Vol. 1, *Euthyphro, Apology, Crito, Phaedo, Phaedrus*. Translated by Harold North Fowler. Cambridge: Loeb Classical Library, Harvard University Press, 1971 [1914].
———. *Plato*. Vols. 5 and 6, *The Republic*. Translated by Paul Shorey. Cambridge: Loeb Classical Library, Harvard University Press, 1969 and 1970.
———. *Plato: Complete Works*. Edited by John M. Cooper. Indianapolis: Hackett, 1997.
———. *Plato's Apology of Socrates*. Translated by Thomas G. West. Ithaca: Cornell University Press, 1979.
———. *Plato's Republic*. Translated by G. M. A. Grube. Indianapolis: Hackett, 1974.
———. *The Republic of Plato*. Translated by Allan Bloom. New York: Basic Books, 1968.
Postman, Neil. *The End of Education: Redefining the Value of School*. New York: Vintage, 1996.
Press, Gerald A., ed. *Plato's Dialogues: New Studies and Interpretations*. Lanham, Md.: Rowman and Littlefield, 1993.
Prudhomme, Paul. *Chef Paul Prudhomme's Louisiana Kitchen*. New York: William Morrow, 1984.
Silber, John R. *Straight Shooting: What's Wrong with America and How to Fix It*. New York: HarperCollins, 1990.
Solomon, Robert C. *True to Our Feelings: What Our Emotions Are Really Telling Us*. Oxford: Oxford University Press, 2006.
Solomon, Robert C., and Jon Solomon. *Up the University: Re-Creating Higher Education in America*. New York: Addison-Wesley, 1993.
Steele, Shelby. *White Guilt: How Blacks and Whites Together Destroyed the Promise of the Civil Rights Era*. New York: Harper Perennial, 2007.
Stegner, Wallace. *Wolf Willow: A History, a Story, and a Memory of the Last Plains Frontier*. New York: Penguin, 2000 [1966].
Thoreau, Henry David. *Walden and Other Writings*. Edited by Brooks Atkinson. New York: Modern Library, 1992.
Twain, Mark. *The Adventures of Huckleberry Finn*. Philadelphia: Running Press, 1986 [1884].
———. *The Comic Mark Twain Reader: The Most Humorous Selections from His Stories, Sketches, Novels, Travel Books, and Lectures*. Edited by Charles Neider. New York: Doubleday, 1977.
Webb, Walter Prescott. *The Great Plains*. Lincoln: University of Nebraska Press, 1981 [1931].
Welty, Eudora. *The Eye of the Story: Selected Essays and Reviews*. New York: Vintage, 1979.
———. *One Writer's Beginnings*. Cambridge: Harvard University Press, 1984.
Will, George F. *Men at Work: The Craft of Baseball*. New York: HarperCollins, 1990.
Yeats, William Butler. *The Collected Poems of W. B. Yeats*. New York: Macmillan, 1979 [1956].
Young, Mallory. "On Reading John Graves, Slowly." *Texas Books in Review* 6 (1984): 3-5.
———. "The Phaeacians: Pleasure, Poetry, and Tragic Choice." *The Southern Humanities Review* 16, no. 2 (Spring 1982): 145–152.

Zencey, Eric. "The Rootless Professors." *The Chronicle of Higher Education*, June 12, 1985. Reprinted in *Virgin Forest: Meditations on History, Ecology, and Culture* (Athens: University of Georgia Press, 1998).

ABOUT THE AUTHOR

CRAIG CLIFFORD is Professor of Philosophy and Director of the Honors Programs at Tarleton State University in Stephenville, Texas. He is the author of *In the Deep Heart's Core: Reflections on Life, Letters, and Texas* (Texas A&M University Press, 1985); co-editor with William T. Pilkington of *Range Wars: Heated Debates, Sober Reflections, and Other Assessments of Texas Writing* (Southern Methodist University Press, 1989); author of *The Tenure of Phil Wisdom: Dialogues* (University Press of America, 1995); and co-author with Randolph M. Feezell of *Coaching for Character: Reclaiming the Principles of Sportsmanship* (Human Kinetics, 1997). His essays, guest columns, and reviews have appeared in numerous newspapers and magazines.

Born in Louisiana and raised outside of Houston, Clifford did his undergraduate work in Plan II (the liberal arts honors program) at the University of Texas at Austin. He completed his PhD in philosophy at the State University of New York at Buffalo in 1981, writing a dissertation on Plato and Heidegger under Professor Kah-Kyung Cho.

After nine years as expatriates in Buffalo, New York, and Annapolis, Maryland, Clifford and his wife, Mallory Young, returned to Texas in 1983.

INDEX

Absalom, Absalom! See under Faulkner, William
abstraction, 24, 50, 53
Achaians, 108, 110
Achebe, Chinua, 152
Achilles, 108
Addison, Joseph, 52
aesthetic differentiation (Gadamer on), 109
agroikia, 19
Ajax, 108
Albright-Knox Art Museum, 86
Alcinoos, 108
Aleck Maury: Sportsman. See under Gordon, Caroline
Alemannisch, 37, 41
Always Stand in Against the Curve. See under Willie Morris
American Philosophical Association, 84
Amon Carter Art Museum, 87
analytic philosophy, 2, 158
Ando, Tadao, 87
Anglo-American philosophy, 1
Angst, 8
anti-Americanism, 17
aphorism(s), 4, 54
apologia, 26
apology (in the sense of defense), 26
Apology. See under Plato
aporia, 20, 50, 155, 161, 162
Aristophanes, 85
Aristotle, 2, 4, 22, 24, 83
    definition of a human, 53
    Nichomachean Ethics, 83
    on *scholē*, 20
Atchafalaya Basin, 127
authenticity (in Heidegger's sense), 24
autochthonous intellectual, 96
Autocrat of the Breakfast-Table, The. See under Holmes, Oliver Wendell

Bach, Johann Sebastian, 90, 97, 154
Balch, Stephen, 151

balkanization, 137
barbaroi, 67
Bass Performance Hall, 87
Being and Time. See under Heidegger, Martin
Bellow, Saul, 70
Bergman, Ingmar, 91
Bernkastel-Kues, 132, 148
Bernstein, Theresa, 85, 87, 88
Berry, Wendell, 23
    Making of a Marginal Farm, The, 55
bigotry, 18, 19, 36, 131, 153, 154, 157
binary opposition (of good and evil), 19
bios theōretikos, 24
Bourdain, Anthony, 135–7, 142
    Cook's Tour, A, 135, 136
    Kitchen Confidential, 135
boxing, 105–7, 109–11
Bradley, Bill, 109
Brazos River, 26, 115, 124, 126, 149
Broadway, 83, 84, 86
Brooks, Cleanth, *Language of the American South, The*, 38–39
Brooks, Mel, 17

Callicles, 19, 24, 51, 106
Camus, Albert, 70, 110, 145
canon, literary, 71–72, 153
Casals, Pablo, 97
catch and release, 125–6, 129
Centennial, 32, 78, 101, 115
Cézanne, Paul, *Lac d'Annecy*, 87
Chagall, Marc, 85
Chaucer, Geoffrey, 38
Chesapeake Country Life, 139
chthōn, 96
Circe, 23, 67, 110
Clark, Guy, 89, 90
Clark, James Wesley, *Daughter of the South County*, 139
Cliburn, Van, 87
colere, 95–96
Coleridge, Samuel Taylor, 39, 51, 52

colonialism, 19, 72
competition
　intellectual, 54
　in sports, 106–8
　of wit, 52
Conrad, Joseph
　Achebe, Chinua on, 152
　Heart of Darkness, 152
continental cuisine, 22
continental philosophy, 158
conversationalist(s), 51–52
Cook's Tour, A. See under Bourdain, Anthony
cosmopolitan intellect, 55
cosmopolitan intellectual(s), 19, 23 53, 54, 70, 94, 95, 106–8, 137, 151, 152, 155, 156, 159, 161, 162
cosmopolitanism, 22, 24, 26, 70, 128, 131, 155, 158
cosmopolitan prejudice, 26, 131, 140
cosmopolitan(s), 22, 39, 70, 88, 156, 159
cosmopolitan stage (of intellectual life), 22, 36, 40, 41, 65, 155, 156
Cotton Club, 87
Courtauld Collection, 86
cultura, 95–96
culture
　being cultured, 17, 95
　centers of, 95
　Eurocentric, 72
　high, 16, 67, 83, 85, 91, 95, 97, 107, 129, 134
　indigenous, 72, 142
　intellectual, 134, 158
　local, 157, 159
　opposed to nature, 95, 96
　origin of word, 95
　popular, 134
　sports, 106
Cyclopes, 95–96, 108

Dante, 67, 154
　Divina Commedia, La, 68
Dartmouth, 161, 162, 167
Daughter of the South County. See under Clark, James Wesley

dead white males, 71
Degas, Edgar, *Two Dancers on the Stage*, 87
Demodocos, 108
Derrideans, 21
dialect
　Alemmanisch, 37
　black, 37
　Dante's Tuscan, 68
　German, 37, 41
　Goethe on, 36
　Goethe's Frankfurt, 36
　local, 22, 40, 41
　Twain on, 36–37
dialogos, 53
Divina Commedia, La. See under Dante
Dobie, J. Frank (on Shakespeare), 68
Doig, Ivan, 37
Dupree, Marcus, 111
Dylan, Bob, 89

Easy Rider, 91
Eliot, T.S., 65
Ellison, Ralph, 124
English
　American, 2, 38, 29, 40, 94
　British, 38, 39
　conversational, 51, 52
　correct (standard), 16, 37, 38, 39, 40, 41, 42, 90
　literary-colloquial, 39, 51
　MacNeil, Robert on, 40–41, 131
　Middle, 49
　Queen's, 22, 38, 39, 50, 155, 156
　Shakespeare, 39, 40, 68
　Southern, 35, 38, 39
ennui, 8
Epstein, Joseph, 5, 52
Essais. See under Montaigne, Michel de
essay, 2–6, 148
　argumentative, 5
　conversational, 52
　Epstein, Joseph on, 5
　familiar, 51
　personal, 52
　ruminative, 5

essayer, 2, 52
Eurocentrism, 17, 72, 152
Europhilia, 17
Euryalos, 107, 108
everydayness (in Heidegger's sense), 24, 26
expressionism, 85, 86

facticity (in Heidegger's sense), 21, 22
fate, 109
    fatedness, 67
    fatefulness, 21, 22, 67, 96
    Odysseus' choosing of, 110
Faulkner, William, 2, 37, 38, 40, 41, 65, 66, 69, 70, 143
    Absalom, Absalom!, 37
Fellini, Federico, 91
finitude, 8, 21, 67, 108, 109, 125
Flay, Bobby, 135, 136, 137
Florence, Tyler, 135, 136, 137
folk music, 22, 88–91
foreign film(s), 91, 92
foreign language
    and liberal education, 93
    snobbery, 93, 94
    study of, 93
France, 9, 46, 94, 132, 133, 136
Francophilia, 17, 161
Frick Collection, 86
Frizzell, Lefty, 84

Gadamer, Hans-Georg, 1, 2, 4, 6, 22, 53, 86, 109, 111
gadfly, Socrates as, 157, 162, 163
German (language), 36–37, 41, 49, 53, 67, 94
Germany, 9, 37, 41, 46, 86, 92, 132
Gershwin, George, 135
Geworfenheit, 21
globalization, 17, 19, 72, 153
God of Small Things, The. See under Roy, Arundhati
Goethe, Johann Wolfgang von, 36, 70
Gogh, Vincent van, 110
    Peach Blossom in the Crau, 87

Goodbye to a River. See under Graves, John
Gordon, Caroline, *Aleck Maury: Sportsman*, 124
Gorgias. See under Plato
Graves, John, 5, 18, 41, 52, 68, 101, 124, 130, 149
    Goodbye to a River, 37, 66
gumnastikē, 107, 108, 112, 163
Guthrie, Woody, 89

Hamlet. See under Shakespeare.
Hard Scrabble. See under Graves, John
Hardy, Thomas, 64, 66
haute cuisine, 131–6
Hawthorne, Nathaniel, 70
Hazlitt, William, 51–52
Heaney, Seamus, 38, 68–69
Hebel, Johann Peter, 37
Heidegger, Martin, 1–8, 21, 22, 24, 26, 37, 41, 46, 52, 66, 70, 96, 158
    Being and Time, 3, 132
    Holzwege, 3
    What is Philosophy?, 54
Heidegger's Ways. See under Gadamer, Hans-Georg
Hemingway, Ernest, 19, 25, 85, 111, 130
    "Big Two-Heart River," 124
    "Hills Like White Elephants," 153
hermeneutic stage (of intellectual life), 22
Hesse, Hermann, 70, 90
Hickey, Dave, 25
High Noon, 91–92
Hochdeutsch, 41
Hölderlin, Friedrich, 52, 70
Holmes, Oliver Wendell, *Autocrat of the Breakfast-Table*, 50
homecoming, 22, 70, 72, 160, 162
Home from the Hill. See under Humphrey, William
Homer, 67, 95–97, 108, 160
horizons (broadening of), 23, 142
Horseman, Pass By. See under McMurtry, Larry

Huckleberry Finn. See under Twain, Mark
Humphrey, William, 37
   Home from the Hill, 37
   Open Season, 124
   Ordways, The, 37
Hyland, Drew, 107

idolatry, 16
Ignorance. See under Kundera, Milan
Illiad. See under Homer
imperialism, 19, 39, 72
In a Narrow Grave. See under McMurtry, Larry
inbreeding (in academia), 158
indigenous culture(s), 19, 72, 142, 152
indigenous language(s), 39
indigenous people, 17, 72
indigenous writing, 72
intellectual life, 22, 24, 26, 35, 36, 55, 65, 92, 152, 159
intellectual(s), 12
   autochthonous, 96
   cosmopolitan, 19, 23, 54, 70, 94, 95, 106–8, 137, 151–9, 161–2
   dogma of, 16, 18, 155
   phronetic, 23, 72, 96
   prejudices of, 16–24, 26, 35, 41, 65, 83, 85, 88, 91, 106, 131, 143, 152, 154, 155, 163, 168
   rooted, 23, 26, 161
   rootless, 24
   urban, 23
Ireland, 68, 69, 70, 89
Italian (language), 68
Italy, 132–3, 141

James, Henry, 65, 143, 155
Johnson, Hugh, *World Atlas of Wine*, 131, 132
Johnson, Samuel, 51, 52
Joyce, James, 38, 69, 70
Julius Caesar. See under Shakespeare
Kahn, Louis, 87
Kant, Immanuel, 33, 66, 91, 92, 154
Keats, John, 39

Kimbell Art Museum, 87
Kimbell, Kay, 87
King, Larry, *Best Little Whorehouse in Texas*, 94
Kipling, Rudyard, 70
Kitchen Confidential. See under Bourdain, Anthony
Kundera, Milan, *Ignoranc*e, 160

Lac d'Annecy. See under Cezanne, Paul
Lagasse, Emeril, 135
Lamb, Charles, 51
Language of the American South, The. See under Brooks, Cleanth
Last Picture Show, The. See under McMurtry, Larry
Levine, David (cartoon of Larry McMurtry), 64
Lichtung, 3
life of the mind, 19–22
   first principle of, 19
   second principle of, 21
Locke, John, 50
logomachy, 55
logos, 53
London, 17, 52, 69, 95
Lonesome Dove. See under McMurtry, Larry
love(r) of wisdom, 20, 21,152, 162
Love's Knowledge. See under Nussbaum, Martha

Maclean, Norman, 52, 59, 65, 124–6
   River Runs Through It, A (book), 123, 167
   River Runs Through It, A (movie), 125, 126
MacNeil, Robert, 40–41, 131, 156
Mailer, Norman, 111
Making of a Marginal Farm, The. See under Berry, Wendell
Marc, Franz, *The Wolves*, 86
Marxism, 106
McMurtry, Larry, 15, 37, 64–65
   Horseman, Pass By, 37, 64
   Last Picture Show, The, 64

McMurtry (*continued*)
   Levine cartoon of, 64
   Lonesome Dove, 63–65
   Narrow Grave, In a, 37
   Texasville, 63, 64
Medicine Bow Mountains, 8, 16, 25, 32, 46, 79, 102, 131,
Melville, Herman, 38, 70
Mencken, H. L., 38, 52
Meno. *See under* Plato
Metropolitan Art Museum, 86
metrosexuals, 108
Meyerowitz, William, 85
Mill, John Stuart, 151, 154, 155
Milton, John, 83, 84, 154
Modern Art Museum of Fort Worth, 87
Modern Language Association, 24, 152
Montaigne, Michel de, 2–3, 5, 6, 51, 52
   Essais, 2–3, 4
Morris, Willie, *Always Stand in Against the Curve*, 111
Moulton, Sara, 135
Mozart, Wolfgang Amadeus, 22, 84, 88, 90
multiculturalism, 137
musikē, 107–8
muthologiē, 54
mysticism, 2
mystics, 53

naïve prejudice, stage of, 22, 74
narrative(s), 1, 2, 5, 22, 54
Naval Academy. *See* United States Naval Academy
New York Review of Books, The, 64
New York-ophilia, 16, 17
Nicholas of Cusa, 132, 148
Nicomachean Ethics. *See under* Aristotle
nomos, 96
nostos, 160
Nussbaum, Martha, 1–4
   Love's Knowledge, 1

O'Connor, Flannery, 12, 71, 90
O'Connor, Frank, 69–70, 148, 149
Odysseus, 67, 160, 167

Oedipus, 110
Open Season. *See under* Humphrey, William
opera, 9, 12, 16, 17, 83, 84, 90, 92
Ordways. *See under* Humphrey, William
orthodoxy, 163
   academic, 24, 152–3
Osborn, Carolyn, 65

paideia, 96
Passover, 137
pathos, 25, 108, 109, 111
Patroclos, 108, 109
Peach Blossom in the Crau. *See under* Gogh, Vincent van
perplexity, 20
Phaeacians, 67, 95, 96, 107–10
Philoctetes, 108
philosophy, 1–5, 11, 20, 32, 47, 49, 51, 55, 93, 139, 148, 155, 158
phronēsis, 22, 93, 156
phusis, 96
Plato
   Apology, 20
   dialogue form, 3–4, 53
   Gorgias, 51, 53, 131, 148
   Greek terms in, 93
   and Heidegger, Martin, 3–5
   Meno, 20, 160
   nature and culture, views on, 96
   Republic, 4, 107
   Seventh Letter, 4
   Socrates and Socratic life, portrayal of, 20
   Symposium, 4
   teaching of, 160
ponos, 110
Porter, Katherine Anne, 71
Poseidon, 96
post-colonialism, 72, 152
Postman, Neil, *The End of Education*, 137
postmodernism(ists), 18, 21–24, 51, 152–3
prejudice(s)
   academic, 151–163

prejudice(s) (*continued*)
  childhood, 17
  of culture-vultures, 84–5
  food, 131–143
  intellectual, 9, 16–26
  linguistic, 36–41
  literary, 5
  as membership card, 17
  music, 88
Proust, Marcel, 133
provincialism, 37, 67, 70, 72, 91, 133
pseudo-intellectual(s), 19, 22, 35, 51, 84, 89, 91, 106, 108, 110, 123, 125, 131, 151, 163

Queen's English, 22, 35, 38, 39, 50, 155, 156
questioning, self-questioning, 4–6, 11–21, 96

Redford, Robert, 125
redneck(s), 15, 17, 18, 19, 20, 108
  intellectual, 21, 121, 125
Re-education
  in English language, 40–41
  in food, 131, 133, 143
regionalism, 70, 131
relativism, 24, 39, 95
rituals, 84, 129, 137–9
River Runs Through It, A. See under Maclean, Norman
rootedness, 16–24, 71–72, 90, 130, 133, 159, 161
"Rootless Professors, The." *See under* Zencey, Eric
Roth, Philip, 37
Roy, Arundhati, *God of Small Things, The*, 72

Sache (Gadamer on), 53
scholē, 20
Seventh Letter of Plato. *See under* Plato
Shakespeare, William, 38
  Elizabethan vernacular, use of, 68
  Hamlet, 68
  Julius Caesar, 68

Shelley, Percy Bysshe, 39
Sid Richardson Museum, 87
Silber, John, 91
situatedness, 21, 22
Smith, Logan Pearsall, 40
snobbery
  fly fishing, 123, 125
  food, 134, 136, 142, 143
  intellectual, 20, 24, 91, 93. 95
  language, 38, 94
  sports, 110
Socrates, 19, 21, 24, 51–54, 107, 110, 152, 155, 157, 162–3
  Socratic life, 20
  Socratic wisdom, 20, 50
sophia, 20
sophist(s), 19–20, 24, 51, 52, 53, 96, 155, 157, 162
Sophocles, 85, 110
Stein, Gertrude, 85
Stevens, Wallace, 46, 70
sublime (in nature), 33
Symposium. See under Plato

Tchaikovsky, Pyotr Ilyich, 90
Texasville. See under McMurtry, Larry
Thoreau, Henry David, 18, 130
  "Life Without Principle," 18
  Twain, Mark contrasted to, 52
Todtnauberg (Heidegger's cabin there), 37, 41, 52, 66
Trier, 2, 45, 47, 132, 139
Troy, 108
Truth and Method. See under Gadamer, Hans-Georg
Twain, Mark, 35, 37–38, 52, 54, 55, 70, 124, 143
Two Dancers on the Stage. See under Degas, Edgar

United States Naval Academy, 50–51, 69, 160
University of Wyoming, 78, 101, 102, 168
Van Gogh, Vincent. *See* Gogh, Vincent van

vegetarians, 129, 135–6,
Venice, 141
Verdi, Giuseppe, 90–91, 97
vernacular, 37, 38, 41

Wagner, Richard, 9, 90, 91
Welty, Eudora, 66–67, 71
Wertmüller, Lina, 91
Western civilization, 21, 72
Western Literature Association, 92
What is Philosophy? See under Heidegger, Martin
Will, George, 52, 105, 154
Williams, Hank, 17, 88
wisdom
   love of, 152, 162
   Socratic, 20, 50

Wolves, The. See under Marc, Franz
Wordsworth, William, 39
World Atlas of Wine. See under Johnson, Hugh
worldliness, 67, 90, 108, 131, 142, 143
world literature, 67, 70
Wyeth, Andrew, 88
Wynette, Tammy, 83

xenophilia, 16–17, 22, 72, 136, 141, 142, 153, 155, 157

Yeats, William Butler, 68, 69, 70

Zencey, Eric, "The Rootless Professors," 156–9

VIBS

The **Value Inquiry Book Series** is co-sponsored by:

Adler School of Professional Psychology
American Indian Philosophy Association
American Maritain Association
American Society for Value Inquiry
Association for Process Philosophy of Education
Canadian Society for Philosophical Practice
Center for Bioethics, University of Turku
Center for Professional and Applied Ethics, University of North Carolina at Charlotte
Central European Pragmatist Forum
Centre for Applied Ethics, Hong Kong Baptist University
Centre for Cultural Research, Aarhus University
Centre for Professional Ethics, University of Central Lancashire
Centre for the Study of Philosophy and Religion, University College of Cape Breton
Centro de Estudos em Filosofia Americana, Brazil
College of Education and Allied Professions, Bowling Green State University
College of Liberal Arts, Rochester Institute of Technology
Concerned Philosophers for Peace
Conference of Philosophical Societies
Department of Moral and Social Philosophy, University of Helsinki
Gannon University
Gilson Society
Haitian Studies Association
Ikeda University
Institute of Philosophy of the High Council of Scientific Research, Spain
International Academy of Philosophy of the Principality of Liechtenstein
International Association of Bioethics
International Center for the Arts, Humanities, and Value Inquiry
International Society for Universal Dialogue
Natural Law Society
Philosophical Society of Finland
Philosophy Born of Struggle Association
Philosophy Seminar, University of Mainz
Pragmatism Archive at The Oklahoma State University
R.S. Hartman Institute for Formal and Applied Axiology
Research Institute, Lakeridge Health Corporation
Russian Philosophical Society
Society for Existential Analysis
Society for Iberian and Latin-American Thought
Society for the Philosophic Study of Genocide and the Holocaust
Unit for Research in Cognitive Neuroscience, Autonomous University of Barcelona
Yves R. Simon Institute

Titles Published

Volumes 1 - 161 see www.rodopi.nl

162.   Arthur Efron, *Expriencing Tess of the D'Urbervilles: A Deweyan Account.* A volume in **Studies in Pragmatism and Values**

163.   Reyes Mate, *Memory of the West: The Contemporaneity of Forgotten Jewish Thinkers.* Translated from the Spanish by Anne Day Dewey. Edited by John R. Welch. A volume in **Philosophy in Spain**

164.   Nancy Nyquist Potter, Editor, *Putting Peace into Practice: Evaluating Policy on Local and Global Levels.* A volume in **Philosophy of Peace**

165.   Matti Häyry, Tuija Takala, and Peter Herissone-Kelly, Editors, *Bioethics and Social Reality.* A volume in **Values in Bioethics**

166.   Maureen Sie, *Justifying Blame: Why Free Will Matters and Why it Does Not.* A volume in **Studies in Applied Ethics**

167.   Leszek Koczanowicz and Beth J. Singer, Editors, *Democracy and the Post-Totalitarian Experience.* A volume in **Studies in Pragmatism and Values**

168.   Michael W. Riley, *Plato's* Cratylus: *Argument, Form, and Structure.* A volume in **Studies in the History of Western Philosophy**

169.   Leon Pomeroy, *The New Science of Axiological Psychology.* Edited by Rem B. Edwards. A volume in **Hartman Institute Axiology Studies**

170.   Eric Wolf Fried, *Inwardness and Morality*

171.   Sami Pihlstrom, *Pragmatic Moral Realism: A Transcendental Defense.* A volume in Studies in **Pragmatism and Values**

172.   Charles C. Hinkley II, *Moral Conflicts of Organ Retrieval: A Case for Constructive Pluralism.* A volume in **Values in Bioethics**

173.   Gábor Forrai and George Kampis, Editors, *Intentionality: Past and Future.* A volume in **Cognitive Science**

174.   Dixie Lee Harris, *Encounters in My Travels: Thoughts Along the Way.* A volume in **Lived Values:Valued Lives**

175. Lynda Burns, Editor, *Feminist Alliances*. A volume in **Philosophy and Women**

176. George Allan and Malcolm D. Evans, *A Different Three Rs for Education*. A volume in **Philosophy of Education**

177. Robert A. Delfino, Editor, *What are We to Understand Gracia to Mean?: Realist Challenges to Metaphysical Neutralism*. A volume in **Gilson Studies**

178. Constantin V. Ponomareff and Kenneth A. Bryson, *The Curve of the Sacred: An Exploration of Human Spirituality*. A volume in **Philosophy and Religion**

179. John Ryder, Gert Rüdiger Wegmarshaus, Editors, *Education for a Democratic Society: Central European Pragmatist Forum, Volume Three*. A volume in **Studies in Pragmatism and Values**

180. Florencia Luna, *Bioethics and Vulnerability: A Latin American View*. A volume in **Values in Bioethics**

181. John Kultgen and Mary Lenzi, Editors, *Problems for Democracy*. A volume in **Philosophy of Peace**

182. David Boersema and Katy Gray Brown, Editors, *Spiritual and Political Dimensions of Nonviolence and Peace*. A volume in **Philosophy of Peace**

183. Daniel P. Thero, *Understanding Moral Weakness*. A volume in **Studies in the History of Western Philosophy**

184. Scott Gelfand and John R. Shook, Editors, *Ectogenesis: Artificial Womb Technology and the Future of Human Reproduction*. A volume in **Values in Bioethics**

185. Piotr Jaroszyński, *Science in Culture*. A volume in **Gilson Studies**

186. Matti Häyry, Tuija Takala, Peter Herissone-Kelly, Editors, *Ethics in Biomedical Research: International Perspectives*. A volume in **Values in Bioethics**

187. Michael Krausz, *Interpretation and Transformation: Explorations in Art and the Self*. A volume in **Interpretation and Translation**

188.   Gail M. Presbey, Editor, *Philosophical Perspectives on the "War on Terrorism."* A volume in **Philosophy of Peace**

189.   María Luisa Femenías, Amy A. Oliver, Editors, *Feminist Philosophy in Latin America and Spain.* A volume in **Philosophy in Latin America**

190.   Oscar Vilarroya and Francesc Forn I Argimon, Editors, *Social Brain Matters: Stances on the Neurobiology of Social Cognition.* A volume in **Cognitive Science**

191.   Eugenio Garin, *History of Italian Philosophy.* Translated from Italian and Edited by Giorgio Pinton. A volume in **Values in Italian Philosophy**

192.   Michael Taylor, Helmut Schreier, and Paulo Ghiraldelli, Jr., Editors, *Pragmatism, Education, and Children: International Philosophical Perspectives.* A volume in **Pragmatism and Values**

193.   Brendan Sweetman, *The Vision of Gabriel Marcel: Epistemology, Human Person, the Transcendent.* A volume in **Philosophy and Religion**

194.   Danielle Poe and Eddy Souffrant, Editors, *Parceling the Globe: Philosophical Explorations in Globalization, Global Behavior, and Peace.* A volume in **Philosophy of Peace**

195.   Josef Šmajs, *Evolutionary Ontology: Reclaiming the Value of Nature by Transforming Culture.* A volume in **Central-European Value Studies**

196.   Giuseppe Vicari, *Beyond Conceptual Dualism: Ontology of Consciousness, Mental Causation, and Holism in John R. Searle's Philosophy of Mind.* **A volume in Cognitive Science**

197.   Avi Sagi, *Tradition vs. Traditionalism: Contemporary Perspectives in Jewish Thought.* Translated from Hebrew by Batya Stein. A volume in **Philosophy and Religion**

198.   Randall E. Osborne and Paul Kriese, Editors, *Global Community: Global Security.* A volume in **Studies in Jurisprudence**

199.   Craig Clifford, *Learned Ignorance in the Medicine Bow Mountains: A Reflection on Intellectual Prejudice.* A volume in **Lived Values: Valued Lives**

www.ingramcontent.com/pod-product-compliance
Lightning Source LLC
Chambersburg PA
CBHW021828300426
44114CB00009BA/367